Grace and Gratitude

Updated Edition with New Chapter

Miranda Young

'Phenomenal Woman' is a glorious and important poem by Maya Angelou, first published in 1978. 'The poem rejects narrow societal expectations of women and proposes an alternative perspective on what defines real beauty. Confidence and comfort in one's own skin, the speaker insists, are the markers of true beauty.' [1]

Men themselves have wondered
What they see in me.
They try so much
But they can't touch
My inner mystery.
When I try to show them,
They say they still can't see.
I say,
It's in the arch of my back,
The sun of my smile,
The ride of my breasts,
The grace of my style.
I'm a woman
Phenomenally.
Phenomenal woman,
That's me. [(2)]

This poem sang to Olivia in the time of her passing. Olivia released a single Phenomenal Woman, based on this poem by Maya Angelou with the lyrics running very close to the original poem. This anthemic song, was produced (and previously recorded) by Amy Sky and features Olivia Newton-John with additional vocals by Patti LaBelle, Delta Goodrem, Mindy Smith, and Diahann Carroll. It was the first single off her 2005 album *Stronger Than Before* which promoted breast cancer awareness, with the proceeds going to breast cancer research.

Acknowledgments

Thank you to the memory of Olivia Newton-John.

Thanks Jeffie Jenkins and MW and all the Wilkinson Publishing staff and James Young.

Thank you to the Olivia fans especially the Brazil Olivia Fan Club for their magic and Only Olivia.com for keeping the fires burning.

Dedicated to my Granddaughter Ruby.

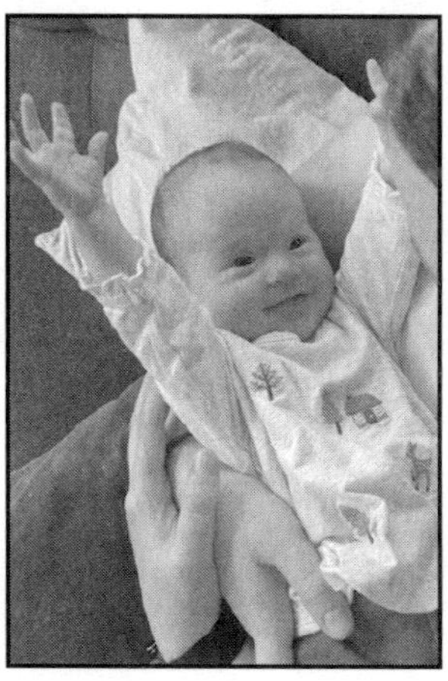

Be who you want to be.

Published by:
Wilkinson Publishing Pty Ltd
ACN 006 042 173
PO Box 24135
Melbourne, Vic 3001
Ph: 03 9654 5446

enquiries@wilkinsonpublishing.com.au
www.wilkinsonpublishing.com.au

Title: Olivia – Grace and Gratitude (Updated edition with new chapter)

ISBN: 9781923259027

eBook ISBN: 9781923259010

A catalogue record of this book is available from the National Library of Australia.

Cover design by Mike Bannenberg & Spike Creative

Page Design by Spike Creative Pty Ltd
Ph: (03) 9427 9500
spikecreative.com.au

Printed and bound in Australia by Ligare Book Printers.

An unauthorised biography and tribute commissioned by Wilkinson Publishing.

Part of the proceeds of this book is proudly donated to the Olivia Newton-John Cancer Wellness & Research Centre.

Contents

Olivia's Afterlife Impact

November 2024. It's another sweet night in Melbourne, Australia's certified home of live music. Guitars are being tuned, makeup applied, and microphones around town are echoing with – *One-Two, One-Two.*

A journalist for the *Herald Sun*, Australia's most prominent newspaper, is doing a cover story for the weekend edition headlined, "*Rock's New Hot Shots. Meet Melbourne's all-woman band Hot Machine – the fresh young faces being acclaimed as the next big things in Australia's rock 'n' rock scene*".

Standing backstage in a green room, the writer captures this moment, watching the band get ready to blow the roof off of the lucky venue that hired them for the night.

"As they ready themselves for a heavy rock set on stage, they break into their pre-show ritual, belting out Olivia Newton-John's 'Hopelessly Devoted To You' … Once the ballad is finished, they're ready to go on stage".[1a]

They are pure authentic rock 'n' roll, and in the space of one year, they are the band you need to see. The article quotes Cherry Bar owner and manager James Young, who was a hard man to shock after 25 years of wrangling the world's greatest rock 'n' roll bar. The first time he saw them, his jaw dropped, and he had to have them headline the iconic

Cherry Rock Festival, saying, "Rock 'n' Roll is not a genre or something to be bought – it's a way of life, a state of mind, it's not a costume". [1b]

I could not say Olivia Newton-John was heavy rock, but she certainly spanned many different musical genres. Now her flags are being flown as an inspiration to the next generation of musicians. Music was simply her lifeblood.

Olivia Newton-John's footprint on the music world is easy to see. Her music means many things to many people. Her songs are anthems for girls to rule the world, a song you grew up with, always open to reinvention, and appealing to all generations and across a sea of genres.

So, what has changed since Olivia's death? It's only been a few years, but her name is still so relevant and admired, and the legacy plans she cleverly put into place in her last living years are flowering like wild roses.

When Dame Olivia sadly passed away on August 8, 2022, the worldwide outpouring of grief was viral and intense. A great woman had passed, and so many people stopped everything and acknowledged her.

Fans and new recruits bowled over by the international media coverage of Olivia's death and the genuine heartache at her loss began to download her massive music catalogue, bonding as they watched her videos and movies. And I wrote a book.

The book was created as a tribute to Olivia's long and exciting life. Along the way, I discovered what a seriously astounding impact this woman had made in her time on earth and that this impact was growing every year.

Her posthumous titles included Australia's Sweetheart, Icon, Health Warrior, and National Treasure. But all her followers, friends, and family loved her most for her two important traits of '*wholesomeness and optimism*', both in her on-stage and private life.[1c]

August 2022 also saw the world reel as we lost Queen Elizabeth II. Society could not believe that such a constant in our lives had gone.

Queen Elizabeth reigned for nearly 71 years, and Olivia performed for nearly 60. They were two very different women, but both left a legacy that shows no sign of slowing down.

It's a strange fact that when someone dies, you start to find out so much more about them than when they were standing right in front of you. It's as though you get to meet them all over again – their younger selves, their hidden worries and all the achievements that they kept to themselves or got lost in time.

When my dear little Mum passed away last year, I thought I had her life history sorted. Not even close. I knew Wendy Macdonald graduated from Melbourne University Medicine at a time when not many women attended university, yet alone became doctors. Her parents were divorced, and her Mum and sister were the ones she relied on. I knew she boarded at Sacré Coeur, a small Catholic girls school in Melbourne, and still had those school friends by her side at the age of 80. She spoke Latin and was a voracious reader. No plant would not grow under her green fingers, and in the '60s she had a beehive hairdo that Priscilla Presley would have been proud of. She fell in love with my Dad, who was also in her graduating class. He lost a game of two-up on the local church steps, and the result was he had to help his mate out at his country practice for a few weeks in the Victorian country town of Stawell. Six kids later, they moved the brood back to the big smoke, and she moved from the work arena of GP into mental and women's health – demanding and creating change in those areas before her time.

I did not know that, apparently, my Mum wrote a book exposing the mental health world, and it was "made to vanish". I did not know that she always wanted a pet monkey, as one had lived downstairs from her in London. She was very proud of being an educational and fiction-published author. I did not know she was a headstrong and naughty child as she was always so prim and proper to me – the only thing approaching a swear word I ever heard her say was "you cheeky piece" when she was very cross. Later in life, she battled the scourge that is Parkinson's, discussing future cures with clever doctors until she couldn't anymore, and she was still teaching the local priest Latin into her 80s.

What did the world find out about Newton-John when she passed away on the very day that was supposed to be a celebration of the 42nd anniversary of her *Xanadu* album? This date is now forever a fine day for celebrating the good thing that was Olivia Newton-John.

One thing is startlingly clear in these few years after her passing – that a star like hers does not fade!

It is also evident that Olivia's charity work and brilliance as a role model really flew under our radar while she lived. When you look beyond the accolades, her forceful ability to change things in the music and wellness industries was remarkable.

ONJ's wellness legacy continues to give back to the world in extraordinary ways. International magazine *Hello* recently looked back on Olivia's life and concluded, "Diagnosed with the disease at age 44, Olivia became one of the world's most high-profile campaigners for advancing cancer treatment. It was Olivia's bravery and honesty amid her 30-year battle with breast cancer that quite literally saved and improved the lives of women around the world."[2]

Veteran entertainment reporter Peter Ford said a year after her passing that he *"can't think of any other celebrity who has done it like she did"*.[3] Posthumously, ONJ's massive and magnificent music catalogue is still being updated and bouncing into album and digital charts worldwide.

ONJ's cancer advocacy is thriving, and her passionate 'promise-keeping' family has dedicated themselves to keeping her brand of positivity alight – like a lighthouse on a rocky shore.

The definition in online Oxford Languages for the term 'Pay It Forward' is to respond to a person's kindness to oneself by being kind to someone else. Olivia did this on such a scale that her support for her wellness centre is being paid forward annually, and grows in size and importance in the hands of survivors, her handpicked ambassadors, and the dedicated medical staff at the Austin Hospital in Melbourne. Olivia put into play such systems that when she passed away all the wealth and celebrity she had enjoyed would continue to keep her dream of a cure for cancer paying forward.

If you have an urge to sing on the world stage or be an actor, or if you have a girl unsure what she can do in this world, it is worth reading about what one Melbourne girl did – and did entirely her way.

Perhaps now we can take the time to truly see this *"trailblazer in the art of pop reinvention"* [4b] and marvel at *"how ably – and convincingly – the chameleonic British-Australian musician shape-shifted between genres and rode the changing moods of pop to become one of the biggest hit-makers of her era and an enduring cult icon."* [4c]

Icon is a big word, but it fits like a glove on the hand of this Dame. Fans worldwide polish her image every day, and one of the nicest rare facts about Olivia that's still valid today is that not one bad word has been said or published about her.

Since 2022, ONJ's immortal 60-year music catalogue is still sought after, while new songs are being found and created in her honour, and old songs are being remastered, digitalised, repackaged, and uploaded.

This luminary's *"powerful, crystalline vocals"*[5] are much sought after and can be heard everywhere. Back in 2022, music charts all over the planet were crammed with her songs when the news of her passing filtered out. Her fans pushed seven of her songs into the iTunes Top 10, with 'Hopelessly Devoted To You' at No.1 on the US Top Songs chart. 'Magic' followed at No. 2, then the John Travolta *Grease* duet classic, 'You're The One That I Want' was at No. 4. And 6 to 9 was 'Let Me Be There', 'Physical' (the remastered 2021 version), 'Have You Never Been Mellow', and my personal favourite, 'Xanadu'. The album charts followed suit, with the *Grease* soundtrack taking the top spot and the *Xanadu* soundtrack hot on its heels at No.3. [6]

So many of ONJ's songs continue to stand the test of time; they are prime candidates for remixes and movie soundtracks and will be singalong classics forever. Other releases over the years were slow burns – yes, some flops – and some lucky tracks have been given two chances at the top of the charts due to an October 2020 deal with Primary Wave Music Publishing, which now handles Olivia's back catalogue.

Before she passed, Olivia began working with Primary Wave, the 'Home of Legends', setting in motion new deluxe editions on CD, Vinyl, and Digital formats. They hired producer Vinny Vero to curate these releases and collect some obscure tracks to feature on bonus discs.[7] Extraordinarily, you can now listen to nearly all her recorded work through online music platforms, which alone is a huge development for preserving her legacy.

Olivia always made it clear in her final years that she saw her cancer centre as her desired legacy – her musical achievements being the engine that could power the dream! Her forward planning worked, as new re-releases emerged fresh and ready to engage a new generation of fans.

Her posthumous album releases have included *Just the Two of Us: The Duets Collection (Vol. 1 & Vol. 2)*, and her back catalogue will show Olivia loved Christmas. "On Christmas Eve, my Mum would make German cookies and cakes and then we'd sing around the piano. There were live candles on the tree, and my Dad would lead us in singing hymns like 'Silent Night' or 'Away in a Manger'." [8a]

Olivia released many Christmas albums during her life. Her 2007 *Angels in the Snow* holiday album has been 'newly imagined' with an updated duet by Jane Lynch (*Glee*) and is the perfect way to hear Livvy's angelic voice soar again in 2025 and beyond.

Multi-platinum songwriter and producer Sam Hollander said while working on the *Angels* album, *"Her voice had this rare ability to express emotion in a way that felt both intimate and universal … it's such an honour to help preserve and carry her legacy forward."* [8b]

Other albums that have received a revitalising remastering have included *If Not For You 50th Anniversary Deluxe Edition,* out days after her passing, and *Olivia Newton-John's Greatest Hits 45th Anniversary (Deluxe Edition)* in late October of the same year.

Her fans wanted more, so in January 2023, *Olivia's Greatest Hits Vol 2 (Deluxe Edition)* hit the download and album racks. These 14 classic songs were released 40 years ago and now, in a new updated form, are keeping her memory alive.

Grace and Gratitude (Deluxe Edition) followed in June 2024. This one was celebrated Olivia and her husband John's wedding anniversary and had always been John's favourite. It's all about relaxation through the healing power of music, with each track aiming to target a different emotional state. Music healing was a serious science to Olivia, and is recognised worldwide.

Olivia's posthumous singles are unearthed treasures of the highest degree. Firstly, a new version of country classic 'Jolene', a duet with Dolly Parton and part of the *Just the Two of Us: The Duets Collection*.

Dolly, the Queen of Country, wrote and released 'Jolene' in 1974. Olivia covered the song on her album *Come On Over* in 1976. Finally, these two ladies re-recorded it – not knowing it would be the last music video and song ONJ would ever record, as she passed away a short time later. The original version of 'Jolene' (by Dolly) was ranked No. 63 on *Rolling Stone* magazine's list of "the 500 Greatest Songs of All Time".

Dolly Parton said of Olivia, *"I loved every moment that I ever got to spend with her. I've always been inspired by her grit, tenderness, willingness, and determination."* [9]

If that wasn't enough, 'My Dream', an unreleased song with Olivia's vocals, was found on a cassette by her long-time friend Jim Brickman. They wrote the song together 15 years ago with American country singer Victoria Shaw.

A renowned songwriter and pianist, Brickman was Olivia's old friend and collaborator. They first met long ago when he was invited to open for her on a concert tour. He reunited with the four-time Grammy winner for a popular remix of a live version of his 1997 classic 'Valentine', released on February 22, 2022, the year Olivia lost her battle with cancer.

'My Dream' emerged in September 2024 with Brickman wanting "the song to be shared on a global level, and it needed an extremely passionate performance. Il Volo, an Italian pop opera trio, also came on board, and Brickman said they "brought such an emotional and cinematic quality to it. It just feels intimate, yet epic." [10] The song was bejewelled and restored.

Raising money for Olivia's Foundation was the primary reason Brickman worked on 'My Dream', but he also hoped that the song would be "a balm for fans who miss her dearly".

"Like so many of us when I hear one of her songs on the radio," he says, "it makes me smile and reminds me how beloved she is, and always will be." [11]

Another single, 'Phoenix', released in 2024, must be included in her post-mortem release list. Even though Olivia didn't sing on it, she was there for its creation and wanted it out in the public arena.

The self-healing-themed new song, 'Phoenix', was co-written by her daughter Chloe Lattanzi. This single was released on what would have been Olivia Newton-John's 76th birthday (26 September 2024), but Chloe began working on the song a few years ago. Olivia told her daughter, "*Please finish this; it's the most beautiful song you've ever written.*"[12] Chloe was so happy to release this song in her mother's honour.

Chloe has always been open about her struggles with mental health and said her mother once told her that "*the most important thing to her more than anything in the world is that her child, me, shared her gifts with the world and was happy.*"[13a]

Live theatre tributes worldwide have also been instrumental in keeping Olivia's music front and centre. Australia hosted a national tour titled *The Life and Music of a True Aussie Legend – Hopelessly Devoted*, combining 22 songs and artists with state orchestras. Livvy's niece Tottie Goldsmith, a proud Goodwill Ambassador of the ONJ Cancer and Wellness Centre and 2019 recipient of an OAM for her contribution to charity and the performing arts, also joined the tribute show and was quoted saying that Olivia was her "*mother heart, my 'go to' and my confidant, as I was hers.*"[14]

In the States, the *Always Olivia* touring show won Best Tribute Artist of 2024 at the prestigious Josie Music Awards (the world's largest independent artist award show).

Beginning with the response to her 2023 State Memorial, it is clear that Olivia has a powerful and ongoing influence on fellow performers.

"Newton-John's legacy endures: as one of the earliest women in pop to embrace different eras, genres, sounds and even self-presentation, she lives on in the DNA of every female pop star's self-reinvention."[15]

Women in music received a boost when Sandra Dee evolved into 'Physical' Olivia. Suddenly, here was a woman in charge of her own music and showing how it could be done. When her 'Physical' video was released, it was a massive step into the future; with MTV at the helm, it proved a game changer.

"Olivia was always herself. And her career became a blueprint for all Australian performers who followed." [16a]

Olivia's personal life, icon trajectory and compelling career decisions are a roadmap for musicians everywhere – it should be printed and handed out with earplugs, train cards home, and water bottles at all gigs.

Olivia followed the Paying it Forward concept with her fellow entertainers, constantly mentoring those who came after her. Australian stars Kylie and Dannii Minogue, Delta Goodrem, Sia and many more acknowledged Olivia's influence on their careers. [16b]

"Since I was 10 years old, I have loved and looked up to Olivia Newton-John. And I always will," – Kylie Minogue [17]

Looking at her life retrospectively, an interesting pattern of pairing traditional and non-traditional methods has always been evident in her health advocacy, music, and personal life. These pairings are well thought out and part of her long-term plans, which are only now coming to fruition.

I do believe Olivia was a bit of a glorious troublemaker – but in such a polite, powerful force-of-nature way. She actually left a serious trail to be followed as she wove her way through this world, asking people at all times to look at things a little differently.

The world now looks differently at women in music. ONJ has had something to do with this. Her fearless image changes and pivots are inspirational, as are her more straightforward career goals of having a few home bases to escape to, surrounding herself with good people, and always remembering to be grateful for what she has and her loyal fans. She urged people to be open-minded and to look outside the drawn lines when it came to love, and her motto, "Love is love", helped to force change for gay marriage in Australia.

Olivia changed the perspective of what advocacy means. She showed how much could be achieved when she created the Olivia Newton-John Cancer & Wellness Centre in 2012 at a cost of A$271m – it is a brilliant combination of state and federal and philanthropic support. Then, in a full-on left-of-centre move, she started selling off most of her properties after her cancer diagnosis – all to invest in the foundation. She donated music money and her time and finally made her family promise to keep it going.

She talked about sensitive things before these conversations were 'de rigueur'. She told the world to have regular breast examinations and, interestingly, she has been named as someone who "drove a change of the language around cancer.

She avoided terms like 'fighting', 'battle', or 'war'. She wasn't 'surviving' ('That sounds like someone clinging to a lifeboat,' she said at the time); she was 'thriving'."[18]

Olivia pushed for medicinal marijuana to be used in conjunction with traditional cancer treatment. Saying her idea was "*to fund research into kinder ways such as the use of medicinal cannabis to treat pain, to treat cancer, to prevent cancer, and to live well with cancer."* [19]

Most importantly, she cited positivity as a key to healing, believing that one's mindset is vital to the healing journey. She wanted the medical world to embrace alternative healing and use non-traditional medicines alongside life-saving scientific methods. Her daughter Chloe believes that her "*mom far outlived what most people expected because of these medicinal properties."* [20]

"The Wellness Centre is very important to me as it has been my dream to create a healing place within the hospital grounds — a sanctuary of peace, beauty and relaxation for cancer patients" [21] *–Olivia Newton-John*

And she did it – this place exists in Melbourne!

The main centre is funded by the Olivia Newton-John Foundation, and every year thousands gather to raise money at her annual October 6 Wellness Walk. Now in its 11th year in 2024, it has raised $12 million so far and supported more than 30,000 people. With her niece and daughter at the head of the crowd, flying the flag for her through their tears. "I have been part of this journey with Olivia every step of the way, turning the first sod of dirt to build the Centre to doing art therapy classes together. I have always shared her passion and understood her vision" – Tottie Goldsmith. [22a] Officially, the ONJF confirmed that "*as custodians of Olivia's dream and legacy, we all share a commitment to honour her vision and work to make it a reality*". [22b]

Chloe Lattanzi also walked alongside her support system, including her husband, James Driskill, her father, Matt Lattanzi and her stepfather,

John Easterling." *I could never imagine letting my mom's dream die, and I feel her inside of me, guiding me, like, 'This is your job. This is what you're supposed to do.'"* [23]

A universal truth is that when people are grieving they look for signs from the departed. They need help dealing with the loss and look for symbols of hope and comfort. These symbols are often in the form of saints, superstitions, and positive role models. Since her passing, Olivia has become such a fighting symbol.

Olivia once said her church was the Church of Nature. A lifelong supporter of animals and the environment, she also spoke quietly about being open to afterlife contact.

Slipping into discussions of the traditional norms of death, ONJ raised conversations about what defines the afterlife. That someone could sense a passed one around them is not new. Still, she and her family have made it an open chat about their feelings and that she sometimes manifests herself to her daughter and husband as a lovely blue orb light. Even suggesting to her daughter that she would come back as that light while she was alive. Some fans have reported hearing her songs playing in unusual circumstances as if she was sending a message.

"Chloe's unflinching belief in the afterlife and in communication with her departed mother – also supported by Olivia's ex-husband John Easterling – is a clear advocacy of a spiritual link with departed souls." [24a]

I can believe in an afterlife as taught in Catholic churches, but I also believe that I can sense my mother's presence when I see sunflower yellow, and my Dad when a magpie gives me a knowing nod in my garden. Is it a need to manifest comfort? Is it them? Sometimes, it's too strange to think it could be just me willing the signs. But these conversations sit quietly and comfort Olivia's family and fans. Each to their own, and love is love!

In conclusion, this Dame was no ordinary Melbourne girl. She experimented, she stuck her neck out, and she had an unflinching spirituality system built in, which has spilled out to fans and family everywhere.

She was cited as *"a perfect role model"* at her State Memorial [24b]. Although there are a multitude of reasons Dame Olivia Newton-John was widely admired, "*her kind heart and genuineness were the foremost reasons*". [24c] She really was the total package, and as time passes, she grows in stature.

A tribute article in *Hello* magazine for 2023's International Women's Day was headlined *"How the legacies of Olivia Newton-John, Whitney Houston, and Ronnie Spector go far beyond their music"*. Stating the true but unheralded fact that *"Olivia and these ladies made an impact far beyond the stage and studio, cementing a women-first legacy that will last generations."* [25a]

What has changed since Olivia's death "is that she is now not just celebrated for her discography, but because she utilised her fame to help lift others — especially women." [25b]

Her husband, naturopathic entrepreneur John Easterling, has been dedicated to upholding her legacy. Recently, he posted that he has been "*staying very busy with the Olivia Newton-John Foundation Fund and the research that's going on there. We're sponsoring plant medicine and cancer research. And the beauty of that is that we're seeing stunning results in the early stages."* [26]

Finding that he has been travelling a lot since his love Olivia passed in June 2024, he put their Santa Ynez estate up for sale, saying that it was "*time to let somebody else enjoy that peace and serenity and beauty" of the home they shared.* [27a] He added that "*aside from the items that he and Newton-John's daughter, Chloe Rose Lattanzi, were keeping, many of the Grammy winner's personal belongings would be sold at a Julien's Auctions later this year*", with part of the proceeds going to Olivia's Fund. [27b]

Olivia's absence sees her next generation rising up! Chloe's struggles with her grief of losing her mother have started to heal, and her latest single sees a woman stepping up into the limelight as a more mature singer with purpose and hope.

ONJ's image constantly evolves from a living icon to a woman whose career roadmap should be studied and emulated.

We need a statue now – her city of birth, Cambridge in the UK, is lobbying for one. Surely, Melbourne, her self-proclaimed 'heart home', can do the same. Emblazoned with a touch of orange (her favourite colour), pop it next to Ian "Molly" Meldrum and down the road from the much-missed man of Melbourne music, Michael Gudinski. Perhaps we could also slip Chrissy Amphlett in there and Michael Hutchence, Ron Peno, Shirley Strachan, Marc Hunter and industry legends Warren Costello and Glenn Wheatley, and many more. All these departed music lovers could lead us to the heart of a city filled with live stadiums and little music venues that incubate the next big things, taking Australian music to the world.

I hope there are many, many more albums to be remastered. Let Chloe do a daughter version of the 'Physical' single, and maybe a CGI/AI-generated Olivia in *Grease 3*. Olivia Newton-John's life was a masterclass in the Frank Sinatra classic 'I did it my way', and her wings spread much further than we could have imagined. What a stunning role model for the modern musician and, more importantly, for the modern woman in music.

Spread positivity and pay it forward.

Part One

Heritage to Legacy

'I live my life in gratitude.'
Olivia Newton-John

A phone rings in the late afternoon in Melbourne, Australia.

'Hi, I am calling on behalf of the Olivia Newton-John Cancer and Wellness Centre. How are you today? Do you have a moment to talk?'

'Oh, what a lovely woman. Yes, l do have time.'

(Actual call. Early 2022)

The thousands of calls and positive responses that the Cancer and Wellness Centre has made and received since opening in 2012 are just part of the incredible legacy Dame Olivia Newton-John leaves behind, like the bejewelled train of a glamorous ball gown.

'Olivia was so much bigger than her showbiz career.' [1]

Everything important to her she planned, she backed with all her star power and carried out with intelligence and positive thinking. The perfect example is how Olivia, as the patron and figurehead, opened her $189 million Wellness Centre in Melbourne.

Angela Ceberano, Flourish PR Founder, worked on the centre with Olivia for many years and said, 'Of all the celebrities I've ever worked with, Olivia was the most selfless and genuine.' [2]

Olivia partnered with The Austin Hospital because it would be part of the public health system and accessible to all. It meant all aspects of cancer care were in one place, reducing patient travel time and stress and broadening their access to the types of care they needed.

Olivia's mission statement was clear: 'In 1992, I was diagnosed with breast cancer. The diagnosis came the same weekend my father died of cancer, so you can imagine the shock. I learned very quickly how important it was for me to think positively. The whole experience has given me much understanding and compassion, so much so that I wanted to help others going through the same journey.'

'And that's exactly what the Olivia Newton-John Cancer Wellness & Research Centre is – a positive healing centre to support people on their cancer journey.' [3]

The *New Yorker Magazine* stated: 'Her most lasting legacy might be as the rare celebrity who was almost universally well-liked and thought of as an essentially kind and warm-hearted person.' [4]

This statement really distils the magic and super-rare essence of Olivia down to single sentence. There is a saying that goes, 'When you do a good deed on earth you get a jewel in your heavenly crown.'

Olivia's crown must be a resplendent one indeed.

A recent NBC Think Piece on Olivia said, 'Olivia Newton-John was that rare creature, a genuine girl-next-door in Hollywood. A pop-star parents approved of and a role model to young girls everywhere. It was no surprise when Queen Elizabeth officially made her a dame in 2020 for services to charity, cancer research and entertainment.' [5]

On the 8th of August 2022, Dame Olivia, the beloved icon and role model, succumbed to cancer at the age of 73 after first being diagnosed with the disease 30 years ago and battling three recurrences during her life. Her much-loved husband John Easterling announced via her social media channels 'that she had passed away peacefully at her ranch in Southern California this morning, surrounded by family and friends'.

Veteran Seven Network entertainment report Peter Ford described her death as Australia's 'Princess Diana moment'. A moment everyone stopped and tried to take it in that such a woman had passed. A moment that everyone will remember where they were when they heard the news that Sandra Dee had left this mortal coil. The emotional impact was worldwide and affected celebrities and the public alike.

Most celebrities whether good and bad press, but it's almost impossible to find a bad word written about Olivia – that in itself speaks volumes.

Olivia became Australia's first big silver screen export, paving the way for many Australian performers to follow. 'Yet despite her stratospheric superstardom, she led a humble, quiet life, all the while navigating extraordinary challenges, with steely grace.' [6b]

For more than five decades she was our most successful and much-loved artist. Her true gift was her versatility. She happily tried

and succeeded in so many different musical genres, dominating the US and worldwide country music charts, soundtrack charts, pop charts and, later in life, holistic healing music avenues.

'[Olivia] was a fearless fighter for traditional and alternative cancer research and a vibrant warrior princess for the art of positive thinking in the face of fear. In her later years, music was healing and positive and recorded to help and aid other women suffering as she did.' [7]

Olivia was a master of the art of transformation in both her film and musical career. She loved taking chances and trying on new characters, but underneath it all, she was the same forthright, graceful and sweetly generous woman her whole life.

She must have had an iron inner core to remain always grateful for her wonderful life in the face of all her health trials and tribulations.

At the Australian Women in Music Awards in May 2021, Olivia was inducted into the Honour Roll. Tina Arena stood on the AWMA stage and sang Olivia Newton John's '*I Honestly Love You*', one of her signature songs, co-written by Peter Allen.

AWMA Founding Executive Producer Vicki Gordon said that this song expressed 'what I think we all feel about what Olivia gave to us – in our childhoods, in our adolescence, in our lives – a radiant positivity that she expressed in song. This positivity in the face of adversity is her incredible legacy to all who knew her.'[8]

With her incredible legacy in entertainment and philanthropy, can we ask: Where does Olivia stand in the pantheon of Australian music history?

The answer is clear: she is undeniably one of the stars at the top of the tree. Some might even say that she's the Queen! As her dear friend John Farnham introduced her to 70,000 people who had gathered at Sydney's ANZ Stadium: 'Would you please do me a favour and welcome to the stage my friend Dame Olivia Newton-John?' Turning around, he asked, 'Where are you, Your Highness?' [9a]

As if confirming her uncrowned status, Olivia Newton-John was backstage at Oprah Winfrey's Opera House show in 2010 talking to Nicole Kidman and Keith Urban when Bono walked in. He did a sweeping bow and said, 'You are the Queen of Australia.' [9b]

Although born in England and not an official Australian citizen until 1981, Olivia would always say that she considered herself an Aussie.

Despite living most of her later years in California, Olivia grew up in Melbourne, Australia where she began her lifelong entertainment career. She also called Byron Bay in New South Wales her spiritual home and was a very special place to her.

In a recent newspaper article about Melbourne's long-running bid for a Rock and Roll Hall of Fame, fearless music guru Ian 'Molly' Meldrum (Music TV superstar and one of the greatest ambassadors for Australian music) said of Melbourne's role in Oz music: 'The Music Industry was born here.' He cited *Countdown* being filmed in Melbourne, and local legends, including Olivia Newton-John, The Seekers, Ross Wilson, Skyhooks, Paul Kelly, Air Supply and Kylie Minogue, 'all started their careers here'. [9c]

These legendary artists, like Olivia, showcase Melbourne as an elite place to hone musical skills then take on the world!

To acknowledge that fact that Olivia remained proudly Australian when she was such an international superstar, the Australian Women In Music Awards (AWMA) noted that 'genius of [her kind of] brilliance can grow in this soil, on this land and in this culture. That we lift up in value and esteem the Australian women singers, songwriters and cultural leaders who gift us so much beauty and creativity by using their talent to create music.' [10]

Olivia Newton-John was typical of the folklore character - an 'Aussie Battler'. She was inextricably tied to the Great Southern Land with 'her infectious smile, angelic voice and humble nature – all of which made her a beloved cultural emblem'. [11]

Olivia was our sweetheart Australian Ambassador, with the silky blonde hair, translucent vocals and shatterproof wish to succeed. Once she championed a cause, she literally gave it her all. Once she was your friend, she remained so for life.

Being such a powerful figure in the entertainment industry made her the perfect role model for women in music. Projecting her central qualities of grace and gratitude, Olivia climbed the superstar ladder and her journey was something to be proud of, to absorb and to emulate.

Her influence on the worldwide tribe of women in music has many offshoots into a myriad of important industry arenas. Olivia Newton-John was a songwriter and live performer. She smashed years of sold-out world tours, made pioneering record and film deals, management manoeuvres and dedicated charity campaigns. She survived and conquered the world stage for more than 50 years, fought off cancer for 30 years and never faltered in striving to present who she was and what she stood for.

'One of the keys to Olivia's longevity was her versatility.' [12]

When her career began to slow down touring-wise, her versatility kicked in again and she turned to charity work and championed the environment, animal rights and the merits of blending alternative and scientific medicine in the fight against disease, which included playing a key role in legalising medicinal cannabis in Australia in 2016.

Unstoppable in speaking her truth, unstoppable in lending her name to a 'good cause' and, right up to the end, fearlessly willing to try something new, just to see where it could go. Versatile and adventurous, curious and not afraid to voice concerns and advocate change. These characteristics were all part of the rare genetic makeup of this unique woman. She was also a much-loved early accepter and supporter of the LGBTQ community, always repeating the valuable message: 'Love Is Love'!

The Aussie music scene was frankly devastated in 2022 by the loss of three of our icons in a short space of time. Judith Durham, the Seekers leading lady; Archie Roach, our heart-wrenching Indigenous truth-teller; and Dame Olivia Newton-John, the visionary. All irreplaceable, all masters in their own fields and timeless. The AWMA announced that they were 'so humbled that Olivia was the most recent inductee on our Honour Roll and we join with everyone whose lives she touched in tribute to all she offered to the world through her music.' [13] How amazing and fortuitous that she got to receive this accolade and feel all the serious industry love for her while she was alive.

In history, the date August 8 marks the loss of country music great Glen Campbell in 2017; Australia's iconic female saint Mary MacKillop, the patron of abuse victims, in 1909; and in 1959 one of Australia's dearly loved Indigenous painters Albert Namatjira; and now Dame Olivia in 2022. Olivia Newton-John now rests amongst a sea of creative, intelligent and gifted souls. When the news of her demise had spread, global media erupted in torrents of tear-stained print articles and the internet was crowded with online stories and grieving video laments for her passing.

Tributes and articles and essays flooded the world media pages – all desperately trying to capture the silken essence of this multitalented woman's mortal life. Trying to capture all the facets and impact of her mortal reach and how dearly she would be missed by family, celebrities and the public alike.

Her achievements have to be listed, and the list is brobdingnagian in its length and reach. Dame Olivia – so named and recognised by Britain in 2019 for her services to music, cancer research and charity – also received the Companion of the Order of Australia in June 2019, 'which is awarded for eminent achievement and merit of the highest degree in service to Australia or humanity at large.' In 2021, Japan bestowed on her their highest accolade, The Order of The Rising Sun, in recognition of her long music career and philanthropic works.

This superstar sold more than 100 million records and is one of the best-selling music artists in the second half of the 20th century to the present day. Her stellar musical career included being a four-time Grammy Award winner. Five No. 1 hits and ten Top 10 hits on the *Billboard* Hot 100. Two No. 1 albums on the *Billboard* 200 chart, including *If You Love Me, Let Me Know* (1974) and *Have You Never Been Mellow* (1975).

In the 1970s, Olivia made a name for herself in the country music genre, charting several Top 10 singles on country radio and even earned the title of CMA Female Vocalist of the year in 1974.

Olivia is survived by her husband John Easterling; daughter Chloe Lattanzi; sister Sarah Newton-John; brother Toby Newton-John; nieces and nephews Tottie, Fiona and Brett Goldsmith; Emerson, Charlie, Zac, Jeremy, Randall, and Pierz Newton-John; Jude Newton-Stock, Layla Lee; Kira and Tasha Edelstein; and Brin and Valerie Hall. [14]

Way back in 1978, she starred in the musical film *Grease*, with the movie soundtrack still one of the most successful in history – featuring major hit duets with co-star John Travolta (*'You're the One That I Want'*, which ranks as one of the best-selling singles of all time, and *'Summer Nights'*).

Her iconic solo recordings include the Record of the Year Grammy winner *'I Honestly Love You'* (1974) and *'Physical'* (1981) – *Billboard*'s top Hot 100 single of the 1980s – *'Hopelessly Devoted to You'* (also from *Grease*), and, from the 1980 film *Xanadu*, *'Magic'* and *'Xanadu'* (with Electric Light Orchestra).

On celluloid, she strutted in black leather pants and roller skated into our hearts, immortalised in two cult classic films *Grease* and *Xanadu*. Her character Sandy, the sweetheart from *Grease* is universally iconic, adored by the LGBTQ community and part of the constant question for all genders in the entertainment industry: Do you have to master two sides of your personality to survive? The seductress and the sweetheart. Her gentle character Kira, the ancient muse on roller skates in *Xanadu*, opposite Golden Age screen icon Gene Kelly, took some time to grow on the public perhaps, but is as iconic now as *Grease*.

ONJ was a fantastic performer in so many other films and TV specials, legendarily appearing in the iconic *Wonder Woman* series with Lynda Carter. Her video clips became classics. Her sexy *'Physical'* instructor character in the '80s music clip was a worldwide smash and won the 1983 Grammy Award for Video of the Year and a nomination for an Emmy Award for Outstanding Art Direction for a Variety or Music Program.

'*Physical*' also served to double down on her daring *Grease* image. She was having fun being the bad girl!

Like the mythical gypsy, Olivia's life and career kept her travelling the globe from the tender age of 5 years old, blazing a path in the music industry and doing it like the great man Frank Sinatra's signature song championed – '*I Did it My Way*'.

In amongst all this colour and movement, Dame Olivia took time to find and lose loves, make friends from all walks of life and create her own dear family.

'Inspiring us as she squared up to her mortality and leaving behind a loving family and beautiful and caring daughter who was the pride of her life. She often said her greatest achievement and her greatest joy was motherhood. A gift and honour and something Olivia never stopped talking about. The bond between her and her daughter Chloe was and is unbreakable, incredible and touching.' [15]

This three-part tribute to Oliva's 'Grace and Gratitude' hopes to explore her complete celebrity and personal journey.

Part One will follow her career timeline from the age of 5 when she moved to Melbourne through to the TV screen of 1960s Melbourne, to performing live and on international TV in the UK, to superstardom as an actress on the silver screen and as #1 on the US charts as a singing star. Touching on Olivia's major launching pads to fame, *Grease, Xanadu* and that fantastic '80s single '*Physical*'. As she battled her own recurring bouts of breast cancer, her quieter years were still jam-packed with touring and establishing herself as a serious cancer research advocate.

Part Two will follow her right up to the day she passed and then look at the blinding light that is her massive legacy. Trying to see all sides of this multi-faceted woman, we touch on her loves and her passions such as animals, her daughter, her partners and friends. Highlighting her health and wellness legacy and her memories as a wife and mother which are both vital to her total superstar makeup. Then we will jump off the yellow brick road of her life journey and discuss her place in the music Industry as a woman and artist and shine a light on her place in the world as an entertainer and activist and fierce supporter of the LGBTQ community worldwide. We will read a chorus of praise from her worldwide friends and industry experts close to home such as Ian 'Molly' Meldrum, Richard Wilkins and Melbourne University and RMIT resident Musicologists. Her life story would not be complete without a dive into the aqua blue pool that is her love of the Great Southern Land and how this love enhanced her life.

A lovely tribute in the *Sydney Morning Herald* read: 'Meeting one's idols is usually a bad idea, but Olivia was exactly as I had imagined her. She was funny, kind and generous, and wore her fame lightly. Beneath the Las Vegas sequins, there was an Aussie girl who loved nothing more than being surrounded by animals on her farm.' [16]

We won't look for secrets or tales behind closed doors; to be honest, her doors were always firmly swung open and she lived her life joyfully and with a sense of humour and adventure. We see her through the lens of two of her most magnificent personality traits – 'Grace and Gratitude'. And highlight the fact she was a rare being and an icon in the industry – she was the total package!

With the crown of greatness firmly on her head, she has always simultaneously been real. Australia claims her, the world claims her, Australian women claim her and we all bow to the claim of her dear family. Wanted in life, revered in death … she truly is an immortal.

'Thank you for life
Thank you for everything
I stand here in Grace and Gratitude
And I thank you...' – Olivia. [17]

In a 2007 overseas interview, Olivia was asked how she would like to be remembered. She answered: 'I hope my music makes people feel something and makes them think about their lives. I would love to feel they felt something for my music, whether it's good or bad, as long as they feel something. I hope I leave a legacy with the hospital (Olivia Newton-John Cancer Centre in Melbourne) and with environmental things, to encourage people to do the same, to encourage people to give back. And I hope I leave behind something worthwhile.' [18]

She has achieved this and so much more.

'The world is out of balance when we lose these magnificent people.' [19]

Chapter 1

Childhood, Cambridge and Heritage Blood

'I respect my parents' opinion very much. No matter how old you are, what your parents think is very important. If they like your boyfriend or if they like some work you've done. And if they don't, it's more shattering than anybody else telling you because they're the most honest.'

Olivia Newton-John. [1]

When Olivia released her touching and deeply personal autobiography *Don't Stop Believin'* in 2018, one reviewer shouted in print: 'That's Quite an Interesting Family You've Got There, OLIVIA!' Olivia already knew this, stating her family certainly was 'a lot to live up to!' [2]

Heritage, gene pool, environment and nurture can all play a massive part in who we are and who we can become. Then the one-in-a-million humans come along, the special ones. The latter has a sprinkling of fairy dust, heads off in a different direction to their family's traditional occupational lines, and becomes exceptional in their chosen field. These are the immortals. They can be from the pantheons of science or the arts: the survivors, the adventurers, and the ones who go down in history.

Olivia Newton-John's family is fascinating, and even more interesting is how she turned her parents' and grandparents' genetic gifts into the basis for her stellar career. Looking back at the parental influence on her life in 1994, Olivia recalled, 'My mother was very sensitive to nature, and she was very anti-violence and was very caring about things, and my father was very academic and brilliant, and I didn't spend as much time with him, but you know I got the genes, I guess.' [3]

This iconic slip of a woman was so much more than just an entertainer. Olivia was independent; she zigged when other people zagged, she worked hard. And Olivia thrived on change and collaboration, incorporating it into her career and lifestyle. She was defined by and, in some cases, defined the musical trends in every decade she lived through. She was constantly learning, adapting, and looking for ways to make 'positive change' possible in her music and life.

She was passionate about her family, respectful and grateful for her parents and siblings and euphoric about her one true love – her child Chloe.

ONJ was born to intellectual parents Irene and Brinley (Brin) Newton-John in post-WW2 Cambridge, England, on the 26th of September 1948. This was the year then Prince Charles now King Charles III was born to Princess Elizabeth on November 14th. When King George VI died the throne passed to his 25 year old daughter Elizabeth in 1952. Elizabeth would rule for the whole of Olivia's life. Britain opened its first Supermarket, and The Olympics were held in London. "The Invincibles", the Australian cricket team, toured England that year and did not lose a match. Sir Laurence Olivier's film of Shakespeare's *Hamlet* was the first British film to win the Academy Award for Best Picture, and Post-war bread rationing had just ended. *If You Ever Fall in Love Again* written by Irish songwriter Dick Farrelly was a hit and T.S.Elliot won the Nobel Prize for Literature.

The phenomenally historic university town of Cambridge was Oliva's first home, as her father, Brin (1914–1992), spent more than a decade of his life in Cambridge, eight of those as the Headmaster of the Cambridgeshire County High School for Boys (today it's known as Hills Road Sixth Form College) before emigrating to Australia in 1954. [4]

A university city, Cambridge was founded in 1209 and is still among the best universities in the world. During the WW2, Cambridge was an important centre for defence and became a military centre. Oliva's father was appointed Headmaster of the CC High School for Boys in 1946; apparently the year before his arrival, he got himself fined for a couple of minor motoring offences – by which time he held the WW2 rank of Wing Commander.

Brinley's life spanned both World Wars as he was born on 5 March 1914 in Wales, in the New Market Tavern in the Hayes, Cardiff, where his mum worked behind the bar. The son of Welsh parents: Oliver John, council schools manual instructor, and his wife Daisy, née Newton.

Olivia said of her grandmother: 'Daisy was a strict Quaker woman who would wash my dad's mouth out with soap if he ever swore or said anything close to blasphemy.' [5] Interestingly, Daisy had been a singer in the Royal Welsh Ladies Choir.

Educated at Canton Municipal Secondary School, Cardiff, Brin won a scholarship to Gonville and Caius College, University of Cambridge (BA, 1935; MA, 1939), where he achieved a double first in the modern and medieval languages. After graduating, he became an assistant master at Christ's Hospital (1936–38) and Stowe School (1938–40). He was a prolific academic and a natural-born teacher. Olivia described her dad in glowing but realistic terms: 'My father was charming, charismatic, and devilishly handsome, and demanded the best from himself and his family. A 'well done' was a compliment of the highest order from him, and not easily attained. Dad believed in hard work, discipline, and doing things on your own merits.' [6]

On 5 April 1937, at the registry office in Kensington, he married Irene Helene Käthe Hedwig Born, daughter of the physicist Max Born and Olivia's much-loved and inspirational mother. Together they had three children: Rona (1941–2013), Hugh (1939–) and Olivia, the baby who was seven years younger than her sister and nine years younger than brother Hugh.

A year after he graduated in 1940, Brin was off to war, commissioned in the Royal Air Force on 30 September 1940 and drafted into intelligence. His educational prowess was impressive. He aced everything he had a crack at. He fought like a hero in the air and made a massive difference with his exceptional code- breaking mind on the ground.

He spent two years interrogating captured German pilots, using his language skills and familiarity with upper class German society to gain their confidence and elicit information. Olivia described his wartime life in her memoir: 'He was a brilliant man who spoke French and German fluently. His German was so perfect that when he became a wing commander and later an intelligence officer for the Royal Air Force, he spoke Hochdeutsch (high or perfect German) and interrogated German prisoners of war. (Future warning: I would never be able to hide anything from him!).' [7]

Brinley was involved in the critical authentication and capture of Rudolf Hess in May 1941. In 1942 he was seconded to the top-secret Ultra project at Bletchley Park, the intelligence unit that, among other things, broke the German Enigma codes. [8]

Olivia's dad was a 'big force of nature and former MI5 agent'. [9] He was a high achiever and a multi-tasker, a traveller and constantly curious about the world around him. All these character traits are evident in his baby daughter and her long and cosmic entertainer career.

Olivia's father also bestowed another genetic gift on her – a singing voice! Welsh 'Brin' Newton-John was a talented singer endowed with a beautiful bass-baritone voice. The Welsh are renowned for being great singers, and Wales has had a strong tradition of choral and folk singing, alive since the 12th century. Sir Tom Jones, one of the greatest singers of our time, is also a Welshman – there must be something in the water!

Brin also played the violin during his school years; for a brief time, he had considered a career as a professional singer. At Bletchley Park, he sang in opera performances, gave recitals of German lieder, and took part in revues. This literary scholar and university administrator was also a well-respected TV presenter in the years 1956-58 in Victoria and 1958-62 in NSW and a radio announcer from 1981-1992 in NSW. [10]

Olivia was immensely proud that 'music was a big part of my home and family as well. My mum said I could carry a tune as young as two years old, and soon I knew the words and would sing harmonies to every song on the radio.' [11]

Olivia's singing prowess and progression in the world was due to her hard work, natural ability and a touch of magic. She said, 'I got this gift from my father ... he could have been an opera singer but chose to become an academic because he was so critical of himself and didn't think he was good enough. He had one recording of himself on an old black acetate disc but destroyed it because there was one bad note. (I wonder where I got my perfectionism from?).' [12]

Olivia often paid tribute to her mother, Irene Newton-John, praising her intelligence, fortitude and help with her career. In a pivotal future move in Olivia's career, Irene took a chance and moved countries so her 15-year-old girl could give her singing dreams the best shot. 'My beautiful mother, Irene Newton-John, was strong, fierce and independent – the perfect female role model with a deep sense of social justice. Mum taught me about eating healthily and the importance of treading lightly on our planet. She was an activist before it was even 'a thing' ... I guess I have inherited that gene, as I have always been instinctively passionate about our planet, nature and animals. Mum always told me, 'If you can help someone, do it.'' [13]

Going back even further into Olivia's geology, her grandfather Max Born's wife was a renowned mathematician named Martha Emma Hedwig (Ehrenberg) Born. She was the daughter of German Jewish jurist (an expert on jurisprudence) Victor Ehrenberg and Helene Agatha von Jhering, his Lutheran wife. Incredibly by way of Helene Agatha's family tree, Olivia was a descendant of Martin Luther – the 16th-century monk and theologian, considered one of the most influential people in Christian history, in that his beliefs gave rise to Protestantism. Going back even further, Helene Agatha's father, Olivia's great-great-grandfather, was jurist Kaspar Rudolph Ritter Von Jhering, best known for his famous 1872 book *The Struggle for Law*. The family accolades keep coming for Olivia – through her mum's line, she was also a third cousin of comedian Ben Elton.

Irene Helene Käthe Hedwig Born – Olivia's mother and world travelling companion – was born on 25 May 1914 in Berlin, Germany. She was the eldest daughter of Max Born, who won the Nobel Prize in 1954 for Quantum Mechanics. Irene's sister was Susanne Margarethe, an artist and teacher living in Bath, England. Olivia's much-loved uncle was the German-British Professor of Pharmacology at King's College London.

Asked about her relationship with her famous grandfather Max, ONJ said, 'I kind of feel that he's my guardian angel. I've always felt that.' [14]

Her grandfather was a master in Physics and was one of the founders of quantum mechanics, but his best mate was the GOAT (Greatest Of All Time) of Physics – Albert Einstein!

Olivia recalled, 'Albert Einstein was a close friend. When my mother was a young girl, Einstein spent many evenings in her family house playing the violin while my grandfather played the piano. My mother would later translate a book of letters between Albert Einstein and Max Born called *The Born–Einstein Letters*.' [15]

Olivia's family was part of the mass exodus from Germany in the 1930s as Hitler's hideous Reich grew more assertive. Sensing the danger, 'In 1933, my Jewish grandfather fled from Germany with his wife, Hedwig, to escape Hitler's regime. He was a brilliant mind and a humanitarian who helped Jews escape Germany. I'm extremely proud of my peace-loving grandfather.' [16]

They chose England as their new home because, as a student, Max Born had studied at Cambridge University. 'My German grandfather (Max) was the first person to sign an anti-nuclear proliferation treaty because he was strongly opposed to war. He was also a good friend of J. Robert Oppenheimer, the physicist credited with being the father of the atomic bomb. Still, my grandfather refused to collaborate with him on anything that was destructive or would hurt people.' [17]

Max was forced to leave his chair in Physics at the University of Gottingen in 1933 due to laws enacted by the Nazi Party. After working briefly at the University of Cambridge and Bangalore, Born accepted the position of Tait Professor of Natural Philosophy at the University of Edinburgh in 1936, where he promoted the teaching of mathematical physics while continuing his research into the behaviour of electrons. He became a British subject and chose to stay in Edinburgh until his retirement in 1952, dying in Göttingen on 5 January 1970. [18]

Olivia told *Saga* magazine in 2012: 'I'm so proud of him – he was never allowed to speak of his work when we were young, but he made the family a tape about all he did in the war.' [19]

Max Born's only son, Gustav Victor Rudolf, was also a famous scientist. He played a key role in developing drugs that stopped heart attacks and strokes after witnessing the horrors of Hiroshima during the Second World War. He also narrated, and stored for history at Göttingen University, the moving story of how Max Born and his family fled Germany. 'Recognised as a leader in the new physics, our father received invitations from countries worldwide. Then came the offer of a lectureship in Cambridge, which he gladly accepted at the end of June 1933. Life in Cambridge was bound to be strange at first: everything in another country is the same and yet astonishingly different, from the bread you eat to the people you meet. So it was in England. The overriding fact was the welcome and warmth with which we refugees were received by the British people.' [20]

So with all the chess pieces of her family history in one place, her parents met at Cambridge when Irene heard 'a man singing in a deep baritone voice, and she couldn't take another step. She followed the voice. Mum always said she fell in love with the voice first before she even saw him.' [21]

The two 17-year-olds locked eyes. Irene was an elegant brunette and classically beautiful, and he was 'six foot three, blond, handsome and had a mesmerisingly 'aristocratic voice'. [22]

Olivia's parents were married 5 April 1937 (to 1958) in Kensington, London, and divorced in 1959. Their first-born, Hugh, became a respected doctor in Melbourne; their second-born, Rona, became a mother of four, model and actress. And their most famous offspring was singer and actress Olivia Newton-John, born in 1948.

Irene's husband, Brin, was away a lot due to WW2. As a father, Brin only managed to get home to witness Olivia's birth and not that of the two elder children. Before Olivia was born, being German, Irene did not have an easy time in England during or post-war while her German-speaking husband was away so much. Olivia would later say, 'Two kind Quaker women would bring eggs and vegetables to her doorstep to help her and the children. They were her only friends. In turn, Mum would speak kindly with the German prisoners of war. One of the many things my mother taught me was that no matter what you're going through in life, kindness is what will sustain you.' [23]

Rumours that her husband had an affair while away in the air force also left Irene untrusting, insecure and broken-hearted as she had loved Brin since she was 17. But she was stoic and held the family together, having another dear baby – Olivia – their last child.

In 1953 things changed again. Brin Newton-John got a new job in Melbourne, Australia.

Her father, impressed by Australia and 40 years old, had been offered the significant Master of Ormond College position at the University of Melbourne – an academic accolade he was happy to accept. Olivia recalled in her memoir, 'l was five years old when my parents, Hugh, Rona, and I boarded a massive ship called the Straithard to cross the ocean to Australia.' 24. As a five-year-old girl, Olivia embraced the spirit of adventure thrust upon her by her parents. 'Travel for what you love, for what you want to achieve' – all life lessons she took to heart.

They landed in Melbourne, Australia, in 1954 after a long sea voyage, with their hopes and dreams pinned like tickets to their chests as part of the glorious immigration wave to Australian shores.

With such a brilliant and dangerous family history coursing through Olivia's veins and the pressure of post-war life sitting heavily on her family's shoulders, it all added to some severe pros and cons regarding the mental baggage she and her family had brought with them. Melbourne is Olivia's for the taking, and a new chapter begins in her life that will change her forever.

She becomes Australian!

Chapter 2

Address All Newton-John Mail to Melbourne, Australia

The City Of Melbourne, Australia, wants its own internationally recognised Rock and Roll Hall of Fame. A destination for music lovers to celebrate homegrown talent.

This ten-year wish project was initially the brainchild of Michael Gudinksi (an architect of the Australian music industry), Glenn Wheatley (musician and music manager) and Ian 'Molly' Meldrum (Oz music guru). 'Their reasoning was simple. Melbourne is famous for its live music scene and the birthplace of many celebrated acts that went on to wow the world.' Gudinski said, 'People in this city have always supported artists and original music, and we have great venues … We are the music capital of Australia.' [1]

Since 2018, the City of Melbourne has been declared the world's live music capital. THE WORLD! 'Melbourne is a music town. Just wandering the streets at night, you can hear bands bursting through the walls of pubs, acoustic sessions wafting out of small bars, or CBD buskers so good.' [2]

Melbourne boasts one live music venue for every 9503 residents, making Melbourne the live music capital of the world on a per-capita basis. [3] The capital city of Victoria has arguably been the centre of Australia's music scene since the '60s.

Researchers claim a striking factor is 'how passionate audiences are here … Melbourne audiences have always been engaged.' [4] There is a touch of mystery and magic to learning your music craft in lovely Melbourne town. It's what Melbourne does best! Due to the fantastic acoustic engineers trained here, music is literally in the air.

Books like *Roots* talk about 'how Melbourne became the live music capital of the world' (2019, by Craig Horne), delving 'into the history of live music in Melbourne, and the stories of those musicians who played what they wanted, when they wanted, without a damn'. [5]

Melbourne's 'music badges of honour' are dazzling and plentiful. Starting with our expertly curated Australian Music Vault, housed in the Arts Centre 'just a drumstick's throw from ACDC Lane'. The game-changing 2010 Save Live Australian Music (SLAM) demonstration was held to save and protect live venues. A 20,000-strong crowd marched through the streets, the Victorian Government listened, and the result was The Live Music Accord/Agent of Change, which states that if an apartment block appears near an existing live music venue, the apartment must take responsibility for soundproofing measures because the music venue was there first. [6] A seemingly simple yet stunning change that London adopted soon after, and the knock-on effect of this will shore up our musical heritage for generations to come.

'This city has produced ARIA and Grammy award winners, rock stars and pop stars, chart toppers and contemporary singer-songwriters, and they all continue to lead successful careers today.' [7a]

Creative souls grouped in Melbourne share houses, rehearsing and playing live in the plethora of pub band rooms until they got picked up by our great record companies and touring agencies and TV stations and introduced to the world. Olivia was such a star, and her story resonates with so many other celebrities, such as her dear friend John Farnham who, like Olivia, was born in England, moving to Melbourne in 1959. John's career has lasted more than 45 years and still going. Australian of the Year in 1987 after his 1986 album *Whispering Jack* became the highest-selling album in Australian history. Nick Cave – The Dark Lord and international everything – was born in Victoria. While at Caulfield Grammar, he and a group of friends formed the band The Boys Next

Door, later known as The Birthday Party.

The Little River Band is a rock band originally formed in Melbourne in 1975, going on to sell more than 25 million records and achieve 13 US Top 40 hits, Michael Peter Balzary – Flea, the bass player for the Red Hot Chili Peppers – was born in 1962 in Burwood, Melbourne, while Crowded House, a world-recognised band, formed in Melbourne in 1985 and lead singer Neil Finn tours with Fleetwood Mac in his downtime.

'The health of the Melbourne scene has been a beacon … really diverse; a real melting pot of different influences. The level of experimentation was inspiring … Melbourne, culturally, has been able to facilitate that kind of sustained rehearsing and playing and language development between individuals.' [7b]

Then there are the Melbourne ladies, ladies influenced and impressed by Olivia's journey, and ladies who were role models for Olivia herself. The Seekers are an Australian folk-influenced pop quartet, formed in Melbourne in 1962. They were the first Australian pop music group to achieve major chart and sales success in the United Kingdom and the United States. Lead singer Judith Durham is an icon who sadly passed away in 2022. Helen Reddy was born in Melbourne to a show business family and started her career as an entertainer at age four. She sang on radio and television and won a talent contest on the television program *Bandstand* in 1966; her prize was a ticket to New York City and a record audition. Reddy arrived in NYC as a single mother to a three-year-old, with just $200 in her pocket, before becoming the world's top-selling female singer in 1973 and 1974.

'Helen's ethos and legacy created a space for women in music to use their voice and platform as a change for good.' [7c] A great mentor to Olivia, who also adopted her life message and spread the word of support and positive change for women in the music industry.

Years ahead of Olivia, Melbourne can claim another Dame, the great opera singer Nellie Melba, who was born in the suburb of Richmond and was the first Australian classical musician to achieve international recognition.

Twenty years or more after Our Livvy, international pop princess Kylie Minogue and her stunning sister Dannii, both born in Melbourne, adored Olivia Newton-John and honed their craft in Melbourne's music streets as Olivia did on TV and talent shows. Global singing sensation Filippina Lydia Arena – known as Tina Arena – was born in Melbourne, as were songbirds Kate Ceberano, Missy Higgins, and Vanessa Amorosi. Let's not forget Chrissy Amphlett, whose 'career was launched in Melbourne. In 1975 she lived in Prahran's Greville Street, and it was at the Station Hotel that she first saw AC/DC, inspiring her own school uniform look.' She helped put Australian rock on the map, and now her name is permanently marked on Melbourne's CBD grid.' [7d] Olivia Newton-John Lane should be next on the Melbourne city planning table.

That Melbourne is such a creative community is not an accident, 'it is the product of inspired and eager storytellers, risk-takers and entrepreneurs that compel governments to listen eventually. There are profound lessons to be gained from understanding why cultural Melbourne punches so far above its weight. It is a story of rebellion, risk-taking and rule-bending.' [8a]

A special mention to our biggest risk-taker, Michael Gudinski, without whom much of the scene would never have happened. 'It is also impossible to celebrate our rock'n'roll credentials without saluting Ian 'Molly' Meldrum – the man who brought Australian music to the world through the ABC TV show *Countdown*. The role of community rule-bending radio stations 3RRR and 3PBS could not and cannot be overlooked as hothouses of musical talent as well as providing the first airplay for countless musicians.' [8b]

Melbourne brought in Australia's first Night Mayor role in 2021. A globally recognised position taken up by James Young, the owner and booker at Cherry Bar, Yah Yah's and Hotel Westwood, to get the nightlife community back on its feet post-Covid. James says: 'Music is who we are. It is a cornerstone of Victoria's identity as a creative state. It is something we are known for worldwide, and it is a huge economic driver. Our state nurtures emerging artists.' [9]

All this passion in one place: how could the chosen home of the great man Michael Gudisnki AM be anything but pumping live music every day and night? The founder of the Mushroom Group in Albert Park, he made it Number #1 globally. Even though he sadly died on March 2, 2021, all the tendrils of this incredible, thriving company flourish today, with its 50th anniversary in 2023.

Having worked at Mushroom for many years and witnessed M.G.'s passion for music in person, it was electric and extraordinary. He loved music in all its varied forms, perhaps his favourites being Rock and Roll and, of course, Ed Sheeran. The bond between these two was an example of the incredible loyalty and love Gudinski inspired here and internationally. Sheeran's song '*Visiting Hours*', written for his friend and mentor and sung so beautifully at his memorial, was pure poetry and broke every heart in the massive Rod Laver Arena. Gudinski's energy was infectious and always reciprocated in droves by Melbourne punters, venue owners, tour managers, songwriters and singers – great and small.

'Michael lived and breathed all things Melbourne,' read a statement from his family. 'He was a global ambassador for our city and beamed with joy showing it off to many world-famous artists and business leaders, hosting them in our great town over the years. He tirelessly fought tooth and nail to ensure Melbourne was seen as the live music capital of Australia and known as one of the great music cities of the world, which it indeed is.' [10]

How dearly we miss this man. An incredibly lifelike statue of Gudinski now stands outside Rod Laver Arena, smiling and looking over the packed crowds coming to hear Australian and international musicians play. Give his tummy a rub for luck, leave him a gig T-shirt – he sees it all.

M.G. might even agree that Olivia – brought here by her singing-loving, academic father as a young girl – was raised and trained in the best rock and roll school in the world: Melbourne.

'Livvy' grew up in the suburbs of Ormond, Parkville and Jolimont. She started writing songs at school and playing folk-style live gigs, aged 14, in the little coffee shops and venues that encouraged live music. Perhaps she always knew she wanted to sing and, in return, Melbourne wrapped its loving musical-infused arms around her during her formative years and laid the groundwork for the great entertainer she would become.

This combination of genetics, environment and essential passion, all in one young girl, added to the fact that Olivia Newton-John was in just the right place to write music, get up stage and practise her God-given talent.

As a child, Olivia said she 'used to wait for my father in the afternoons under this gorgeous tree in the middle of the driveway (of Ormond College, Melbourne), and I used to write stories and poems about birds and trees and the sky. This began both my songwriting and a deep, personal connection with nature.' [11]

When the Newton-John family of five stepped off the boat in 1954, they moved straight into the grounds of Melbourne University, 'unpacking boxes at our fantastic new home on campus, a beautiful stone mansion with endless bedrooms and our own housekeeper. I couldn't believe my eyes as I navigated those long hallways that were perfect for hide-and-seek.' [12]

Sadly, the marriage that had weathered a war was now finding it hard to navigate a new country. 'Our home looked perfect from the outside, but inside was another story …' When Olivia was about 9, her parents told her they would design a new bespoke house for them all on the

Ormond property. Unfortunately, they never got to move in as her father told her one night that she was going to go and live with Mum in an apartment in Parkville, not far from the campus, and he would live apart from them. The marriage was over. [13]

Olivia and her mother moved to 'lion-roaring' distance from the Melbourne Zoo. Unfortunately, her father was asked to leave his university job as the rule was he had to be a married man. Brinley had served Ormond College for five years, and during his time there, he initiated an extensive building program, made the school co-educational and allowed alcohol on campus (which made him very popular).

In 1959 he applied and was accepted for the position of associate professor of German and Head of the Department of Arts at Newcastle University College. This move to Newcastle made visits to his family very hard due to distance and expense. He retired from the College in 1974 and was awarded the impressive title of professor emeritus. He spent his retirement indulging his love of classical music, lecturing on everything from Bach to Wagner. After moving to Sydney in 1981, he served as a regular presenter and board member on the fine music radio station 2MBS–FM.

Brinley, like his daughter, was considered a pioneer in television broadcasting in Australia. He served as moderator of the 1958 Australian Broadcasting Commission program, Any Questions, and was the creator and host of the popular program *Forum* for Newcastle TV station NBN 3 in 1962. In short, like his wife, children, parents and grandparents, Brin Newton-John was an outstanding academic who packed a lot into his life.

To this day, the University of Newcastle celebrates his achievements with the Newton-John Award, which included him choosing the Uni's colours and motto: 'Universitas Novocastrium, I look ahead.' [14]

This is a motto to live by, and one I feel Olivia adopted, as she was always looking ahead and striving to think positively.

Olivia spent her summers in Newcastle, NSW and embraced her half-siblings Sarah and Toby, who were born to her father's second wife, Valerie Cunningham – the university librarian and a very accomplished pianist. Olivia's memoir records her saying of her new step mum, 'Val would play the piano, and Dad would sing … From the start, I adored them all.' [15]

In later years, Brinley spent all of his time in his daughter Olivia's flat in Manly in Sydney, and a beautiful portrait painted by Bill Leak hangs in Ormond College, the University of Melbourne, to this day in memory of this man who passed on July 3, 1992 (aged 78) in Sydney.

Olivia mused in her memoir, 'My father is doing a radio program – classical music. He has a beautiful speaking voice, and that's his passion in life, his music. My mother lives in Melbourne and is an avid photographer. She's also started writing for a magazine out there, and she submits poems, very funny ones, and articles. In some way or other, my family is always doing something with the media.' [16]

Meanwhile, Olivia's mother Irene's life changed dramatically due to her divorce. She had to get a job out of the home, and with her son, Hugh, at university and daughter Rona getting married, Olivia was on her own. Olivia became a 'latchkey' child. Remembering those times for her mother, Olivia stated: 'In those days, women didn't fare very well in divorce settlements, and watching my mother struggle financially taught me how strong women rally to take care of themselves and their children.' [17]

Mother and daughter moved to a little house in Jolimont, and Olivia found she was missing her father more and more and that she didn't feel drawn to the academic life but one of singing. Every young child wants to be so many things before they find the one that fits. Very early on, growing up in Australia, little Olivia decided that because she 'was so crazy about animals, that I wanted to do something associated with them, and I thought of being a vet'. However, she soon gave up the idea when she realised it would involve going to medical school. [18] Another occupation she considered was becoming a mounted policewoman. Her profound love of animals has always remained a priority throughout Olivia's life. 'I love animals,' she explained. 'They give so much to you and demand so little. And you can trust them.' [19]

Education-wise, Olivia went to primary school at Christ Church Grammar School in the Melbourne suburb of South Yarra with another famous Australian musical icon, Daryl Braithwaite (future lead singer of Australian band Sherbet and fortuitously also managed by Roger Davies – Olivia's future manager). Olivia's confidence was growing, and at 12, she appeared in Green Pastures at a Melbourne theatre and her older sister, Rona, entered her into a competition to find a lookalike for British child star Hayley Mills. She won, and it gave her the confidence to perform more in public.

ONJ found deep solace in music and always would. She was a talented, pretty young girl who dreamed and talked about – even way back then – of becoming a famous singer. At age 13, she was enrolled at University High School in Parkville where she spent the next four years, from 1961 to 1964. At 15, she was described in the student newspaper as 'a lively fifth-form student with noteworthy eyes'. And it painted a clear picture of a girl who was deeply passionate about music and theatre from a very young age and a school that nurtured her talent at every opportunity. This school seemed to cater to the artistic student. Past students also included Crocodile Dundee director Peter Faiman and the playwright David Williamson. [20] Olivia's memories of her school days were 'I scored very high on intelligence tests but had trouble concentrating on my lessons … Luckily for me, singing didn't require a degree.' [21]

The singing bug had bitten this young Melbournite, and Olivia said that her mum would often tell her that, as a little girl 'I sang perfectly in tune. 'You sing like an angel,' she said. I always made my mother and my sister cry when I sang, but in a good way (hopefully).' [22]

The music world in Melbourne was heating up. It was a fertile place to get a chance to sing on stage or TV. In 1958, Johnny O'Keefe had the first rock and roll radio hit in Australia with '*The Wild One*', and in 1959, rock music first appeared on Aussie TV.

At only 14 years old, Olivia met three local girls, Carmel, Freya and Denise and formed a short-lived girl group called 'Sol Four'. They often performed in a coffee shop owned by her brother-in-law Brian Goldsmith. Although working full-time, Irene was always watching Olivia and made her stop singing with the Sol Four group because her schoolwork was being neglected, and she was concerned about her daughter becoming too involved with her first boyfriend, Ian Turpie (future Australian actor and famous T.V. host). This did not deter Olivia from publicly performing or dating Ian. Her mother gifted her an acoustic guitar, and with the help of Ian, she learned to play and sing folk music on her own. Olivia recalled this epiphany moment in her memoir: 'Brian had a folk singer in his restaurant on the weekend, Hans Gorg, and I was allowed to go watch him perform, with Rona keeping a close eye on me. One day, Hans invited me onstage actually to sing with him and his guitar. Heaven. Pieces clicked into place. I had found my everything.' [23]

On Saturday morning T.V., there was a show called *Kevin Dennis Auditions*; the format was standard: a contestant would sing, dance, or perform their 'talent', and a panel of judges would either give them a thumbs-down, or a gong, which was a thumbs-up.

Livvy's biggest supporter, her sister Rona, encouraged her to go on the show, with then-boyfriend Ian playing the guitar for her. She sang one of her favourite songs, '*Summertime*'. In her own words, the story of how she officially became a singer went like this: 'Three resounding gongs later, it was a victory. Evie Hayes, one of the judges and a famous American TV personality in those days, phoned my mum to ask if she could manage my career … 'All of a sudden, just like that, I had a career and a manager.' [24]

Olivia had been noticed, and the work started flooding in. Channel 7's *Tarax Happy Show*, hosted by Happy Hammond, asked Olivia if she would take over for the Christmas holidays 'as one of the girls was getting married, which she did, and after that, they offered me a permanent position there, so that's how [she] started working in television'. [25]

On the *Happy Show* she was billed as 'Lovely Livvy', a name that stuck forever, and it was on *The Go!! Show* that she would meet her future singing partner, Pat Carroll, and music producer, John Farrar. [26]

This little girl's performer resume was blossoming. At just an innocent fifteen, naturally beautiful and confident, she took part in Johnny O'Keefe's ten-week Sitmar Talent Quest on the show *Sing Sing Sing* in April 1964. She chose to perform the song '*Anyone Who Had a Heart*' and then won after a performance of '*Everything's Coming Up Roses*'. The life-changing prize was £150 (around $200) and a return trip to England.

'As Olivia told *The Sydney Morning Herald* at the time, she planned on finishing her high school degree before taking the trip. However, she ended up dropping out of school, much to the disappointment of her parents and moved to London instead.' [27]

'There's a kind of a line between music and math, so I guess I got the music gene, thank goodness. But my mother wasn't too thrilled. She wanted me to go to university and get a degree or do something, and my father, he liked opera, so he wasn't too thrilled either.' [28]

The advice she received at the time from friends and teachers was that if she was thinking about being a singer, it would need her full attention. What a massive decision to make – leave school, her family, her boyfriend and all her friends and go to London.

Olivia did not go straight away! She did not want to yet. She loved her singing and T.V. career in Melbourne. In May 1965, ONJ was the opening act on an episode of *Boomeride*, a new live music show on Channel Nine. She was given a risqué song to sing, the lyrics of which said that although she was '16 now ... One of these days, when I grow up, I'm gonna make love to you.' Known for her 'Miss Goody Two-Shoes' reputation, her performance was totally opposed to her innocent looks. [29]

In her small screen debut, ONJ starred with Pat Carroll in a made-for-television film *Funny Things Happen Down Under* (1965), which didn't make any impact publicly but was a vital film experience for her.

On the cusp of womanhood, Olivia had tasted how exciting an image change from innocent to risqué can be, and she had a taste of the film world. It was time to look for more!

Although happy in her newly adopted town of Melbourne and gifted 'with a crystal-clear soprano voice. Her great talent, however, was to inhabit a song and deliver its emotional message authentically'. [30] Irene knew her girl could sing and that she had a bigger future in store.

Nearly one year after she won the ticket-to-London prize, her mother finally convinced her to broaden her horizons and leave her boyfriend for a trial few months in London in the swinging sixties.

When she does leave to go back to the U.K. in 1965, she is not the same shy Cambridge girl. She has weathered her parents' divorce, had a first love, and become far more independent. During her formative music training years, in such a short time, she went from strumming a guitar as a budding folk singer to belting out winning T.V. show tunes.

Her psyche has changed – she is Australian!

Growing up in Melbourne, she may only have been a teenager, but she had the blood of old souls coursing through her veins, the blood of whip-smart survivors, thinkers, and creatives. She already knows what she will and won't do and embraces change as a good thing. But her roots, her core beliefs and the moral compass within would never change and never did. Olivia was a soft-spoken Melbourne teenager who had discovered ambition, and now, with her mother in tow, she was travelling down a road to stardom.

Time to take over the UK. And then the US beckons.

Chapter 3

The UK Sixties World Beckons

'When's it my turn?
Wouldn't I love, love to explore'
'Part of Your World'
Song by Olivia Newton-John

No matter how far she roamed Melbourne would always be home to Olivia, but London was the place to be if singing for a living was to become a reality. As her mum rightly said at the time, 'If you want to sing, then take this chance. There might never be another.' [1]

Olivia wept at the ships dock, waving goodbye to her heartbroken boyfriend Ian – he had given her an ultimatum: be back in three months or he would have to move on. She promised she'd be back sooner than that.

London in the 'Swinging Sixties' … what a time to be alive! What a time to be in the music industry and what a time to be a teenager.

Olivia was unsure of what would eventuate in England, saying: 'I don't know what my path is yet. I'm just walking on it.' [2]

London in this brilliant decade was all about the hedonistic pursuit of pleasure; it was the vortex of a worldwide explosion of art, music, literature and fashion. Flower power, love beads, peace signs, groovy art and rock 'n' roll music ruled everything and the newly liberated planet could not get enough of it. 'One of the biggest, defining aspects of the 1960s was music … If the Fifties were in black and white, then the Sixties were in Technicolor.' [3]

The British Invasion's soundtrack counted in The Beatles, The *Rolling*

Stones, The Who, Cliff Richards, and the Small Faces. The mini skirt was in, mod culture reigned supreme, and eclectic Carnaby Street was the place to shop.

Everyone joined protests for the anti-nuclear movement, feminism and sexual liberation. Pirate radio ruled the airwaves and experimental films played in the burgeoning British cinema industry. Magazines attracted creative photographers and writers and adventurous publishers. London metamorphosized from a post-war, gloomy city to a brilliant epicentre of style and the epitome of cool. It was filled with young people due to the post-war baby boom and this new generation did not bear the restrictions of their parents' time, and the parents wanted the kids to play in the sun, to be part of this new movement with all its freedom and possibilities.

Into this UK world of endless possibilities Olivia Newton-John landed, guided by lady luck and her mum. She was plunged into this melting pot, with talent and good looks to spare – a sure-fire recipe for success.

Mother and daughter moved into a tiny one-bedroom flat in Hampstead where Olivia slept on a fold-out couch. Her sister Rona was also living in London, and in 1972 Olivia remarks, 'Rona and I recorded a song together – '*Just Us Two*'. That was such a fun time. I loved singing with my sister – she always inspired me to be the best performer I could be. Rona had style and impeccable taste and taught me about [fashion] and decorating houses and mostly about not being afraid to be yourself.' [4]

In those first few months, all Olivia wanted to do was go home to her boyfriend and the life she had back in Australia. She actually went as far as applying to become a ward of the court, so her mother was not in charge, but her plea was denied. Then the breakup letter came from Ian – he had waited three months and now started seeing someone else (his future wife, whom he would marry in 1968).

ONJ decided to make the best of it and she recorded her first single in 1966 at just 18 years old for Decca Records titled '*Till You Say You'll Be*

Mine'. Things really changed when her girlfriend Pat Carroll, whom she had worked with on the *Go!! Show* in Australia, joined her.

'We became friends straight away,' Pat recalled. 'She went to England, and then I won a radio award and I was sent to England as well, so she picked me up at the airport.' [5]

The flat rented for Pat by her agent was in a scary part of town, so she moved in with Olivia and her mum. The girls combined their mutual dream and became a double act. Olivia laughed at the memory of them together: 'She ended up moving in with me and my mum for two years … Sleeping on the floor on a blow-up mattress. It was great because you don't know any different. We were young girls. We were having a blast, we're in London in Carnaby Street in Beatles days. Can you imagine? It was fantastic.' [6]

The left-behind Ian Turpie and Olivia always remained friends and Ian said when asked about her early work, 'The improvement in her singing since she went to England has been remarkable. She told me Shirley Bassey has been a big influence on her. After hearing Bassey, she worked at developing her 'head voice' to sound like a chest voice, the way Bassey used hers. The power she's developed is amazing.' [7]

The 'Pat and Olivia' duo toured UK clubs and army bases and contributed backing vocals to recordings by a number of other artists, notably the song '*Come In, You'll Get Pneumonia*' by The Easybeats. Olivia's first UK manager was Peter Gormley (who represented both Pat and Olivia). He also managed Cliff Richard; Frank Ifield; The Seekers; Hank B. Marvin, Bruce Welch and John Farrar (known as Marvin, Welch and Farrar). But suddenly, Pat, not being English-born, discovered that her visa had expired, in December 1969, and she had to go home to renew it.

Olivia continued to work solo and gained enough momentum to record her debut album. When Pat returned, she brought her husband with her – John Farrar.

John Farrar played a massive role in Olivia's global career. He was a music producer, arranger, singer, guitarist, and member of several rock and roll groups, including The Mustangs (1963–64), The Strangers (1964–70), Marvin, Welch & Farrar (1970–73), and The Shadows (1973–76). He worked hand in hand with Olivia during the highlight years of 1971 to 1989. He was the legend who wrote her American number-one hit singles: '*Have You Never Been Mellow*' (1975), '*You're the One That I Want*' (1978 duet with John Travolta), '*Hopelessly Devoted to You*' (1978), and '*Magic*' (1980).

Farrar also produced most of Olivia's recorded material during that time, including her number-one albums, *If You Love Me, Let Me Know* (1974), *Have You Never Been Mellow* (1975), and *Olivia's Greatest Hits Vol. 2* (1982).

He was a co-producer of the global hit soundtrack for the film *Grease* (1978) and produced Olivia's first American number-one hit single, '*I Honestly Love You*'. [8]

But back then John was just her best mate's talented new hubby and they all bunked in together to save money in London as Livvy's mum Irene had moved out to leave the girls to conquer their new world.

Olivia's international career would not have been the success it was without Irene's help. Irene said at the time: 'I felt I had to take her to Europe, so she'd get a proper sense of proportion, because people here (in Australia) tend to make too much of young stars. I felt she might have got a swollen head which would have ruined everything.' [9]

Irene stayed in the UK for a while, going on to explore the art of photography, which she found that like her daughter, she was good at. 'This led to a change of career and Irene was able to concentrate on this and writing on a freelance basis. Irene did not marry again, enjoying her own independence and freedom.' [10]

Irene wrote for travel magazines in Australia, where she lived out her life and watched all her children's careers with pride and loved being a grandparent, having eight grandchildren. Her grandmother Irene passed away on 29 Aug 2003 (aged 89) in Melbourne and was cremated, with her ashes scattered in Byron Bay, Australia. Olivia sadly said, 'She was, and remains, the inspiration behind almost everything I do.' [11]

In 1967 Olivia fell in love again – this time with the founding member of the UK band The Shadows, Bruce Welch and they became engaged quickly, which caused an uproar as he was technically still married. During the court case for the divorce, Bruce's then-wife named Olivia as the 'other woman', a problematic time for Olivia whose public image was under scrutiny. They were both in the public eye especially with Bruce a founding member of hugely popular group The Shadows who became the backing band for Sir Cliff Richard from 1958 to 1968.

Engaged and living with Bruce along with newly married Pat and John, they became an awesome foursome. Olivia proved to be very musically adaptable over the years. She didn't drive these changes so much as she navigated them, adapting to different sounds and styles with the aplomb of a showbiz natural. 'That innate sense of show was cultivated in her native Australia and recognised by Don Kirshner, the American producer who helped bring the supergroup the Monkees to air.' [12]

Kirshner was an American music consultant, called 'the Man with the Golden Ear' by *Time* magazine and well known for managing pop bands.

He asked Olivia to star in the 1970's Sci-Fi film titled '*Toomorrow*'and to bring to life the music group '*Toomorrow*' formed in the film and take it public. 'it was said Kirshner was trying to repeat his earlier TV and music group creation successhe had with the Monkees). [13]

Teaming up with Harry Saltzman (the maker of the popular James Bond movies), *Toomorrow* the film was to be launched via the cinema and the group would release an album and single. The whole project did not go well. In an interview in 1983, Olivia said she had been asked to do one scene in her underwear but refused and burst into tears at the very thought! [14]

The film *Toomorrow* soundtrack was technically Olivia's first major release debut album (not solo but group). '*You're My Baby Now*' was released as a 7' single with picture sleeve on RCA Records, with '*Goin' Back*' as the B side. The movie ran for one week in London theatres and the soundtrack didn't really sell, but the creative juices were flowing.

Despite this setback, within a short space of time, Olivia's popularity soared and she was named Best British Female Vocalist for two successive years by *Record Mirror* magazine. [14] And, along with her increasing list of hit singles, Olivia appeared on Cliff Richard's weekly television show It's Cliff Richard (1970-1974), often joined by her fiancé Bruce. 'She had an early go at English folk-pop stardom in the Sixties — with her angelic chirp, blonde hair, blue eyes, and blinding white teeth, she was like a G-rated version of Marianne Faithfull.' [15]

Her early UK career was closely tied with Cliff Richard's – her association with Cliff and the Shadows brought her music to a wide audience, touring Europe with Cliff and the band in 1971 and appearing on his later TV show *Get Away With Cliff.*

ONJ released her first solo album, *If Not For Yo*u, in 1971 with Festival Records, and the single of the same name was her first No.1 hit, modelled on a previous remake by George Harrison. The second single, '*Banks of the Ohio*', a murder ballad previously recorded by folk idols Joan Baez and Arlo Guthrie, also went to number 1 in Australia and number 6 in the UK.

'*If Not for You*' was a song written by Bob Dylan and originally recorded for his 1970 album *New Morning* and the Olivia version was produced by Farrar and Bruce Welch. It was this song's success that persuaded Olivia to up traps and move to the good old USA in 1975 and pivot her musical style and give country music her heartfelt attention.

1972: Olivia released her second album, and was invited to be Cliff Richards' resident guest on his ridiculously popular national BBC-TV musical variety show for 13 weeks in a row.

Perhaps without even knowing it yet, Olivia was keeping illustrious company. Her next single, '*What is life*', was written by George Harrison and then John Denver lent a hand with writing the single '*Take Me Home Country Roads*', which she recorded for her album *Let Me Be There*. This became her first Top 10 single in the US. Again, the US is beckoning as the next step in her career.

1973: ONJ released her third album in three years, titled *Music Makes My Day* and then – high praise, indeed – she was asked to represent the UK at the world's biggest and most decadent singing competition, *Eurovision*!

Eurovision is one of the greatest song contests in the world. It is a competition that brings together nations, genders and sexual orientations. And to top it all off, the voted winners are always catapulted onto the world stage and rightly so.

Olivia chose to sing a sentimental ballad called '*Long Live Love*', which was picked by the British public. They also chose her costume –a hippie-style, flowing baby-blue dress.

Imagine getting this chance to sing on a world stage and you come up against ABBA singing '*Waterloo*'! Not even the power of Olivia could knock this magnificent pop music-altering, Swedish foursome off the winner's podium, but she did come in a very respectable fourth.

All six song candidates from the contest were recorded by Olivia and included on her *Long Live Love* album, her first for EMI Records.

The public was starting to notice, especially in the US, UK and Australia, that Olivia was reinventing herself as a country music singer.

In the earlier phase of her career, Ms. Newton-John beguiled listeners with a high, supple, vibrato-warmed voice that paired amiably with the kind of swooning middle-of-the-road pop that, in the mid-1970s, often passed for country music. [16]

1973's '*Let Me Be There*' also charted high on *Billboard's* country singles chart. She hit the country Top 10 six more times, winning the Best Female Country Vocal Performance Grammy for '*Let Me Be There*' and the Academy of Country Music's Top Female Vocalist prize in 1974.

'The popularity of Olivia Newton-John opened up country music to new audiences, including international ones, while Newton-John's success in country helped create a foundation under her career, and facilitated her move to the United States.' [17]

Now became the time to fully appreciate Olivia and her colossal impact on country music here and abroad.

Chapter 4

Country Music Star

'There's questions we're always hearing everywhere we go
Like how do I cut a record or get on a country show?
Well, it takes more than just ambition and three chords on an old guitar
There's a few more things you ought to learn to be a country star'
'How to Be a Country Star'
1979 song by The Statler Brothers

Country music lovers embraced Olivia Newton-John's music when it landed in the United States of America. Her 'more folk-oriented early sound meant she was categorised 'as country in North Americana', and she turned out to be a formidable artist in the country music realm.' [1]

Seven of her singles were Top 10 Hot Country Songs hits between 1973 and 1975, including her signature tunes '*Have You Never Been Mellow*' and '*I Honestly Love You*'. These magnificent tunes were also hits on the pop and adult contemporary charts. A three-way chart slam – Olivia's sweet, non-intimidating disposition and her unique and delicate voice meant her songs travelled where they were liked and where they fitted, not just down the one musical trail.

She dominated various charts for so many years because her music crossed many genre borders. The versatility and dynamism of the Adult Contemporary (AC) genre included . Adult Contemporary music has serious longevity and long-time listeners. It's ranks are full of the great music ballads of many generations, whether it's from soft rock to. Famous musical artists in this genre include Frank Sinatra, Rod Stewart, Diana Ross, Elton John, Paul Kelly, Air Supply, George Michael, Leo Sayer, Savage

Garden, Bryan Adams, Amy Winehouse, Garth Brooks, Shania Twain, Sam Smith, Lady Gaga, Adele, Indigo Girls and, of course, our Olivia.

Olivia knew the secret to longevity in music is changing your metaphorical and actual image – not so you are unrecognisable but so you move and glide with the times.

'The impact and influence that Olivia Newton-John left upon country music in the mid '70s would be criminal to resign to a passing footnote or afterthought.' [2] Olivia's contribution opened up an entirely new world within the genre.

Music is a global energy force: pop music in the UK and USA is pop music in Australia, and so is country music. Australian country music is heartfelt and born from living on the land. It's a melting pot of American, British and Irish folk music and the works of our traditional Australian poets like Henry Lawson and Banjo Paterson.

Olivia's impact on country music was not just in the US but here in Australia. 'Hers is a seminal Australian voice that has broken down barriers (and brick walls), paving the way for a more diverse sound and representation within country music and beyond in Australia.' [3]

The Australian Country Music Hall of Fame is home to stars like Slim Dusty, Olivia Newton-John, John Williamson, Keith Urban, Lee Kernaghan and Kasey Chambers, with a splash of the great Nick Cave and Paul Kelly. Kasey Chambers' incredible country music career includes five number one albums to date (the most number one albums by an Australian female artist, equalled only by Kylie Minogue and Olivia Newton-John over all musical genres). [4]

It has been suggested that two changes in pop music helped Olivia achieve her domination of country music: firstly, the rise of 'soft rock' in reaction to the harder rock and punk of the late 1960s, and secondly, the 'mainstreaming of country music, also epitomised by stars like John Denver and Anne Murray. [5]

The sanctity of country music was brought into question as 'mainstreaming' became an issue in 1973 when Olivia won the Country Music Association's Most Promising Female Vocalist and in 1974, after she was chosen as the CMA's Female Vocalist of the Year over the more traditional stars like Loretta Lynn and the Queen herself Dolly Parton. 'Here she was a non-American whose material blurred traditional genre lines.' [6]

The Country Music Association's founding premise in 1958 was to keep country music pure and to prevent the infiltration of rock 'n' roll. *Rolling Stone* magazine labelled the win a 'flat-out scandal when this Aussie interloper won the Country Music Association award for Female Vocalist of the Year. George Jones and Tammy Wynette were so outraged, they organised 50 other Nashville veterans in a CMA boycott and founded the Association of Country Entertainers.' [7]

Purists were fed up with so-called 'non-country' artists infringing on their charts and winning their awards, they wanted country music to remain a'separate and distinct form of entertainment'. [8]

To add insult to injury, Olivia recorded her country tunes in London and not the Holy Grail city of Nashville. Thankfully, the anger towards Olivia and her win didn't last long, and she moved on with much grace and gratitude. After winning the Grammy Award for Pop Music in 1974, she offered to give her statue back, but the board would not have it.

In her autobiography, Loretta Lynn (*The Coal Miner's Daughter*) provided her candid perspective on Olivia's CMA win. 'I've got no complaints. Look, she walked off with the Grammy Award for 1974 pop music. When you're hot, you're hot, that's all.' [9]

Olivia was gracious throughout the whole affair, and the day after the Grammy award ceremony, she offered to give her statue back, but the board wouldn't have it.

In 1975 Olivia said, 'I've never claimed to be a country singer; to call yourself that, you'd have to be born in that background. I simply love country music and its straightforwardness. And since the records have also sold well outside of the country audience, it seems to me that we're broadening the acceptance for country music.' [10a]

'This was a perfect response from a star who was fundamentally polite and positive, but far from a pushover.' [10b]

Through it all, Olivia Newton-John listened to all this criticism and worked even harder. She released her second country album, *Have You Never Been Mellow* in 1975. It went on to become #1 in the country charts and spent six weeks on top.

Her next country album, *Don't Stop Belivin'*, was recorded in Nashville in 1976, and her team hired long-time A-list session musicians such as Charlie McCoy on harmonica, and Weldon Myrick on steel guitar. Her move to Nashville 'and finally moving to the US full-time was another Country music pacifier'. [11]

This move and the whole public spat inspired Stella Parton, Dolly's younger sister, to record '*Ode to Olivia*' and release it to the public in 1975. Stella was a country singer in her own right whose biggest hit was the 1975 classic '*I Want to Hold You in My Dreams Tonight*'.

Stella's '*Ode to Olivia*' contains references to a number of Olivia's songs and was a response to the criticism she had received from the American country music community for allegedly not being a 'true' country singer.

'I was trying to apologise to her [Newton-John] ... I thought it was embarrassing that they got so irate that they had gone to such trouble ... I never will forget I played that song ['*Ode to Olivia*'] in the studio for [my sister] Dolly and she said, 'Oh Lord, Stella, don't let Porter hear that.' I said, 'Screw Porter, I don't care what he thinks.' ... They just got all ticked off because none of them won that year.' [12]

Porter Wayne Wagoner was an incredible country music singer, well known for his stunning handmade ornate Nudie suits and blond 'pompadour' hairdo. He first introduced Dolly Parton on his US television show in 1967. Thankfully, Dolly (who initially aligned herself with the old schoolers) later contacted and supported ONJ. As a thank you to Dolly, Olivia went on to record a cover version of Dolly's magnum opus '*Jolene*' for her 1976 album *Come On Over.*

Ode to Olivia
By Stella Parton and Bob G. Dean

Nudie makes rhinestone suits
I guess he's made a million
But nobody can copy you
There's just one Olivia
But you've built the bridge
and crossed over into country
And we ain't got the right
To say you're not country

We ain't got the right to say
to say you're not country
You've just a country girl
It's so plain to see
We Honestly Love You

To date, Olivia Newton-John remains the only non-American singer to win a CMA Award for Female Vocalist of the Year. She actually went on to make several more country albums before moving into the pop and film soundtrack arena. Then, in 1998, ONJ made a welcome comeback to country music after two decades with the album *Back with a Hear*t, released in the US and critically reviewed as 'thoroughly winning'. [13]

In 1974, Olivia broke up with her long-time boyfriend Bruce Welch. She went on a tour and a holiday in the South of France where she met Lee Kramer. Lee was working for a business with his brother, importing and exporting cowboy boots to and from London, but after he met Olivia he ended up following her to the US and becoming her manager 'who managed her crucial leap to Los Angeles to capitalise on her deal with MCA Records in the early '70s.' [15]

They spilt in '76, got back together a few times, but eventually split again after a decade together – perhaps the intrusion of business pulled them apart romantically.

Olivia's single '*I Honestly Love You*', from the *If You Love Me, Let Me Know* album (1974) became her lifetime signature song. Written and composed by Jeff Barry and Peter Allen, this ballad became her first pop number one. The album also scored at the 1975 Grammy Awards for Best Female Pop Vocal Performance and Record of the Year.

The lure of cowboy boots and country music was starting to fade for Olivia as the pop music and disco era softly called to her. 'Olivia made a career out of fitting in wherever she went.' [14]

It was time for Olivia to relocate to the USA to fully realise her potential in the entertainment world.

Since the age of14, Olivia had always strongly believed in the power of the TV media and that it was the best way to build your profile and get your songs known. She hit the US TV circuit, running with one of her first appearances on *The Dean Martin Show*, then *The Andy Williams Show* and then the megastar Bob Hope's show. She was crooning with legends and loving it. She found them all to be so kind and encouraging and later, when her only child Chloe Rose was born, Bob Hope sent her a baby gift.

One night in Florida Olivia went to a concert by Australian singer Helen Reddy and when backstage, Helen said these prophetic words to her: 'If you want to make it in America, you must live here.' From that moment ONJ knew what to do. She said, 'The seed was planted. This trip wasn't just a visit, I was relocating.'

Helen Reddy already had a #1 single in the United States under her belt, a Grammy Award, and was the host of her own variety show on US television. Born and raised in Australia, Reddy became a naturalised American citizen in 1974. Reddy really played an important part in furthering Olivia's career because it was through her that Olivia met *Grease* film producer Allan Carr – the meeting that completely changed Olivia's life.

When Helen Reddy sadly passed away in September 2020, Olivia posted on Facebook: 'Helen Reddy encouraged me and paved the way for my success in the USA. Thank you Helen for your friendship, your voice and your passion for women's rights – you will be missed.' [17]

ONJ was only 27 when she went to live in America in 1975. With John Farrar's help she pulled a great band together and took up residence with Lee in Malibu, near Los Angeles. Her sister Rona and Rona's son Emmerson came to stay and soon it was off on tour on the back of the '*I Honestly Love You*' single.

The rapturous welcome for her next album, *Have You Never Been Mellow* – with both the single and album going to number one in the US – was confirmation her relocation was a good idea.

'Seventies AM-radio soft-rock Olivia, when she kept finding new ways to get her heart broken on hit after hit. No happy songs for these lass. She was the star of the Mellow Era who actually had the gall to use the word 'mellow' in a song title – her Number One therapy.' [18] Clearly *Rolling Stone* agreed – she had cracked the American market and her fan base was growing every day.

For 45 years, Olivia held the Guinness World Record for the shortest gap (154 days) by a female between new Number 1 albums (*If You*

Love Me, Let Me Know and *Have You Never Been Mellow*) on the US *Billboard* 200 album charts until Taylor Swift in 2020 (140 days with *Folklore* and *Evermore*). [19]

Albums that followed were *Clearly Love* (1975), *Come On Over* (1976) and *Don't Stop Believin'* (1976), which she took on tour in Japan. The trade mag *Cashbox* named her Top Vocalist of 1975 – in both singles and albums (Helen Reddy came second in both). *Billboard* stated that Olivia and Elton John were the top-selling artists for the year.

The late '70s were a cavalcade of great moments for Olivia: she finally hosted her own US TV show, *A Special with Olivia Newton-John*. This was her first time in control and a life goal achieved; it must have seemed a world away from *Sing Sing Sing* in Australia.

Have You Never Been Mellow was considered the best of her '70s solo albums. Olivia was slowly phasing country out of her sound and in 1976 the pop world arrived in earnest as she covered the Bee Gees for the title track of *Come on Over* – her seventh studio album, which peaked at number two on the US Country album charts. The lead single and album title was written by Barry Gibb and Robin Gibb and originally featured on the Bee Gees' 1975 album *Main Course*, and came in at number 23 on the US *Billboard* Hot 100. The country charts still loved everything ONJ did and it peaked at #5. This clever girl was getting in early with the Brothers Gibb and that classic sound!

Cashbox magazine said, 'The constantly maturing vocals of Olivia Newton-John continue their musical growth … Ms Newton-John puts effective emotion into every song.'

Her US audience had loved her for her delicate delivery of ballads and country songs, which is what made her first compilation, *Olivia Newton-John's Greatest Hits* (1977), a smash hit. The album collected all of ONJ's American Top 40 singles released between 1971 and 1977. It was still classified a country album and was certified double platinum in the

US and platinum in the UK. How amazing to not even be 30 years old and have a greatest hits album!

Never off the top of the charts for long, in 1977 the mid-tempo waltz '*Sam*', from *Don't Stop Believin'*, returned Olivia to the No. 1 spot on the AC chart and she also put out the album *Good Thing Better* and hosted a BBC TV special, *Only Olivia*.

In a very memorable moment, ONJ also made her debut at the legendary NY Metropolitan Opera House – giving each guest a red de-thorned rose. This touch of elegant class highlights the essence of Olivia in her entire life. It shows both her inner gracefulness and her public gratitude to her dear long-term fans.

'I've had many lives in music. I've had country when I started, then I crossed over into pop ... I have such a large repertoire to choose from,' Olivia Newton-John once told CNN. [20]

If Olivia had slipped down to Santa Monica Pier to have her fortune read at this time, surely the gypsy would have said, 'You think you are a star now, STRAP IN, here comes *GREASE!*'

Each step in her performer's journey was needed to set up the next. Each step demanded a change in method, and often a change in place, and she delivered each time enthusiastically. Her folk songs led to the UK; the UK led to world TV, better song writing, touring, and a dedicated team behind her, which all led to Country USA, which was now leading to film domination.

Before Olivia Newton-John was Sandy in *Grease*, Olivia was one of the great country singers of the 1970s. Her pure talent and vocal prowess in country-styled music, was surely why she came to the attention of Hollywood where she was soon jettisoned into movie stardom alongside John Travolta. And what a team they made: those scenes in *Grease* are legendary.' [21]

Historically and politically, the '70s were a tumultuous time in the

US: the Vietnam War had divided the country, African Americans, Native Americans, women and the LGBTQIA+ community were for fighting for equality.

In the music world, hard rock, arena rock, prog rock and new wave were on the rise. Punk and the blues had raised their heads and soft rock and pop were the radio darlings. The Bee Gees were one of, if not the biggest late '70s musical act, dominating album sales, and music charts in so many countries. They spearheaded the disco and pop music scenes … who can forget the 1977 movie starring John Travolta, *Saturday Night Fever*, which changed everything? Disco was King!

John Tavolta was a pivotal musical film actor and only 22 when he won the spot of Danny in the 1978 movie *Grease*, then going on to do the *Saturday Night Fever* sequel, 1983's *Staying Alive*. The hand of fate perhaps, or the magic of Hollywood, saw Australian singer Helen Reddy throw a dinner party/pool party in Los Angeles, inviting the film producer Alan Carr, who was casting around for his new musical *Grease*. He ended up sitting across the table from Olivia. 'As Carr tells it, the moment they started speaking, he knew he had found his Sandy.' [22]

Carr would later say it was Olivia who needed persuading.

ONJ had been burned by her experience in the '60s sci-fi film *Toomorrow* and did not want to jeopardise her successful music career with another roll of the dice on silver screen fame. To persuade her, Carr changed Sandy from an American, as originally written, to an Australian, allowing Olivia to use her native accent.

'She had a brilliant voice,' Travolta would later tell *Vanity Fair*. 'I never let up on it. I insisted that we cast her.' [23]

Olivia was 28 and John 22. Could she play 17-year-old high school student Sandra Dee? Nervously, Olivia headed to London to watch the play performed, with actor Richard Gere in the role of Danny Zuko. She loved the whole fun vibe of the story. But it actually took a visit from Travolta to her home to convince her. In her autobiography she remembered: 'Then Danny Zuko himself walked up my front steps...' And it was that moment that changed everything. Olivia explained how John Travolta had told producers 'there was only one human being on this planet I could see as Sandy'. [24]

So, she took on the role of a lifetime, kept her Aussie accent and demanded and earned equal billing with co-star John Travolta. She was always flexing her girl power – a fantastic model for female liberation.

Interestingly, she was not producer Alan Carr and director Randal Kleiser's first choice for the role of Sandy. They had wanted Carrie Fisher (*Star Wars*) and Susan Dey (*The Partridge Family*). The role was also offered to Marie Osmond, who passed because she was uncomfortable with Sandy's transformation from sweet to sexy.

Sadly, Elvis Presley was considered for the role of The Teen Angel, but died in 1977 before production. I believe John Travolta harnessed the spirit of the King in his luminous *Grease* performance.

'Once Olivia Newton-John starred in *Grease* opposite John Travolta in 1978, the entire world changed for her, including her music. She became exclusively a pop performer, and an international superstar.' [26]

'I solve my problems and I see the light
We gotta plug and think, we gotta feed it right
There ain't no danger we can go too far
We start believing now that we can be who we are
Grease is the word'
'*Grease*', lyrics by Frankie Valli

Chapter 5

Grease – Ms Sandra Newton-John

'We take the pressure and we throw away
Conventionality belongs to yesterday
There is a chance that we can make it so far
We start believing now that we can be who we are
Grease is the word'
Grease lyrics – Frankie Valli

For Dame Olivia, the prophetic song lines above could not ring any truer. It was time to (publicly at least) shed her 'Good Girl' image and try something unconventional.

'Olivia Newton-John guaranteed her place in pop culture history when she purred 'tell me about it, stud' at the end of *Grease*, the 1978 musical film that has become part of each subsequent generation's childhood.' [1]

The chance she took playing the film character 'Sandra Dee' propelled her into the realm of mega stardom and all because she believed she now really was the entertainer she had worked towards all these previous years.

Dancing from one stepping stone to the next, Olivia's luck and hard work continued to amaze even her. In her memoir, '*Sandy Newton-John*', as some called her then, admitted: '*Grease* lifted my career into the stratosphere'. [2]

The role in *Grease* would come to define Olivia Newton-John's career.

Behind the scenes, Olivia had become somewhat disillusioned with the music industry in 1978 when she came up against MCA Records.

In 1975, ONJ and MCA Records signed an initial two-year, four-album deal where she had to deliver two LPs a year. MCA also had the option of extending the contract if the artist did not deliver on time. Her fourth album, *Making a Good Thing Better*, was late. So MCA – which obviously wanted to keep her – filed a breach-of-contract case. Newton-John countersued for $10 million and claimed that because, in her opinion, MCA did not adequately promote and advertise her product, this freed her from their agreement. MCA's countersuit requested $1 million in damages and a promise Newton-John couldn't work with another record company. The result was Olivia was forbidden from offering her recording services to another label until the five-year pact had run its course. [3]

One positive was that as a result of this case, record companies changed their contracts, with them based on a set number of albums recorded by a musician and not a specific number of years. A hard lesson, but Olivia made it easier for those who followed – as was her lovely nature. But it did leave a nasty taste in ONJ's mouth and she was looking for a change in career direction.

The famous pool party at the home of the 'godmother to Hollywood's Aussie colony' [4a] (Helen Reddy) happened, and film producer Allan Carr(who revived the art of musicals) noticed Livvy's' 'inherent it-factor', saying he was 'knocked out' by his dinner-party companion. 'I told her immediately she was everything a movie star should be.' [4b]

Allan Carr based *Grease* on the 1950s Broadway musical, which John Travolta was already familiar with as he had played Doody in the earlier Broadway production.

Three other *Grease* stars also appeared in the Broadway production: Jeff Conaway (Danny on Broadway and Kenickie in the movie), Barry Pearl (Sonny on Broadway and Doody in the movie) and Jamie Donnelly (Jan on Broadway and in the movie).

New to the musical game, our Olivia signed on as the leading female 'who in 1978, the year of the film's release, was a kind of early Taylor Swift figure, melding country and pop – this was a testament to the quiet authority of the Australian'. [5]

With the play's original American Sandy Dumbrowski now changed to Sandy Olsson – an Aussie who had holidayed, and then moved, to the US with her family – production began.

Spoiler alert for those who have not seen the film, Sandy was the stereotypical 'nice girl' who falls in love with a '*grease*r' named Danny (John Travolta) and at the end of the film they reverse their roles – Danny changes to squeaky clean and Sandy – resplendentin skin-tight blank pants and a leather jacket – becomes a 'bad girl'.

Off screen, Olivia was getting her 'swagger on' confidence-wise,and from now on she would always 'stand by who she was and not bend to industry whims … Here was a calm, self-possessed, poised young woman swimming in the big Hollywood shark tank, and unlike her transformation from good girl to vixen in *Grease*, she didn't need black skin-tight leggings, sky-high heels or a cigarette dangling from her siren-red lips to get her way.' [6]

At only 28, she'd always had an inner-strength, but she was now an established singer who had sold millions of records before stepping into the role of Sandy. She knew who she was and what she could do. She'd fought for recognition outside Australia and won. And she did all this 'at a time before *Crocodile Dundee* gave American audiences a compass (albeit a shaky one) for Australian culture'. [7] Olivia was a pioneer and a success story in both the well-trodden fields of music and film with background help from her manager/boyfriend Lee Kramer, and her John Farrar-led team who helped steer Olivia through the transition from country singer to mega-star actress, navigating this upcoming successful period of both musicals, *Grease* and *Xanadu*.

Grease was originally released in the United States on June 16, 1978, and was an immediate SMASH HIT at box-offices all over the world. 'Olivia Newton-John was that rare thing: a wonderfully unselfconscious star' who became 'Queen of the movie soundtracks'. [8]

The cold hard sales facts and sheer reach of this film are quite extraordinary and still punching well above their weight 45 years later!

After 66 days, *Grease* had grossed $100 million to become Paramount's second-highest-grossing film, behind *The Godfather*, and was the highest-grossing film in 1978. *Grease* became one of the highest-grossing movie musicals ever, 'besting even *The Sound of Music*.' [9]

It remained the highest-grossing live-action musical until 2012 when it was overtaken by *Les Misérables*, and it remained the US champion until 2017 when it was surpassed by *Beauty and the Beast. Grease* is now the seventh-highest-grossing live-action musical worldwide. [10]

The iconic soundtrack is one of the highest-selling albums of all time and includes songs such as '*You're the One That I Want*' and '*Hopelessly Devoted To You*', written and produced by John Farrar.

Years later, in 2006, Olivia ended up suing, claiming that Universal Music International owed her more than $1 million in royalties for the album, which was originally released in 1978. The matter was settled out of court.

Not everyone was a *Grease* fan. Famously, in October 1978, 'Bob Geldof yawned and tore up a photograph of John Travolta on Top of the Pops … but there was still a sense that Bob was desecrating an icon.' *Grease* was bigger in the UK and Ireland than anywhere else. And songs from the soundtrack were at the top of the charts for nearly a third of the year. [11]

John Farrar's incredible songwriting and music production was so much a part of Olivia's success, it's hard to separate the two. He was so tuned into her sense of identity and pivoted every time she needed a change. They were family. Famously at the Sydney, Australia premiere of *Grease*, on Aug 3 1978, 'because Olivia was unable to attend the Melbourne premiere or in fact fly down to her former home city she flew many of her friends to Sydney for the night, including John Farrar's mother, who, when Olivia lived in Melbourne, was like a second mum'. [12]

This epic soundtrack was nominated for a Grammy for Album of the Year in 1979, with Olivia's best-known ballad ever, '*Hopelessly Devoted to You*' also scoring a Grammy nomination for Best Pop Vocal Performance, Female. This classic song also received an Oscar nomination for Best Original Song, which she performed live at the 1979 Academy Awards.

Other just as well-known singles from the *Grease* soundtrack –'*You're the One That I Want*' and '*Summer Nights*' – shot to number one on both sides of the Atlantic.

Olivia's character of Sandy was ranked number 89 on *Premiere* magazine's 100 Greatest Movie Characters of All Time and the soundtrack became the most successful musical movie soundtrack in history and spent 12 weeks at Number 1, with Olivia nominated for a Golden Globe Award as Best Actress in a Musical.

Grease was re-released for its 20th anniversary in 1998 and ranked as the second highest-grossing film behind *Titanic* in its opening weekend.

Olivia explained: 'I think the songs are timeless. They're fun and have great energy. The '50s-feel music has always been popular, and it's nostalgic for my generation, and then the young kids are rediscovering it every 10 years or so, it seems. People buying the album was a way for them to remember those feelings of watching the movie and feelings of that time period. I feel very grateful to be a part of this movie that's still loved so much.' [13]

Carr's film, based on the original musical written by Jim Jacobs and Warren Casey, was so named *Grease* after the 1950s United States working-class youth subculture known as *grease*rs, with the musical set in 1959 at fictional Rydell High School.

The musical score models itself on the enduring sounds of early rock and roll, and the plot bravely looks at many social issues that are still prevelant today, like teen pregnancy, conflict, peer group pressure vs friendship, and the politics of being in a gang. The *Grease* storyline follows the traditional literary exploration of the fall from innocence to experience.

Production was mapped out in five weeks and shot over two months. They were given a $6 million budget by Paramount CEO Barry Diller, 'who dismissed the whole thing as so much cinematic cotton candy. Its leading lady was foreign and untried, there were so many reasons *Grease* should not have worked.' [14]

The mood of the film strives towards being light, and the culture and lyrics borne from it still appeal to the public today. It's a rollickingly great love story that starts out in high school with Sandy, a sweet 17 years old, moving schools only to find her mysterious summer love is King of Cool in the new school and quite the different lad to who he pretended to be.

The film was shot in 1977, starting in June at Venice High School in Los Angeles. LA that summer was brutally hot, making the dance sequences – particularly the famous National Bandstand scene, filmed over five days inside – a nightmare.

The opening beach scene was shot at Malibu's Leo Carrillo State Beach, a clever reference to the classic flick *From Here to Eternity* about another controversial love affair. Who can forget Burt Lancaster and Deborah Kerr and those bathers on the beach! Just as no one can forget Olivia's skin-tight black disco pants at the end of *Grease*. It is incredible how iconic a costume can become and how fashion can represent and challenge the changing of sexual freedoms and ideas.

The race was filmed at the Los Angeles River, between the First and Seventh Street Bridges, and the final scene, where the carnival took place, used John Marshall High School.

'Allan would come in standing on the dolly cart in his caftan, with his arms outstretched like Moses, and he would say, 'Children, children, gather round,' and then give us the reports on the dailies and how they were being received,' recalls Dinah Manoff, who played Marty, one of the Pink Ladies. [15]

Let's not forget to mention the extraordinary choreography and costumes that gave *Grease* its timeless edge. That final vivid change of Sandy Newton-John – from Sandra Dee to one of the greatest vamps of all time.

John Travolta was the perfect Danny. He has an original strut all his own and, bolstered by his 1977 film success with *Saturday Night Fever*, he was positively on fire cinematically.

While filming *Grease*, Travolta was actually still coping with the loss of his great love, the actress Diana Hyland, who had died that spring, losing her battle with cancer. Suffering from insomnia during much of the *Grease* shoot, 'it acted as a giant distraction for me,' Travolta says of doing *Grease* during his mourning. 'Probably the healthiest thing I could have done was to be in back-to-back movies, because I was very sad.' [16]

In cinematic history there have been those rare diamond entertainers who straddle both the film and music worlds successfully – Judy Garland, Doris Day, and Barbra Streisand and now Olivia, and after her, Cher and Lady Gaga.

There are 'few talents that can force the entertainment industry machine to accommodate them as they are', [17] which is definitely why Olivia was the Queen for so many decades.

Grease had brought together a double threat – Olivia as both singer and actress, sweet and serious, and John as the up-and-coming movie male star who could dance and sing and smoulder. John and ONJ's authentic chemistry was another reason this movie went ballistic.

'Summer lovin', had me a blast
Summer lovin', happened so fast
Met a girl crazy for me
Met a boy cute as can be
Summer days drifting away
To, uh oh, those summer nights

He got friendly holding my hand
Well, she got friendly down in the sand
He was sweet, just turned eighteen
Well, she was good, you know what I mean
Summer heat, boy and girl meet
But, uh oh, those summer nights'

'Summer Nights'
(from *Grease* soundtrack)

Grease co-star Didi Conn – who played Frenchie – said that it was no secret that Travolta was secretly infatuated with Olivia. But ONJ said in later interviews that their timing was never right for a romance. 'We were both with other people when we were filming,' she said in 2018. 'I think, respectfully, it just didn't happen.' [18a]

They were always close in real life, and on hearing of her death, a heartbroken Travolta wrote: 'Yours from the first moment I saw you and forever! Your Danny, your John!' [18b] In the 2023 Academy Awards' In Memoriam segment, Travolta also paid a tearful tribute to his Grease co-star saying, "They've touched our hearts, they made us smile and became dear friends who we will always remain hopelessly devoted to."

What a combination and it worked. As Olivia said, 'As for highlights, of course *Grease* changed my life and I will always be grateful for that experience.‘ [19]

The film's world premiere was June 2 1978 at the Mann's Chinese Theatre on Hollywood Boulevard. It was a recorded night of glorious pandemonium, screaming fans, poodle skirts, slicked-back hair and cinema history.

'The *Grease* premiere after-party was held at Studio 54. Elton John was there, Grace Jones was there, I just remember it was crazy,' Olivia revealed. 'It was wild and fun and a very exciting night.' [20]

The *New York Times'* critic Vincent Canby described the film as 'a larger, funnier, wittier and more imaginative-than-Hollywood movie with a life that is all its own … Olivia's American star was properly lit.' [21]

The *New Yorker* said, 'She was a clever actress, an intelligent chameleon and at heart a real Lady … Newton-John became a household name across the world for playing Sandy in the 1978 musical *Grease*. The movie captures the quintessential American high school experience, with Newton-John its most apple pie character.' [22]

Olivia is a lifelong role model to young girls everywhere – Australian musicians especially. She knew she was the best she could be for her adoring public. But Olivia was never really a bad girl – she was just good at her job! Her good girl 'Sandy Dee personality radiated far stronger than that of her inner provocateur' and 'Olivia Newton-John was that rare creature, a genuine girl-next-door in Hollywood. A pop-star parents approved of and a role model to young girls everywhere.' [23]

In her heartfelt autobiograhy *Don't Stop Believin'*, Olivia describes working on the *Grease* movie as 'as tale of two Sandys'. Sandy #1 is best summed up in the *Grease* song '*Look At Me, I'm Sandra Dee*'

I don't drink (no)
Or swear (no)

I don't rat my hair (eew)
I get ill from one cigarette
(cough, cough, cough)
Keep your filthy paws
Off my silky draws

Sandy #2, in her owns words, was 'deliciously wild' … 'it felt empowering as pre-adrenalin and the idea of claiming my won sexiness rushed through my body'. [24]

Her transformation was groundbreaking because on film it was the character's own idea and, yes, there were some serious new threads involved but Sandy's attitude and, importantly her confidence, changed. Her inner self became her outer self and the result was a lightbulb moment for the character and for Olivia personally. 'Like everyone, I've got different sides of my personality. I've my dominant self, my need-to-be-dominated self, the sane Olivia and the crazy Olivia. Playing these different characters gave me a chance to show strange parts people haven't seen much.' [25]

This debate is a constant when discussing Olivia Newton-John's career: 'The Two Sandys dilemma - Good 'Apple Pie' girl or bad 'Vixen' girl. [26]

The change on screen that took Sandy from pigtails to black leather as well as a much-discussed moment in Olivia's actual life and career trajectory, it was important historically as a female experience. Her new image had people talking.

Olivia came out in defence of her new look in *Rolling Stone* in 1978, saying: 'Innocent, I'm not … People still seem to see me as the girl next door.' Doris Day, she pointed out, had four husbands, yet she was still viewed as 'the virgin'.

But *Grease*, like all previous generation films, must deal with criticisms of their dated sexual politics. Does *Grease* still hold its impact today –

has it aged out, is it working against the evolution of feminism today? In response to *Grease* being called out for being sexist, Olivia said years later 'empowerment comes from calling your own shots and being who you want to be'. [27] She also wanted to remind critics of the original premise and time the film was created. 'I think in this particular instance, it's kind of silly because the movie was made in the '70s about the '50s. It was a stage play, it's a musical, it's fun. It's a fun movie musical and not [meant] to be taken so seriously.'

'I think we need to relax a little bit and just enjoy things for what they are, and I didn't see it like that at all, I think it's just a fun movie that entertains people. That's all.' [28]

Olivia didn't believe the two Sandy's moment was a deeper metaphor for a woman to change to get her man. Both characters change, so perhaps love and compromise is the message. It's simply a girl in love with a guy. 'Everyone forgets that, at the end, he changes for her, too.' [29]

I believe Olivia was showing the ladies out there that you could be both Sandys and this whole makeover succeeded in updating ONJ's public image in the music world as well. Her '80s sex symbol phase was starting to emerge. 'Little did we know that a pair of sleek, skin-tight black pants would set off a worldwide tremor that would last for decades.' [30]

Grease's phenomenal success naturally spawned many spinoffs and sequels and prequels – nothing that captured the original spirit but all serving to boost the vibe of this classic and keep it alive. There is also a prequel in the works titled *Summer Lovin'*.

And the spinoff *Rise of the Pink Ladies* is set four years before *Grease*, focusing on the iconic girl group from the film.

Grease 2 was a 1982 American musical romantic comedy film and the sequel to the *Grease*, with clean-cut British student Michael Carrington (a cousin of Sandy's) and Michelle Pfeiffer as Stephanie Zinone, the leader of the Pink Ladies. The producer proposed an idea that never eventuated that Travolta and Olivia would reprise their characters as a now married couple running a gas station near the end of the film, with Travolta singing a new number, 'Gas Pump Jockey'.

In 2003, Olivia Newton-John confirmed that a second sequel was being developed. 'They're writing it, and we'll see what happens. If the script looks good, I'll do it. But I haven't seen the script, and it has to be cleverly done.'

This script was later adapted into a musical, *Cool Rider*, and modified for the stage.

Rather than reappearing for the sequel, Travolta went quiet for two years from 1981 after the underrated film *Blow Out*, while Olivia was in the midst of releasing her twelfth album, *Physical.*

But she was always grateful for the film that made her a star. 'Forty-one years on, it's still phenomenal,' she said. 'John [Travolta] and I still can't believe it. I'm so grateful to have been part of that movie and to feel all that love – it's pretty incredible, isn't it?' [31]

'*Grease* was as gorgeously innocent as Newton-John herself, and the beguiling niceness of everyone involved made it a rocket-fuelled hit. Newton-John's wonderfully unselfconscious performance as squeaky-clean Sandy gave her a movie star status that she never entirely lost.' [32]

When Olivia passed, around the world *Grease* was revived in cinemas – with money going to breast cancer research, to honour ONJ.

Grease was a pop culture moment, involving discussion, controversy and change. It was a lot for parents of young girls and boys to take in back then: smoking, tight pants, and teenagers having sex. But when Olivia sang '*Hopelessly Devoted to You*', you would have to a robot not to tear up. Even today, fans are just as passionate about this film and Olivia.

Unbelievably, Olivia Newton-John was not among those honoured at the 2022 Emmy Awards on September 12.

Fans spoke out on social media as Olivia was not included in the in memoriam segment at the awards show. She was included online but not on film. An actress who had appeared in shows like *Sordid Lives: The Series, Bette, Murphy Brown* and *Ned and Stacey*, cameos in *Dancing With the Stars, Loose Women, The Talk, RuPaul's Drag Race, The View* and more.

The infuriated public tweeted – 'She is and always will be an icon.'

Olivia's publicist Michael Caprio expressed his frustration to TMZ, saying he was 'personally very disappointed by the snub'. Caprio worked with Olivia for more than two decades, serving as her publicist for 24 years. [33]

Post *Grease*, in the film world, Olivia moved on to *Xanadu*. Andin the music world, her game-changing single, '*Physical*', was only a few years away.

Her music career ran concurrently with her film career – her soundtracks ruled the airwaves. But *Grease* and her on-screen metamorphosis gave Olivia a chance to move into a different musical lane that was nearly as shocking and as exciting and long-lasting as Sandy 2 was.

Applying the appearance of Sandy 2 to her singing career, Olivia titled her next album *Totally Hot*,' and presented herself on the cover in shoulder-to-toe leather.

The album, released at the end of 1978, went platinum, yielding the rock-oriented '*A Little More Love*' with the line, 'Where did my innocence go?'

And although Olivia would not survive a coming onslaught of the far more suggestive pop hits of Prince and Madonna and beyond, 'she showed us a door to a kind of forbidden zone, if you chose to go through it, and naturally, we did'. [34]

Chapter 6

The Magic of Xanadu

'Newton-John was the ultimate 'it' girl.
From cinema's leading lady to pop star, her grip on the world of entertainment lasted for decades.' [1]

Olivia and the silver screen were partners for life. She was both iconic and influential in her celluloid legacy. Her onscreen chemistry with John Travolta, coupled with the genius of Allan Carr in *Grease* 'had started a party that, nearly 38 years later, with every screening, every high-school production, every karaoke sing-along to '*Summer Nights*', shows no signs of dying down.' [2]

ONJ cleverly intertwined both her skills in music and acting, having them reinforce each other and ultimately defining Olivia as more than just a one-trick pony.

'As for highlights, of course *Grease* changed my life and I will always be grateful for that experience.' [3]

Livvy had her up and downs in all her creative pursuits, but after *Grease* played the world's cinema screens, she was jettisoned into the Superstar realm, and even though her next big film, *Xanadu* in 1980, wasn't initially well received, over the years it also grew into a cult classic.

The late '70s were packed with appearances for Olivia. She performed at the famous Music for Unicef concert in New York in 1979, marking The International Year of The Child and singing on stage alongside ABBA, Rod Stewart, the Bee Gees and John Denver. Her 1978 *Greatest Hits* album was selling like crazy, and her *Grease* soundtrack dominated global charts. Her second Olivia TV Special aired in the US and the single '*You're the One That I Want*' went to a magnificent No 1 in Australia.

'Applying the evolution of her *Grease* character to her singing career, Ms Newton-John titled her next album *Totally Hot* and, mirroring her Good Sandy/Bad Sandy in *Grease*, she appeared clad in black leather on the cover. The album went platinum.' [4]

This album 'signalled a change in sound and aesthetic developed in collaboration with her creative team, John Farrar, Steve Kipner, Fleur Thiemeyer and Roger Davies.' [5] *Totally Hot* was not a country-sounding album, but it reached No. 4 on the Country charts. Olivia released the B-side, '*Dancin' 'Round and 'Round*', to Country radio, peaking at No. 29. It became her last charted solo Country airplay single. [6]

Then, in the middle of all this glorious successful chaos, our Olivia was appointed Officer of the Order of the British Empire (OBE) in the 1979 New Year's Honours and Dame Commander of the Order of the British Empire (DBE). Welcome to the roundtable, Dame Olivia Newton-John.

The Dame then swung back to the States and performed at the Oscars, singing '*Hopelessly Devoted to You*' (nominated for Best Song) perfectly on stage. Straight afterwards, riddled with a nasty virus, she spent four days in the LA hospital. It has been said that this song was her moniker tune and 'one of the most effectively saccharine, perfectly sung, love-ridden ballads ever and the crown jewel of the *Grease* soundtrack.' 7.

The new decade opened with Olivia releasing '*I Can't Help It*', a duet with Andy Gibb from his *After Dark* album, and by starring in her third top-rating television special, *Hollywood Nights*.

Returning to Australia for the Royal Command Performance in May at the Sydney Opera House in front of Queen Elizabeth II and Prince Philip was a homecoming highlight for The Dame. What a night – her love of Australia shone brightly here for the entire world to see. She thrived in the company of fellow top entertainers such as Bert Newton, John

Farnham, Peter Allen, Paul Hogan, Julie Anthony and Helen Reddy. She led the grand finale of '*Waltzing Matilda*', joined by a 400-voice choir and the other performers, and out front with Peter Allen, they sang Allen's self-penned '*I Still Call Australia Home*'.

But the big news for Olivia fans was, of course, the upcoming film release of *Xanadu*.

Passing on the offer of *Grease 2*, Olivia Newton-John opted to star in the musical *Xanadu*. 'In the early 1980s, she was seen as part of the 'Australian invasion', a period where Oz culture was particularly prominent on the international stage through acts such as Air Supply and the Little River Band.' Being the clever businesswoman and entertainer that she was, 'Newton-John leaned into the moment.' [8]

Olivia is now firmly in the second phase of her career. She is making 'being Australian' popular, and her movie success has opened some serious career doors for her – time to strap on her roller skates for *Xanadu*, the film.

On the personal front, Olivia and her boyfriend/manager, Lee Kramer, ended their partnership after the filming of *Xanadu*. Olivia had met her future husband, dancer Matt Lattanzi on the film set, and Kramer also decided that it was probably best to end his manager role.

That job was offered to Roger Davies – a wunderkind Australian 'who guided her through the next phase of her career and played an important part in the massive success she enjoyed in the early 1980s, including her multi-million-selling albums *Physical* and *Soul Kiss*.' [9]

Roger Davies, born in 1952, was famous for managing women in the music industry. This titan has an imposing roster, home to acts such as Sherbet (1970 – 1979), Tina Turner (1981 - 2010), James Reyne (1986 – 1990), Tony Joe White (1989 – 2000), Cher (1999 – present), Janet Jackson (1989 – 2002), Joe Cocker (1991 to 2014), Sade (1991 – present), Pink (2001 – present) and, of course, Olivia Newton-John (1979 – 1986). [10a]

Roger also managed Steve Kipner, the singer-songwriter who famously co-wrote '*Physical*'. Davies was working for Olivia Newton-John's then-manager Lee Kramer, and it seemed a natural progression for him to take over. Davies grew up in Melbourne. He left university in 1970 to become a roadie for the band Company Caine. He moved to Sydney and worked for the booking agency Consolidated Rock (set up by Michael Browning and Michael Gudinski). In October 1972, aged 20, with a fellow workmate, Michael Chugg, he set up the Sunrise booking agency and one of their clients included Sherbet. [10b]

Davies translated his early Australian music industry experience and expertise overseas and remains to this day one of the most successful and respected artist managers in the world, and on board for Olivia's *Xanadu* journey and beyond.

Xanadu was initially conceived as a relatively low-budget roller disco picture, but it evolved into a much larger project when a few big stars joined the production. With a budget of $US20 million (approx. $28.6 million), which in the late ‹70s and early ‹80s was massive, the film was dubbed 'a bit of genius'. 11

The film's title references the poem *Kubla Khan*, (or *A Vision in a Dream. A Fragment*) by Samuel Taylor Coleridge, which is actually quoted in the film. The poem was never completed, and *Xanadu* was the name of the Chinese province where Khan established his pleasure garden.

This 'pleasure–garden' musical romance was directed by Robert Greenwald and starred our Olivia as Kira, a magical muse sent from heaven. Her co-stars were Michael Beck and the Golden Age of Cinema film legend Gene Kelly. The soundtrack featured Olivia, Electric Light Orchestra, UK pop idol Cliff Richard, and the San Francisco-based art-rock band The Tubes.

The film's tagline was: 'A fantasy. A musical. A place where dreams come true.' Coupled with Olivia's dreamy voice, the leading song lyrics came alive.

'A place where nobody dared to go
The love that we came to know
They call it Xanadu
(It takes your breath, and it›ll leave you blind)
And now, open your eyes and see
What we have made is real
We are in Xanadu'

Olivia was the first choice to play *Xanadu*'s female lead, but the male star wasn't locked in. She put an Aussie friend forward for the role – an unknown named Mel Gibson, but in the end, the part went to actor Michael Beck, who'd previously starred in *The Warriors.*

Kira was the modern version of the ancient muse Terpsichore who also appeared in the 1947 film *Down to Earth*, played by Rita Hayworth. Film historians love to debate the (unconfirmed by the writers) theory that *Down to Earth* may have inspired *Xanadu* (due to similar plot points).

Terpsichore is one of the nine Muses, the patron of lyric poetry and dancing. Kira (Olivia on roller skates) in *Xanadu* says, 'Have you ever heard the expression 'kissed by a muse'? Well, that's what I am. I'm a muse ... We've been painted by Michelangelo. Shakespeare's written sonnets about us. Beethoven played music for us. We're not supposed to feel emotion or show any feelings. Muses are just supposed to inspire.'

How apt that Olivia portrays a muse to inspire the creative soul inside others. 'If any muses inspired director Robert Greenwald during the making of this thing, it was in casting the semi-divine Newton-John and her sun-kissed, guileless, girl-next-door beauty, as a goddess, and pairing her ethereal Mezzo-soprano, with the wild electro-rock of ELO.' [12]

Filmed in 1979, *Xanadu* opened on 8 August 1980, billed as 'an epic mashup of disco flash and golden age Hollywood glamour'. [13]

The key scenes were filmed at LA landmarks such as Paradise Park (the park scene where Kira first 'bumps' into Sunny), the Main Street district in Santa Monica, Malibu Pier in Malibu and Venice Beach. The outside sequence, right before the animated section, was shot at the Hollywood Bowl, and the building that becomes the *Xanadu* nightclub in the film was the Pan Pacific Auditorium, which was once a popular venue in Los Angeles. Sadly in 1989, it burned to the ground, and today the site is a park.

'It has been said that what *Xanadu* lacked in craft and cohesiveness, it more than made up for in disco style and music.' [14a] Although this film didn't set the box office on fire (Esquire magazine wrote, 'In a word, Xana-don't'), the soundtrack did set the music world on fire.

'*Magic*' scored Olivia a number-one spot on the *Billboard* charts for four weeks. A *Billboard* reviewer described the song as a 'sizzling track … essentially it's Olivia taking Jeff Lynne's usual spot as the lead singer of ELO. The combination is a winning one.'

This soundtrack was fun, joyous and hugely popular. In the US, the album went double platinum and managed five Top 20 hits: '*Magic*', '*Xanadu*', '*Suddenly*', '*All Over the World*' and '*I'm Alive*'.

'The title track, '*Xanadu*', alone would have been enough to kick this soundtrack into crucial classic territory, but it also includes the absolute soul-stealer '*Magic*'.' [14b]

'You have to believe we are magic
Nothin' can stand in our way
You have to believe we are magic
Don›t let your aim ever stray.'
Magic (from *Xanadu* soundtrack)

The powers that be paired the movie release with a TV special, *Making of Xanadu*. This special was a sweet peek behind the scenes, including interviews with Olivia, Gene Kelly, John Farrar, Jeff Lynne (of ELO) and Michael Beck, and finishing up with some great footage of the *Xanadu* wrap party.

As recently as 2020, a BBC article argued that it might be time to rethink '*Xanadu* … Perhaps now, as the film turns 40, we ought to reappraise it. Maybe *Xanadu* is a misunderstood masterpiece?'

The best aspect of the film – universally agreed upon – was that Olivia's 'supernatural, lushly overproduced pop singing' cemented *Xanadu* as a film cult classic, ensuring it still has a modern-day following. [15]

Xanadu did work some serious magic on Olivia's personal life, even if she did break her coccyx while filming the dance number for '*Suddenly*'. She met her future husband and father of her only child, Chloe Rose – the handsome, younger dancer Matt Lattanzi.

Sadly, this flick was the final film role for Gene Kelly (1912 - 1996). Actor, dancer, singer, filmmaker and choreographer, he was known for his athletic dancing style. He sought to create a new form of American dance accessible to the general public, 'dance for the common man'. [16]

On the screen, he was pure faultless dancing magic! In a 2012 interview, Olivia reflected on the memorable experience and likened it to another highlight she'd had so far. 'He was lovely … How lucky am I that I've been in movies where I've danced with two of the greatest dancers of all time – Gene Kelly and John Travolta? I would never have thought that, because I had two left feet growing up.' [17]

Gene explained in a 1985 interview that it was Olivia that got him to trip the floor fantastic one more time. 'I had already decided about a year and a half before I did *Xanadu* that I was through with dancing … In fact, I wasn't going to dance in *Xanadu*, but several journalists told me that Olivia Newton-John kept saying how sad she was that she wouldn't get the chance to dance with me. So I finally said, 'All right, throw in a number." [18]

Kelly himself choreographed his dance number with Olivia, and he reworked some dance moves they performed, similar to ones he'd performed when he danced with Judy Garland in the 1942 film *For Me and My Gal.* [19]

More *Xanadu* magic for the cast was that this film was the first significant dance film for choreographer Kenny Ortega, who was lucky to receive vital mentoring from the master Gene Kelly. Ortega went on to choreograph the dance numbers for *Dirty Dancing, Pretty in Pink*, all three *High School Musical* movies and my favourite, *Ferris Bueller's Day Off.*

Another sprinkle of magic landed on Don Bluth, who did the transformational cartoon sequence in *Xanadu*. Bluth had recently left Disney and went on to direct *An American Tale* and *The Land Before Time.*

Olivia realistically summed up *Xanadu*, saying: 'I certainly wouldn't die of overexposure in *Xanadu*. Not enough people saw it. I don't regret it or anything else I've done ... I learned a lot, and the music was successful. I would've been upset if the music flopped.' [20]

Strangely, when Olivia was in Australia to promote the film, she could only promote the soundtrack because she was a member of the US Screen Actors Guild and they were on strike at the time –she was not allowed to talk about the movie. She didn't want to cancel her trip home, so the soundtrack was the only topic on the table.

After being given the Key to Melbourne, Olivia appeared on the Australian TV talk show with Don Lane in August 1981. Don asked about her relationship with *Grease* producer Allan Carr. He mentioned that they'd fallen out (over her not doing the *Grease* sequel) but made up during a plane flight from LA to Australia for the Royal Command Performance. All Olivia graciously said, after being put on the spot, was that, yes, they hadn't seen each other for a while but ended up sitting on the floor of the plane eating spaghetti! [21]

In the lush and experimental '80s, Olivia 'came to embody the sleek fantasies of pleasure, painlessness and profit. Nothing disturbed her. She disturbed no one.' [22]

Sadly, someone did appear to disturb her. A few years after *Xanadu* was released, Olivia faced one of the scariest experiences of her life at the hands of a stalker. In 1983, Michael Owen Perry, an escapee from a mental institution, became 'obsessed' with Olivia, and struggled to separate the film *Xanadu* from real life. He sent her fan mail from 1980 to 1983, reportedly believing he was a god and that Newton-John was a real goddess. On July 17, 1983, Perry armed himself with guns and embarked on a shooting spree, killing two of his cousins, a two-year-old nephew, and his parents. When police searched his trailer home behind his parent's house, they found a list of names made by Perry, which included 'Olivia'. In 1984 he was convicted of the five murders and remains on death row at Angola State Penitentiary. Speaking to *Entertainment Weekly* in 2007 about the incident, ONJ said, 'I left the country for a while. That was a very scary time.' [23]

When she did pack her bags, Olivia's choice of retreat was Australia. But the quiet time did not last long. The '80s had a lot more to give to Olivia.

Chapter 7

Trailblazing and Heady Years

Olivia Newton-John was a trailblazer in the art of pop reinvention. 'This chameleonic musician shape-shifted between genres and rode the changing moods of pop to become one of the biggest hit-makers of her era and an enduring cult icon.' [1]

Her film and TV biography was abundant and her use of music videos were inventive. In 1982, she released *Olivia Physical*, a VHS offering a video for every song on the album. 'I think this is the way albums will go in the future – visuals with the music,' she told *Billboard* in 1981 (35 years before Beyoncé's 'visual album' *Lemonade*). [2]

Her prolific use and love of making music film clips was a bold move and it always paid off. The clip for the '*Physical*' single broke ground in its obvious hidden message and seriously raunchy choreography – and all before music clips even had award ceremonies!

Fashion was another tool Olivia used to cement her name in the book of idols. She had established herself as 'a household name known for her singing, dancing and acting, and she left a lasting impact on anyone who came across her.' [3]

ONJ was aware that fashion was a game changer in the public eye. Her outfits from *Grease* caused a resurgence of '50s fashion. Her '*Physical*' gym outfit started the athletic fashion craze. Even that *Xanadu* tiger print dress, the Kira muse floaty frock and roller-skates became instant pop culture must-haves – copied and worn around the world. 'Her outfits are the threads for every birthday party, every sleepover, every theme night.' [4a]

Her acting roles were an eclectic mix and never predictable, and her fashion moments were the same.

Funny Things Happen Down Under in 1966 was her first film and it took Olivia Newton-John another 33 years to make another movie in Australia – *A Few Best Men*. Only one other Australian movie followed, and it was her last, 2020's *The Very Excellent Mr Dundee*, in which she acted alongside Paul Hogan, Chevy Chase and John Cleese. She played herself in a hilarious rendition of '*You're The One That I Want*', highlighting the fact that Olivia was a natural and funny comedian. She could slip into a comedy skit at a moment's notice and often played the scene to perfection with some of the greats, from Bob Hope to Paul Hogan.

The '*Physical*' film clip was also very funny and scripted to be so – a sleight of hand to get the censors to look the other way perhaps.

Olivia's first television film was the comedy *A Mom for Christmas*, directed by George T. Miller and produced by Walt Disney Television. Olivia stars as Amy Miller, a department store mannequin who comes to life to act as a mother to 11-year-old Jessica. Over a 50-year career in both comedy and drama roles, ONJ performed on *Murphy Brown, Ned and Stacey, Bette* and *Sordid Lives* and even *Wonder Woman* with Lynda Carter.

In Australia, all throughout her life Olivia must have appeared on every talk show, music show and awards ceremony from *Countdown* to *This Is Your Life* (twice). Olivia appeared on Australian comedian Norman Gunston's (real name Garry McDonald) show a few times and plays along brilliantly.

Norman begins by asking if Olivia made it big in America because of her relation to Elton Newton-John or Patty Newton-John. She was always happy to act along with any comedy skits no matter how long or short. She appeared on the *Dave Allen Show, Dean Martin Comedy Hour* (1972) and the *Bob Hope Christmas comedy special* in 1977 when Olivia starred in a *Star Wars* comedy sketch as Princess Olivia, who with Fluke Sleepwalker (Perry Como) must battle Bart Vaiter (Bob Hope) to rescue Santa Claus. At times you can see Olivia trying not to laugh! The real

Luke Skywalker (Mark Hamill) makes an appearance at the end.

She owned *Saturday Night Live* on May 22 1982 and performed '*Physical*' in the opening monologue, as well as '*Make a Move On Me*' and '*Landslide*'. 'Through the '90s and beyond, her acting career continued sporadically, but with an infectious sense of fun. She was cast against-type as a sketchy bar singer/arsonist in the 2000 indie film *Sordid Lives* and its TV spin-off, and gamely paid homage to her '*Physical*' video in a 2010 episode of *Glee*.' [4b]

As a hilarious tribute, The Goodies wrote and released *Saturday Night Grease-Discotheque* in January 1980 on BBC2. The Goodies were a legendary trio of British comedians: Tim Brooke-Taylor, Graeme Garden and Bill Oddie. The show ruled the comedy world from 1970 until 1982. In the Olivia episode, Tim has developed a crush on Olivia, whose portrait has replaced Queen Elizabeth II on his wall. His obsession prompts him to emulate the mannerisms, hairstyle and fashions exhibited by *Grease* co-star, John Travolta.

Love, Light and Laughter were the three Ls that followed The Dame around her whole life, publicly and privately.

Even her first UK film, 1970's *Toomorrow*, a low-budget sci-fi flick in which a pop group is abducted by aliens, is now viewed as amusing.

Sandra Dee is Olivia's greatest acting nom de plume, then of course she was Kira in the campy *Xanadu*, and Debbie in 1983's *Two of a Kind*, where she teamed up with John Travolta, in a crime movie where the soundtrack was again a huge hit, spawning three hit singles for Olivia and going platinum.

Then she was Lina Bingham in 1996's *It's My Party*, a drama based on the actual events of the death of Harry Stein, architect and designer and previous partner of *Grease* director Randal Kleiser. It was one of the first feature films to address the controversial topic of AIDS patients dying with dignity. Alex Greenwich MP said on his social media page when hearing of her passing, 'Olivia Newton-John was one of the first Australian celebrities to back #marriage equality, and at a time when others found it too 'political'. So sad to lose such an Australian icon and champion of the LGBTIQA+ communities. Vale.' Olivia.' One of her favourite characters to play was the gay country singer Bitsy Mae Harling in *Sordid Lives* (2000). *Vogue* magazine reviewed Olivia in this flick: 'With a shaggy bob, tattoos, a smoky eye, and uniform of low-cut crop tops paired with cheetah-print cowboy hats, the actor is almost unrecognisable in this comedy … Newton-John delivers big laughs and a definitive answer to those who doubt her range.' [5]

She was Hope Gordon in *Score: A Hockey Musical* in 2010, Jasmine Wilde in 2001's *The Wilde Girls*, a TV movie alongside her daughter Chloe. Barbara Ramme in *A Few Best Men* in 2011, and in the hilarious *Sharknado 5* in 2017 she played Orion, again alongside Chloe.

'In the early 1960s, television was the main medium for female performers. Two-thirds of all Australians had a TV in the home, and the small screen presentation of rock and pop culture, which at the time was still suffering a reputation as a threat to the moral fibre of a nation, meant it could be carefully monitored.' [6]

Never one to be concentrating on just one thing, Olivia's love of music clips ran concurrently to her big screen manoeuvres. Music shows were her bread and butter in the '60s in Australia and when MTV emerged, Olivia was ahead of the visual game.

Music Television debuted in August 1981, establishing the fact that music videos could make or break songs. 'She only had to toy with going too far … She knew the power of the art form.' [7]

Olivia was the Queen of the Music Video and she totally revamped herself at the dawn of the music-video era. You name the song – there is a clip for it.

Her first music video was for '*Follow Me*', a promotional single from her 1975 album *Have You Never Been Mellow* and her '*Physical*' video clip earning Olivia the first-ever Grammy for a music video, in 1983. Her complete Videography has over 62 music videos, three concert tour videos, and four music video collections – basically there is a lot of tape with her beautiful face on it. It's all part of her immortal status in music history and confirms what a businesswoman and clever career strategist she was.

ONJ's music video for '*Twist of Fate*' was nominated for a Grammy Award for Best Short Form Music Video and when *The Soul Kiss* video was released in 1985 it featured five music videos for the songs. Some of these videos provided a look behind the velvet curtain. 1994's '*No Matter What You Do*' was filmed at Olivia's house at Byron Bay, Australia. 1998's '*I Honestly Love You*' was filmed in LA and featured footage from Olivia's house in Malibu.

In 2011, the music video for '*Magic*' (Peach & Murphy remix) featured the biggest cast ever for an Australian music video, with more than 300 people, while one of her biggest live moments was 1999's T*he Main Event Tour*, shot live in Melbourne, Australia. [8]

Olivia's TV talk show biography was also extensive and though based in the US, she always made regular visits home to Australia. There is footage of her shining brightly on classic shows like *Australian Music To The World*, *Countdown*, T*he Logie Awards, Australia Live, Olivia Down Under, The Man From Snowy River, Good Morning Australia, Rove Live, Enough Rope With Andrew Denton, Australian Idol*, and *Australia Unites: The Victorian Bushfire Appeal.*

Back in 1994, Olivia travelled the world to host the animal documentary series *Wild Life* that ran for two years on the Nine Network. Her Aussie cameraman, Michael Jackson, said Olivia never complained about 'bad weather, snakes or leeches – she was definitely part of our crew and did everything with us. Legend!' [9a] If you search

Olivia's '90s TV history you can spot the secret cameo she did for Aussie soap *Paradise Beach* (Nine). As Matt Lattanzi's character was departing the series, there was Olivia and daughter Chloe climbing the steps to an Ansett jet at Coolangatta Airport.' [9b]

A few little-known classics are her appearance in Michael Jackson's '*Liberian Girl*' music video and the 2010 infomercial hosted by Chuck Norris, Gena O'Kelly and Christie Brinkley for the *Total Gym* fitness program, and lastly in 2013 as the hostess of an infomercial for TriVita's 'Zamu Gold' wellness drink, with her husband,.

In 2018 the Channel Seven biopic mini-series about her life, *Olivia Newton-John: Hopelessly Devoted To You* was made, starring Delta Goodrem, a young Australian singer. This told a version of her personal and professional journey, through her music. According to Olivia's daughter, Chloe Lattanzi, the series was created without Olivia's knowledge, participation or consent. Chloe told *Woman's Day*: 'What's upsetting is the way it's been done. Not one part of it has come directly from our family, it is completely unauthorised.' [10a]

Olivia later consented to the series, providing the profits went to her cancer hospital. When Delta was approached to play Olivia in the biopic, the young singer said, 'Being an Aussie girl, I did grow up with her being a national treasure.' And Olivia told her: 'I'm the same person on camera as I am off camera and that's important in the film for me.' [10b]

Constantly being in the limelight, Fashionista Olivia blossomed. Featured on the cover of magazines all over the world since she was a '60s singing sensation, she looked stunning in any outfit and was not averse to a game-changing hairstyle. She introduced new styles, which were instantly copied and spread throughout fashion culture.

'The moment she sashayed into frame wearing those skin-tight black trousers and leather jacket, Olivia Newton-John cemented her name in the fashion history books. It wasn›t just her on-set looks that captivated audiences. Newton-John rose to prominence during the late '70s when the fashion scape was steered by eclecticism. While intimate at-home photo-shoots provided glimpses into her personal wardrobe, complete with cherry red flares, silk scarves and denim waistcoats.' [11]

In 1983, Olivia and her old singing partner Pat Carroll took a massive step and launched a fashion label of their own, with the Koala Blue boutique selling Australian fashion and cultural items. Koala Blue — (the initials stood for 'Korner of Australia in LA') was a leisurewear line established by the pair and the name was a nod to their Australian roots. At the time, ONJ said she felt homesick while on tour. Sixty stores opened across the world, including outlets in Hong Kong, Canada, Japan, France, the US and Australia. Olivia's satin day dresses, Missoni harem pants, white-fringed cowboy jacket and dresses designed by Bobbie Mannix, became '80s staples. There was even a *Xanadu* collection of dresses by Jack Mulqueen.

'I love fashion, and watching it go from the drawing board to the finished product,' Olivia told the *LA Times* in 1988. 'We found that only the merchandise that had Koala Blue on it was very successful, so we focused on that.' [12]

Sadly, a decade later, in 1992, the chain collapsed after being placed in receivership a year earlier. 'We expanded so fast [that] when the recession hit, we really got hurt,' Olivia said at the time. [13] This did not stop Olivia and her love of fashion. In 2018, nail polish giant OPI released the *Grease* Collection Summer, featuring 12 nail polish shades including Don't Cry Over Spilled Milkshakes, Pink Ladies Rule The School, Hopelessly Devoted To OPI, and *Grease* is the Word (sparkly black polish with a leather finish).

Also beginning in 2018, the Blue Illusion fashion chain in Australia had the privilege of collaborating with Dame Olivia Newton-John to create beautiful garments that raise money to support her philanthropic work. The collaboration runs to this day.

OliviaNewton-John is hands down one of the great '80s fashion icons. Along with her talents as a singer, songwriter, actress, and dancer, Newton-John always wowed when it came to fashion. Whether walking on a Hollywood red carpet or working out in a music video, the English-born Australian talent never failed to impress with her outfit choices.' [14]

Perhaps the most lasting fashion legacy was Olivia's look for the single '*Physical*' in 1981, 'surrounded by oiled muscle men, Newton-John performs aerobics-inspired choreography in fuchsia tights, a white leotard, knotted blue shirt, white headband and blue legwarmers. Along with Jane Fonda's workout videotapes, the '*Physical*' wardrobe, devised with Newton-John's long-time collaborator costume designer Fleur Thiemeyer has come to represent the body-con workout looks of the '80s.' [15]

'As Ms Newton-John explained in a video posted to her YouTube channel in December, the video 'really helped kick off the entire fitness and aerobic craze of the time. It was the birth of the '80s headband fashion craze. I should have started a headband and leg warmer company or made fitness videos. Jane Fonda beat me to it." [16]

Olivia's video 'crystallised, in a short couple of minutes in visual form, what was happening across culture, manufacturing and consumer habits,' said Sonnet Stanfill, senior curator of fashion at the Victoria and Albert Museum and editor of the 2013 book *80s Fashion: From Club to Catwalk.* [17]

The Arts Centre Melbourne's Australian Performing Arts Collection has a number of prized possessions from the collection of Dame Olivia Newton AC DBE, including two gowns, design sketches, scripts, tour music and a prestigious award. Melbourne-based Fleur Thiemeyer, a dear friend, made many of the gowns and was the designer behind ONJ's style in the 1970s and 1980s.

Olivia was introduced to the glamorous Australian couple, singer Darryl Cotton (Zoot) and costume designer Fleur Thiemeyer at an LA pool party. She was preparing to perform in Las Vegas for the first time as opening act for American country singer Charlie Rich. It was suggested that she wear dresses for the performances, and Thiemeyer agreed to create a range of custom pieces for her. From this point on, the group were inseparable, touring together with John Farrar on guitar, Darryl Cotton on vocals and Thiemeyer designing the on-stage looks.

Fleur Thiemeyer is now recognised as one of Australia's most prolific music fashion designers. She had a career working with Bon Scott, Zoot and Russell Morris in the late 1960s, and in the 1970s and 1980s, she worked in the USA, defining the image of artists as diverse as Rod Stewart, Liza Minnelli, Dolly Parton, Mick Jagger, Mötley Crüe, Van Halen, Helen Reddy, The Jacksons, KISS, Frankie Valli, KC and The Sunshine Band and Spinal Tap

Olivia said 'I am so proud of the costumes and delighted that they will become a permanent part of the Australian Performing Arts Collection. It's wonderful to know that they will be carefully preserved for future generations to see.' [18]

Olivia held a 2019 auction of pieces from her *Grease* and *Xanadu* appearances, along with gowns from her tours and awards ceremonies. The auction raised $US2.4 million, with proceeds assisting the Olivia Newton-John Cancer and Wellness Centre in Melbourne. A kind act. An anonymous fan brought Olivia to tears when they returned the *Grease* leather jacket to her after buying it, saying it should be returned to its 'rightful owner' rather than 'sit in a billionaire's closet for country-club bragging rights'. [19]

'Rather than pushing or shaping trends like her pop peers Cher and Madonna, Newton-John safely embodied the looks of the moment through the girl-next-door filter that stayed with her into her seventies.' [20]

Fashion in check. Music clips in check. Film and TV career bubbling along … now it's time for 1981 – Olivia's biggest year.

Olivia continued her re-invention with the release of *Physical*. It was her most successful studio album, going double platinum, and strongly reinforced her image change by showcasing risqué, rock-oriented material. As the song itself shouted to the world, get ready for earth-shaking, legwarmer-wearing Olivia Newton-John. Her headband was now a modern day crown!

'I've been patient, I've been good
Tried to keep my hands on the table
It's gettin' hard, this holdin' back
You know what I mean
I'm sure you'll understand my point of view
We know each other mentally
You gotta know that you're bringin' out
The animal in me'

'Physical' lyrics

Chapter 8

Let's Get Physical

'Newton-John thrust into the '80s (literally) with her steamy workout anthem 'Physical'...Triggered by her Grease character's transformation from sweet to sexy, Newton-John used the movie's momentum to change her image'. NBC NEWS. [1a]

Olivia has been unmasked here as a genius navigator of change.

She adapted to new sounds and styles with the professional skill of a showbiz natural. She effortlessly evolved musically, never abandoning what she moved past, but internalising them all and building on her overall persona and presentation to the public.

As an entertainer of many facets who played the game, the heady days of 1981 saw Olivia receive one of the most significant stamps of celebrity approval – her star on the Hollywood Walk of Fame. 1981 was also the year she officially became an Australian citizen, with her overdue application expedited by then Prime Minister Malcolm Fraser.

In Australia in 1981, important things were afoot. Funnel-web spider anti-venom was developed. The South Australian Parliament passed the Pitjantjatjara Land Rights Act. The police re-opened the investigation into the missing baby case of Azaria Chamberlain, and Peter Carey's novel *Bliss* won the Miles Franklin Award. Two all-time classic Aussie films were released, *Puberty Blues* and *Gallipoli*, Trevor Chappell bowled his infamous cricket underarm delivery against New Zealand at the MCG and *Countdown* on the ABC, captained by the also infamous and magnificent Ian 'Molly' Meldrum, was ruling the music world.

Molly travelled to where the music was happening and brought it back to Australia. He was wild and loose but had an encyclopaedic music knowledge hidden under that signature hat and an interview style that may have been littered with 'umms' and 'ahhs' but somehow managed to get the guest to relax and quite often spill the beans, such as when John Lennon told him first that he Beatles were breaking up (and he didn't realise until he went home and listened to the tape).

Countdown was a weekly Australian music television program broadcast from 1974 to 1987 out of Ripponlea, Melbourne. Like MTV (whose first song was the prophetic '*Video Killed the Radio Star*' by The Buggles), *Countdown* had a powerful international impact because it was one of the first TV shows in the world to champion the use of music video as a serious taster to overseas and local acts.

Countdown was instrumental in the worldwide success of many major overseas acts such as Madonna, Blondie, ABBA, John Mellencamp, Meat Loaf and Cyndi Lauper. Exposure was everything, and many New Wave acts became household names because of their music videos, such as Duran Duran, XTC, The Specials, Lene Lovich, The Cure, and even the US punk band the Ramones. For Olivia, always at the forefront of musical change – 'the message seemed to be goodbye cream puff, hello heartbreaker … Olivia became part of the New Wave music movement, her hits after 1981 were aligned with the sound of the times. Olivia's singles had a synth-pop sound, from '*Heart Attack*' to '*Living in Desperate Times*'.' [1b]

Let's not forget the rise of Adam Ant and Ant Music, Orchestral Manoeuvres in the Dark with their soundtrack songs on *Pretty In Pink*, Ultravox, Soft Cell, Depeche Mode and who can forget The Human League with the first truly 'Emo' song ever – '*Don't You Want Me*' from 1981's *Dare* album. Homegrown acts flourished on *Countdown*, including Our Livvy. She and Molly had a close friendship, and he interviewed Olivia many times all around the world.

'MTV was the revolution that put the radio star on notice. Our Olivia, as our Molly had taken to calling her, was a natural for the new medium's lofty photogenic standards. Still, it was some kind of genius that engineered the image change to leotard, legwarmers and saucy smoulder.' [2]

Other Aussie acts, like John Farnham, AC/DC, INXS, John Paul Young, Skyhooks, Marcia Hines, The Angels, Men at Work, Icehouse, Australian Crawl and Mental As Anything were *Countdown* regulars and their classic songs ensconced in the public minds, thanks to that critical *Countdown* hour every Sunday night from 6pm.

Into this sonically inventive period to be alive, Olivia Newton-John dropped a bombshell – the single '*Physical*'.

'Newton-John revamped herself at the dawn of the music-video era. She knew the power of the art form — her Grammy-winning 1982 video album, *Olivia Physical*, was the *Lemonade* of its day, inspiring a prime-time network TV event.' [3]

Rod Stewart and Tina Turner initially turned down this song, which became a commercial phenomenon and Olivia's biggest hit. It was songwriter Steve Kipner, a Bee Gees associate from way back, who co-wrote '*Physical*' in 1981. Kipner recalled in an interview for *Songwriter Universe*: 'Terry and I were writing a song about the physical side of love, rather than the emotional side.'

At this time, Newton-John's manager was Australian Roger Davies, and they had timed this explosion perfectly – aiming her new look squarely at the MTV age. MTV was up and running and playing music videos 24 hours a day. Everything came together perfectly – a new fashion look, a new hairdo and a seriously naughty song. It was the perfect musical storm and arguably the biggest song of the '80s.

The beauty of '*Physical*' was you could listen to it, even watch the clip many times and still not clock what it was about, and it wasn't exercise.

"*Physical*' was the hit which would leave her innocent persona behind like a snakeskin.' [4]

Olivia explained, 'I just wasn't in the mood for tender ballads. I wanted peppy stuff because that's how I'm feeling … Roger Davies was my manager at the time; he played it for me, and I knew it was a very catchy song.' [5]

Later on, after '*Physical*' had been recorded, Olivia panicked, thinking the song was too rude to release and called her manager, saying: 'We've got to pull this single!' Davies assured her there was no need to worry – and that, anyway, it was too late. 'It's already gone to radio, and it's running up the charts.' [6]

It was then Olivia's idea to release the video first, so people would think the song was about exercise rather than sex. 'Imply and wink and let you, the public, join the dots.' [7] Of course, the song was about sex, but her plan worked. '*Physical*' received massive airplay, except in Utah and South Africa, where the song was banned. [8a]

In 1981, Olivia released *Physical* the album (dedicated to her then boyfriend, Matt Lattanzi, whom she married in 1984). It was her most successful studio album and went double platinum.

'*Physical* is a cornerstone of early '80s pop'. [8b]

Years later, Olivia said on her website, 'I am so proud of this record as it not only allowed me to try new things musically, but it became a part of pop-culture history.' [9] It was coupled with the iconic picture that adorns the album, which photographer Herb Ritts shot. Ritts would later create a similar image for Madonna's 1986 *True Blue* album.

In 2010, *Billboard* magazine ranked '*Physical*' as the most popular single ever about sex. This song had many different layers – the confident woman, the gay love-is-love message and the let's get fit memo.

For the ladies out there, 'it's a woman taking control of seduction, claiming for herself the tactics usually deployed by men: the flirtation, the dinner, the movie, the horny insistence.' [10]

The original edit of the video showed our 33-year-old Olivia working out in a gym in front of a group of men. In a twist at the end of the story, it was revealed the men were actually gay as they coupled off holding hands. Sadly, the twist caused MTV to cut the ending. 'Who would have thought the legendary film clip would set the tone for music video aesthetics for decades to come? Or that the sex-positive anthem would still be finding its way into pop songs forty years later?' [11]

The important message of '*Physical*' was to bring love out into the open for The LGBTQAI+ community and hopefully start to change the landscape forever. 'Very often, the things that you're most afraid of are the things that you really need to just go for,' Dame Olivia Newton-John said in a 2021 interview with *Today.* [12]

ONJ was not alone in being banned; Duran Duran released the single '*Girls on Film*' in July 1981. Their highly controversial music video, which was censored for airplay on MTV and banned by BBC, became the band's first Top 10 hit in the UK, peaking at number 5, and even today, I could sing every word.

The clip was ground-breaking for another reason – Olivia helped usher in the '80s fitness craze, almost a year before Jane Fonda's *Workout* became a worldwide craze.

It's astonishing what an impact a leotard, leggings and headband designed by Fleur Thiemeyer had. This exercise-themed video was an aerobics anthem. 'Olivia had become the fitness goddess of the 1980s. Leg warmers and spandex and a short haircut somewhere between Pat Benatar and Princess Di.' [13]

The album and single were so successful that Olivia toured with *Physical* all over America to sell-out audiences. The longevity of this song was shown by the 2021, 40th anniversary release *Physical*: *Deluxe Edition*. 'It's hard to believe that it has been 40 years since *Physical* was first released ... I am so proud of this record as it not only allowed me to try new things musically, but it became such a part of pop-culture history.' [14]

This song has 'been covered by everyone from Kylie Minogue (her nearest touchstone), Sophie Ellis-Bextor, and Delta Goodrem. Doja Cat and SZA borrowed ', and Dua Lipa interpolated the lyric 'let's get physical' on her 2022 hit '*Physical*'.' [15]

Along the way, Olivia also transformed into the confident performer she dreamed of being as a child. She told *Entertainment Weekly*, 'In the old days, I was just too nervous to have a good time. It may not have shown, but leading up to when I went out on stage, it was always very nerve-wracking, now I really enjoy it ... Let go and enjoy yourself.' [16]

Sandy #2, the girl from *Grease*, is definitely in charge right now. 'Her success was put down to the combination of great business connections – savvy marketing, her production and writing and design team, 'just that incredible breath of fresh air that she was'. [17]

After reaching the pinnacle of her career with *Physical*, her next album was 1985's sultry *Soul Kiss*. Long-time collaborator John Farrar co-wrote four tracks, and the cover art featured photos of Olivia by famous photographers Helmut Newton and Herb Ritts. All Music editor Joe Viglione found that *Soul Kiss* 'seems a bit contrived' and called 'the album, as a whole, one of the weaker links in Olivia's remarkable chain'. [18]

A little-known fact is that in the video Olivia shot for this single, she was pregnant with her daughter Chloe. The album featured Olivia in tight riding pants and boots, holding a crop on the back cover; it was her last risqué album, as she had decided she wanted to take things easier.

Marriage and motherhood were number one on her list. Olivia married her young live-in boyfriend Matt Lattanzi around Christmas 1984 after they had lived together for four years, and the couple enjoyed a fairytale honeymoon in Paris. Love is in the air, and Olivia's most remarkable work is being planned – a baby!

Chapter 9

Wellness Journey

'A familiar face in entertainment for over half a century, Olivia represented not only an epic time in our memories but the notion that one can remain decent and optimistic, despite our personal battles.' [1a]

History has shown that in 1992 Olivia Newton-John was diagnosed with her first bout of breast cancer. This disease took her life in August 2022 after decades of fighting against it.

Not only did she fight for herself, but she also fought for all people living with cancer. She dedicated her life, resources, voice and time to raising money to support this fight.

'I don't think of myself as sick with cancer,' she said in 2020. 'I choose not to see it as a fight either, because I don't like war. I don't like fighting wherever it is – whether it's outside or an actual war inside my body. I choose not to see it that way.' [1b]

Talking about this wellness journey is important. The weapons that Olivia custom-built and used against this cancer have been left for others to use and for us to remember what actually happened to Olivia Newton-John.

Post '*Physical*', the single, Olivia Newton-John dominated network television as much as the music charts. The next single from the *Physical* album, '*Make a Move on Me*' (co-written by Tom Snow) peaked at #5 and earned the singer another gold single. Tom Snow recalled, 'Olivia brings Olivia to the tune. Ain't nobody else who could do it like she did!' [2]

1982's *Olivia›s Greatest Hits Vol.2* was jettisoned out to the public, and she set off on her first tour in four years across North America. *New York Times* critic Jon Pareles applauded the strength of ONJ's voice on this tour, saying it 'summoned country's quavers, disco's melismas, pop's directness, and hard rock's percussive staccato'. [3]

By December this year, *Billboard* had named Our Livvy 'Top Pop Singles Artist' and 'Top Pop Singles Artist Female'. The American Music Awards (Jan 1983) presented her with 'Favourite Pop/Rock Female Artist', and in February 1983, a Grammy Award landed in her lap for '*Physical*' – 'Video of the Year'.

In Olivia's private life, after dating and living with Matt Lattanzi for five years, they got married on 15 December 1984. Olivia tragically endured a miscarriage before their daughter Chloe Rose Lattanzi was triumphantly born on 17 January 1986. This inspired a welcome hiatus in Olivia's music career. Between 1986 to 1992, Olivia was predominantly a proud Mum.

A lovely little piece of Aussie music history happened in 1987, with Olivia singing uncredited backing vocals on James Reyne's (lead drawl-singer of the iconic band Australian Crawl) song '*Hammerhead*', from his self-titled debut solo album.

While back in Australia, Olivia popped in to sing the national anthem in Melbourne for the VFL football grand final between Hawthorn and Carlton – a very Aussie thing to do, and this marked Chloe's first visit down under. Olivia had a lifelong connection to the Carlton 'Blues' and fronted up in her scarf whenever she could. At Christmas that year, beamed live from Olivia's living room – with her husband Matt and Chloe on the couch – Olivia did a New Year's Eve special titled *It's Always Australia For Me*.

Primarily based on the west coast of the United States with her new family, she decided she wanted to cut back on touring. 'I have so many other things I'm passionate about and involved in, and I love singing, and I love recording, but touring takes a toll, and you're away from home a lot,' she said. [4]

'But in 1992, on the eve of a massive worldwide tour (her first in ten years), Newton-John was diagnosed with breast cancer. It was the start of a long battle for the Grammy Award-winning artist.' [5]

The singer's original plan was to release a hits collection of her stellar catalogue titled *Back to Basics: The Essential Collection 1971-1992*. She hoped it would reintroduce herself to the hit charts. But fate intervened. And, on the same weekend she received her diagnosis, her father Brinley passed away from liver cancer. It was also around the time that Olivia suffered the heartbreaking loss of a goddaughter, who died at age five from cancer. 'It was all at once. Everything just came at me.' The tour was cancelled, as she had to receive treatment. [6a]

In her autobiography, Olivia wrote, 'My blood feels like water. It's like someone drained all the energy from me. In 1992, I was diagnosed with breast cancer … I underwent a partial mastectomy, chemotherapy and breast reconstruction. I did herbal formulas and meditation and focused on a vision of complete wellness.' [6b]

After surgery, Olivia returned to country New South Wales to recover. Thankfully, in February of the following year, she got the all clear and again she went to Australia to recuperate.

'This event changed the course of her musical career … as her new lease on life gave her a dogged determination to only record music that she was passionate about moving forward, commercial considerations be damned.' [7]

This wellness crusade was her story to tell and her memoir *Don't Stop Belivin'* is astoundingly candid; in many places, distressing and, in other areas, so optimistic and helpful. It's Dame Olivia taking the reader gently by the hand, showing them her personal health journey and revealing why she was so dedicated and motivated to eradicate cancer from the world.

Her first step was to get herself well. Her second step was aligning with the Austin Hospital research centre in 1992, which changed its name to the Olivia Newton-John Cancer Wellness & Research Centre in 2012. The third step was her Olivia Newton-John Foundation Fund, an independent charity driving global change through funding cutting-edge research and treatment programs, with a particular interest in plant medicine.

'Throughout her lifetime, Olivia gained renown as one of the most active patrons of cancer research.' [8]

In 2005, she co-founded the award-winning Gaia Retreat & Spa — a health retreat in the Bunjalung Country of Byron Bay, a region often known as the healing heartland of Australia. It became one of Byron Bay's most renowned wellness resorts and the 22-room boutique resort sits on eight hectares of the hinterland and offers a day spa, saltwater pool and walking tracks.

'Everything I do revolves around health and well-being … How can we – as regular human beings – make a difference and help the planet, those around us, and ourselves?' [9a]

Gaia Retreat was recently sold to Tattarang, a private investment group owned by mining magnate Andrew Forrest, for $30 million.

In additional property pursuits, Olivia owned a main residence, ranch and several beach houses in Malibu, California and a multimillion-dollar home in Juniper Inlet, Florida.

She purchased a 12-acre horse ranch in the Santa Ynez Valley outside Santa Barbara, California, and a 187-acre Byron Bay farm. Many of these properties, except the Santa Ynez farm, were sold in the last few years of her life, and the money was placed into her Foundation.

Having experienced recurrent bouts of breast cancer in 1992, 2013 and 2017, Newton-John expanded her pursuits into medicine and wellness. Still, her most significant defensive move against cancer was the patronage of the $200 million Wellness and Research Centre at Melbourne's Austin Hospital in 2012. Her associated Foundation Funds' primary purpose is to sponsor research into naturopathy and cancer after Olivia's self-attested success with cannabis oil as a pain alleviator. In 2019, her *Grease* memorabilia auction raised $3.4m, with the leather jacket from *Grease* garnering $348,500 alone.

The world needs fighters for things we cannot see. We need warriors against things we cannot always see. Warriors come in all forms, and Olivia was a warrior pitted against cancer. Her weapons were raising awareness and money, and the power of 'Love & Light', which is how Olivia used to sign all her autographs to encourage everyone to stay positive and share kindness.

She took a pull-no-punches approach when it came to her 30-year struggle with breast cancer: 'I used homeopathy, acupuncture, yoga and meditation in conjunction with my chemotherapy to help me get stronger again after cancer. I also chanted with Buddhist friends and prayed with Christian friends. I covered all my bases.' [9b]

When Olivia was first diagnosed she said, 'I was in shock.' Then she wanted to help others facing the same battle. 'If you had told me 12, 15 years ago that I would be talking about breasts on a regular basis, I would have said you were crazy. I was quite shy about those things in a public forum.' [10]

Hugh Jackman said, 'Her legacy will only grow stronger in the years to come. A fighter for healing from cancer that knows no bounds.'

The Olivia Newton-John Cancer, Wellness and Research Centre – sits within Austin Health, one of Victoria's major public health providers in Melbourne. Using the $200 million she helped raise with state and federal funding plus philanthropic support, the centre provides cancer treatment, education, training and research. It has a dedicated mind, body and spirit-focused wellness centre. Over 20 years ago, when Olivia was approached by the Austin Hospital and asked to be the patron of its new cancer centre, she agreed but insisted on 'having a real input into the core philosophy and the nitty gritty of design'. [11a]

Olivia's charity work, as Paul Kelly, Australian bard and singer, once wrote – follows the formula of 'From little things, big things grow.'

The chief executive of Austin Health, Adam Horsburgh: 'Without her drive and her commitment, the centre would not be here. It has enabled us to provide care and support to thousands of patients over the past ten years … The Olivia Centre began as an outpatient ambulatory centre, then expanding to provide inpatient wards.' [11b]

In 2013, Olivia's much-adored sister Rona was diagnosed with cancer and while visiting her, ONJ was involved in an accident, which eventually led to the discovery that her own breast cancer had metastasized to her shoulder. This shook Olivia, as she believed she had been cancer-free for more than 20 years. Olivia chose to keep this diagnosis secret (until 2018) to give her time to start treatment again. Sadly, Rona Newton-John, who had been living with brain cancer, passed away aged 70 in 2013. Olivia, in mourning, said, 'Your sister is someone you can share things about the family that no one else understands.' [12a]

In May 2017, it was announced that Olivia's breast cancer had returned for the third time and spread to her back, resulting in the cancellation of a planned tour in the US and Canada. She publicly campaigned for the legalisation of medicinal cannabis to ease the pain and became a big advocate for using medicinal cannabis in cancer treatment.

When interviewed by ABC TV in 2017 about the ONJ Cancer Wellness & Research Centre, Olivia added, 'We're providing music therapy. We have people come in and sing. It just relaxes everyone. The therapist goes to the room — the music therapist is amazing — he goes to the room and sings to the patients.' Music and healing hand in hand was always her ultimate plan. [12b]

After her annual charity fundraiser 'Wellness Walk' in 2018, at age 70, Olivia had to go back to hospital in Melbourne. She was treated secretly – having to learn to walk again after fracturing her pelvis. The first half of 2019 was a recovery process with 'Olivia managing to come off morphine, given to manage her pain, and now using medicinal cannabis, cultivated by her husband John Easterling, a plant medicine expert'. [13a]

Marijuana helped Olivia with various difficulties, from pain to anxiety and even sleeplessness. She said, 'Opiates kill people. Cannabis doesn't.'[13b] Plant medicine was a great help to her, and she used the cannabis her husband grew on their ranch under his enterprise Amazon Herb Company. The Plant Kingdom is the original source of medicine, and current science is proving the potent anti-cancer properties of natural plant compounds.

John Easterling said of his dearly loved wife's Foundation: 'Her healing inspiration and pioneering experience with plant medicine continues … The goal is to take laboratory-based research and translate it into practical changes to clinical care in hospitals.' [14]

Olivia's daughter, Chloe Lattanzi, and her husband, James, run a Marijuana farm for medical purposes in Oregon. Chloe supported her mother's beliefs in using holistic treatments, such as acupuncture and massage therapy alongside nutritional knowledge, by adopting a vegan diet while having chemotherapy, natural medicine, relaxation therapies, a positive mental attitude and medical cannabis alongside conventional medical treatments. [15]

Olivia's strong belief in alternative healing and medicinal marijuana is quite earth-mother-type future thinking, and she was part of a successful public campaign to make medicinal cannabis more accessible in Australia.

'Olivia loved helping people. She spent the last two decades of her life giving back … She wanted to leave behind something that would last and something that her daughter, too, could benefit from.' [16a]

The yearly 'Walk for Wellness' charity drive became a beacon for this dream to help others. This event takes place physically every October in Melbourne, and you can participate online. 2022 was the first year without Olivia leading the pack. Her niece Tottie, daughter of her sister Rona (on the ground) and her daughter Chloe (online) led the way. Tottie said as she led the record-breaking crowd: 'A heart-shaped cloud appeared at the close of the day. That was Liv.' Chloe added, 'This is extremely important. This was my mum's life's work, life's dream, and she really did give her life for it. The Wellness Centre is her passion because my mum had a real way of knowing the connection between mind and body.' [16b]

Debbie Shiell, foundation director at the Austin Health Foundation, said, 'The walk will be a chance to reflect on Olivia's amazing legacy while raising money for people living with cancer. It will be a day of love and positivity! Just as Olivia would have wanted.' [17]

She went on to say in another interview with ABC radio: 'I remember when I was talking with her about it, and she drove around the corner and saw her name up on the building, she said it was better than any billboard she had ever seen.' [18]

The disease finally took Olivia's life on August 8, 2022. She had managed to survive for 30 years beyond her initial diagnosis, she said in a 2020 interview with *Forbes* magazine. 'So, all those things, I believe, we will eventually see a world beyond it where it's just treated as any other illness that you can kind of control and live well with and, of course, hopefully, cure it.' [19]

The Cancer Council Victoria said the entertainer›s impact on cancer research and awareness had been far-reaching. 'Olivia was a pioneer in the cancer field, and her work provided inspiration for many … Olivia's impact can't be overstated, and her legacy will continue in the work of world-leading research, treatment and care.' [20]

Olivia's Wellness legacy is a living, breathing and evolving dream.

In late 2022 medical breakthrough news 'that would make the late Olivia Newton-John's heart sing, a team at the ONJ Cancer Research

Institute in Melbourne, which she helped to build, has announced a breakthrough in a potential treatment of deadly pancreatic cancer.' [21]

Olivia Newton-John's niece Tottie Goldsmith wrote a beautiful letter in *HELLO!* magazine where she makes a heartfelt promise to her late aunt to keep the Wellness Walk and her charity drives for cancer research alive.

'Olivia, 'Liv', was my aunt, my confidante and my guiding light. Liv is, and was, magic. She was a tornado of joy and action, a visionary, and a healer … Every day, in every way, she moved us forward as people and was a passionate advocate for everyone who needed her … Liv never imagined that life would turn out the way it did for her, and she treated that gift with the grace and gratitude it deserved … She maintained relationships with everyone she came into close contact with and gave more than she got, always – which is quite a feat when the world has given you so much. It is that legacy of absolute commitment to both people and to the causes she was passionate about that is front of mind for us now.

'I'll be holding Chloe's hand, and we will do this together and make you proud.' [22]

Chapter 10

Earthmother

'Olivia was an icon, powerhouse, and star – she will forever be remembered for her dedication to wellness, natural healing, and her belief in the healing power of Mother Earth, which has so profoundly helped and will continue to help so many.' [1a]

1988 was a massive year for all Australians – it was our Bicentennial and for Olivia (post having a baby) it was time for a new album, *The Rumour*, with its first single and title track written and produced by Elton John (no relation). In honour of the two-hundredth anniversary of Australia, Olivia came home to make a television special called *Olivia Down Under*, where she performed with Cliff Richard to an audience that included Prince Charles and Princess Diana.

This surge in Australian national pride inspired Olivia's first solo single in nearly three years, '*It's Always Australia For Me*', written by John Capek and Olivia Newton-John. 'It was a sweet autobiographical love letter to her adopted homeland. Its pure and personal sentiment that probably resonates better with those from Australia. But despite her lengthy absence from the recording studio, her vocals are stronger than ever.' [1b]

Early the following year Olivia was voted Businesswoman of the Year in the US for Koala Blue. This was a real feather in her cap. Intelligent and talented – she flew the flag for women performers' ability to multitask seamlessly.

Olivia closed the '80s with *Warm and Tender*, a 1989 album of children's lullabies (recorded mainly for Chloe) and starring, as a mom in the Disney movie *A Mom For Xmas* was how she started the '90s. Appearing in Madonna's 1991 documentary *Truth Or Dare* was spicy and exciting TV.

ONJ had decided to tap into her inner 'earth mother' in the later stage of her career. For Olivia, post-recovery from her first bout with breast cancer, 'many of her albums found her leaning into a gently uplifting new-age sound inspired by her life-changing experience with breast cancer.' [2]

She was, at heart, a nurturing and maternal woman; authenticity was important to her and her fans. This is not to say she hid away. She still travelled the globe, released albums, and tried her hand at select movies and tours, but her health issues and her desire to change the world in a positive way and raising her daughter dominated her last years on earth.

Even amongst all these accolades and 'after reaching the pinnacle of her career with '*Physical*', Olivia wanted to take things easier.' [3]

Olivia turned off the world's spotlight for a while, preferring to work on healing and female empowerment projects. She was starting to think about other directions, such as Koala Blue, her ode to Australian fashion, which was a successful decision at least for a decade.

In a 1994 interview, Olivia explained why she had slowly changed her musical persona again: 'I'm not an outrageous person. I could no longer keep up ... I admire Madonna for what she does; I think she's very brave, and she's very bold. That's just not me. I couldn't do that and be true to myself. Even doing '*Physical*' was ... it was my idea to make the video funny because if I had tried to do it straight, I couldn't have pulled it off, it wasn't true to myself ... I couldn't have been sincerely saying, 'Baby, let's get physical' because it would have reeked of fakeness.' [4]

The Art of Musical Healing was an essential part of Olivia's later work. Her first bout of breast cancer informed the type of music she went on to record. In 1994, she released *Gaia: One Woman's Journey*, which documented her cancer journey. Gaia 'was named for Greek mythology's equivalent of Mother Earth and reflected the environmental and global concerns that would occupy her musically and personally for the next 24 years.' [5]

In a remarkable recording career spanning over two decades, 19 albums, and 15 top ten singles, '*Gaia* is the first time that Newton-John has undertaken to write, record and co-produce an album of her songs.'

'I even paid for this album myself which I'd never done. I wanted it to be mine, my baby. I wanted it to come out the way I wanted it to sound.' [6]

Healing music was her new passion and a vital part of her charity legacy. Everything she did was to raise money for her Wellness Centre. In the 2020's she started selling off her property portfolio to place the money into her charity. Always willing to step up and support women, as far back as 2004 Olivia got behind the Livkit – a breast cancer awareness kit she believed could save lives with early detection.

Olivia was in full earth-mother mode, her healing albums included working with Festival Mushroom Records in 2004 on her 19th album *Indigo: Women of Song*, an album of cover versions of songs previously recorded by female singers and entirely produced by Phil Ramone. Dedicated to her mother, it was a tribute album to female singers, including covers of songs by Doris Day, Nina Simone, Karen Carpenter and Joan Baez. It went gold in Australia, peaking at number 15 on the Australian Albums Chart. [7]

In July 2005, '*Phenomenal Woman*', the first track of the forthcoming album *Stronger Than Before* (October 2005), was released. This album promoted breast cancer awareness, with the proceeds going to breast cancer research. Always searching for answers, Olivia said in 2006: 'I did a CD called *Grace and Gratitude*, which is a healing CD. How can we – as regular human beings – make a difference and help the planet, those around us, and ourselves?' [8]

Right to the end of her life, Olivia Newton-John concentrated on music inspired by her work with her cancer foundation; a lot of her public appearances and 'work was built upon her legacy, such as teaming up with John Travolta for Christmas albums'. [9]

Olivia released her final solo LP in 2008 and a Christmas album with Australian singing marvel John Farnham in 2016, *Friends for Christmas*, which was re-released with three additional tracks in 2017. 2012's *This Christmas* CD with John Travolta supported her foundation and the Jett Travolta Foundation. The line-up on this album was incredible: when Olivia asked people for help, they always seemed to say yes. Stars featured on the album included Barbra Streisand, James Taylor, Chick Corea, Kenny G, Tony Bennett, Cliff Richard and the Count Basie Orchestra.

And on the 2016 album *Liv On*, Olivia collaborated with great friends Amy Sky and Beth Nielsen Chapman. Centred around themes of grief, caregiving, and recovery, the album featured new and reworked songs from the trio, including a version of Olivia's '*Grace and Gratitude*'. [12a]

Touring was also back on the cards in between cancer treatments. After her first treatment, Olivia returned to the worldwide touring groove. And her next years are spent getting some serious awards, recognising her stellar career and the sheer size of her charity-driven endeavours. Inducted into the ARIA Hall of Fame in 2002, appointed an Officer of the Order of Australia (AO) in 2006 and named Companion of the Order of Australia (AC) in 2019. And she was awarded a British Damehood in 2020.

Olivia Newton-John graced the front cover of *People* magazine twelve times throughout her career and in 1998, she was named one of the most beautiful people in the world.

There were many career highlights for Olivia, but a few of her favourites over the years were the year 2000 new millennium invitation from the Vatican, on behalf of Pope John Paul II, to perform at the Jubilee

Celebration for the Sick and Healthcare Workers. Being an integral part of the opening ceremony for the 2000 Sydney Olympics was also a massive honour for Olivia. She sang '*Dare To Dream*', a duet with John Farnham, to an estimated global viewing audience of four billion people after running the route around the Sydney Opera House as a torchbearer.

Olivia's final live stage appearance was the Fire Fight Australia charity concert at ANZ Stadium in Sydney on Feb 16 2020, and her duets with John Farnham were momentous and magnificent.

In a tearful episode of *This Is Your Life* in 1995 (a show she did again in 2004), John Travolta declared, 'I cannot imagine life without you. And I have a feeling you can't imagine life without me either. I think we're stuck with each other, well, for a very long time. And I love you, and congratulations on *This Is Your Life*. Love you, honey.' [12b]

Olivia toured Australia in February and March 1998 with her long-time friend Cliff Richard and then, at the end of this year, teamed with one of her dearest mates and long-time duet partners, John Farnham and theatre legend Anthony Warlow for The Main Event music tour. The live CD of this tour went Top Ten and won an ARIA (Australian Recording Industry Association) Award for Highest Selling Australian CD.

Olivia's 1998 *Back With a Heart* was her first studio album in four years, recorded in Nashville, and she won herself an Emmy Award for song writing.

1999 was another year of touring, this time a Greatest Hits tour in the States and her first in the USA for seventeen years. The next few years was spent travelling the world, kicking it off with a stunning 2002 US tour with a Symphony Orchestra to grant the audience a richer sound to her ballads.

Everything in Olivia's life slowed down again in 2003 when her mother Irene sadly passed aged 89.

Then the classic phase many great singers settle into came upon her

– the Vegas Residency. In 2013, Olivia was booked into the Donny and Marie Osmond Showroom at the Flamingo. Sadly, the start date was postponed due to the May 2013 death of Olivia's elder sister, Rona, from a brain tumour, aged 72. ONJ resumed performing, doing 45 shows, beginning in April 2014. Her legacy works in *Grease* paid off here as she arrived to massive fanfare on the Strip in the flame-painted '49 Mercury Convertible from *Grease*, with a bunch of Chippendales in tow. This successful three-year Vegas run prompted a fourth live album, *Summer Nights: Live in Las Vegas* (2015).

'She devoted her later years to philanthropy and family, along with her long, brave public battle with cancer, but she never abandoned music.' [10]

Olivia then scored her first number-one single on *Billboard*'s Dance Club Songs chart in 2015 with '*You Have to Believe*' with daughter Chloe and producer Dave Audé. The song was a re-imagining of her 1980 single '*Magic*', which she noted was to celebrate both the 35th anniversary of *Xanadu* and as a dedication to her daughter. Olivia stated, 'I met Chloe's dad on the set of *Xanadu*, so, without that film, Chloe wouldn't be here. She was the real 'magic' that came out of that film!' The song became the first mother-daughter single to reach No. 1 on the *Billboard* Dance Club Play chart. [11]

The *Physical* album's 40th-anniversary deluxe edition hit the shops in February 2021. Olivia and Chloe reunited for a second single, '*Window in the Wall*', which debuted at #1 on the iTunes Music Video Chart and the Amazon A/C Chart. A few months later, Olivia scored another #1 hit on the Amazon A/C chart with '*Put Your Head on My Shoulder*', a duet with music legend Paul Anka. [12]

Above all of her career achievements, it was her artistry as a singer that she held in the highest regard. 'I [consider myself] a singer who acts,' she said in 2015. 'I just enjoy it. Singing is a part of me. Music is a part of who I am. I can't do this forever, so I am enjoying every minute that I can still do it.' [13]

As always, Olivia loved having many career streams flowing simultaneously: her acting work never stopped, just as her song writing and recording kept going.

As mentioned previously, the late 80's movie *Two Of A Kind* with John Travolta was not a cinematic success and it was labelled a 'blizzard of flamboyant synth, propped up with production by David Foster'. [14] But as usual, the soundtrack didn't suck, with the singles '*Twist of Fate*' – called her last big hit – and the duet with Travolta, '*Take a Chance*', doing very well commercially.

To celebrate her legacy of thirty years of recording, Olivia released *Magic: The Very Best of Olivia Newton-John* in 2001, and while in Queensland, Australia, she filmed her next TV movie, *Wilde Girls*, teaming up with her daughter Chloe.

On filming this role, Olivia happily said 'I think it'll be fun for me because it's so interesting to do different things.' [15]

For another movie, *A Few Best Men* in 2011, Olivia recorded a new song, '*Weightless*', written by her old producer John Farrar and his son Max. 'The sound of Olivia's voice is unique, I think,' says Farrar. 'It's quite rare when you hear voices that don't sound like anybody else, particularly these days. I feel very privileged to have spent all those years with her. I couldn't have worked with a nicer person. We're still the best of friends.' [16]

A new younger set of fans climbed on board the Olivia train after her guest-starring role in *Glee* (2010). And in 2015, Olivia was a guest judge on an episode of RuPaul's *Drag Race.*

In 2017, Olivia had to cancel tour dates due to severe back pain, which was discovered to be her breast cancer metastasized to her sacrum. Olivia initially recovered well and went back to work later that year. She undertook a cameo in *The Very Excellent Mr Dundee* movie and re-commenced her tour.

Olivia's private love life was constantly evolving behind the scenes during her earth-mother musical phase. Back in 1995, having recovered from her 1992 diagnosis, Olivia and Matt divorced, but one year later, Olivia found a new love and moved in with cameraman Patrick McDermott for more than eight years.

In 2004, Olivia was again surprised by the Australian *This Is Your Life* programme whilst at a fundraiser for her cancer centre in Melbourne. It was jam-packed with friends and family appearances, even her old teacher Mr Hogan who advised a 15-year-old Olivia to pursue her singing career. Patrick McDermott her then-boyfriend also sent a lovely message talking about how the whole world loved Olivia and that the animals loved Olivia. He added that if 'we could all be a little bit more like Olivia, then we'd all be a bit better off.' [18]

But on 30 June 2005, while Olivia was at the opening of her self-owned Gaia Retreat and Spa in Byron Bay, her on-again-off-again boyfriend Patrick McDermott went missing on an overnight sport fishing trip out of San Pedro, California. His body was never found. Many theories abound that he faked his death, but nothing has been confirmed. This mystery plagued Olivia for many years and was a great personal sadness in her life.

But thankfully for her love-life reared its head again, and she met John Easterling in 2007 in Peru. John founded the Amazon Herb Company, which makes products using herbs and botanicals from the Amazon Rainforest. The courtship was quick and in 2008 Olivia married for the second, and last time, to John.

John and Olivia bought a new ranch together in Santa Ynez, California, in 2015 for $4.69 million. The 12-acre property has a main house, guesthouse, barn and many areas for horses, including a stable, arena and large pastures. Olivia filled the property with animals and family and lived there happily until the day she died.

In May 2017, it was announced that her breast cancer had returned.

'Olivia Newton-John, Pop's First Female Chameleon' called herself a 'cancer thriver', 'because the illness that has defined so much of her life over the past quarter century has also led to personal enrichment.'[18] This was the same time the Australian made biopic on her life was released starring Delta Goodrem. Initially Olivia did not support this film but as the proceeds went to her cancer fund, she agreed to it and recorded two songs with Delta for the soundtrack. This look back at her life actually inspired Olivia to publish her long-awaited autobiography, *Don't Stop Believin'* -named after her hit song and a *New York Times* Best Seller.' [19]

When the movie and soundtrack *Grease* turned 40, the celebrations were worldwide. Olivia and John Travolta presented Olivia's dear friend John Farrar, in January 2018, at the G'Day USA Gala, with an Outstanding Achievement in the Arts.

'May 2019, Newton-John's elder brother Hugh, a doctor, died at age 80 – his death left Newton-John as the sole surviving sibling.' [20]

2020 into 2021 was a time when the world was locked down, but never one to sit still, in 2020 Olivia and her husband John set up the Olivia Newton-John Foundation, 'which is committed to realising a world beyond cancer. Funding research into plant-based medicine and other holistic and wellness therapies, we are determined to discover kinder ways to prevent, treat and cure all cancers.' [21]

Olivia Newton-John died on August 8, 2022, at her home in Santa Ynez, California.

John Easterling paid tribute to his wife on the day of her death: 'At Olivia's deepest essence, she was a healer using her mediums of song, of words, of touch.'

Her place as a woman in music towards the end of her life was as a healer and her legacy place in music overall.

Even dressed in black leather or a leotard and purple leggings, Olivia Newton-John was always easy listening, and I think her latest evolution was a culmination of all her facets: she was the Queen of adult contemporary and proud of it.

'To the end, Ms Newton-John firmly believed in her audience-friendly approach to music. 'It annoys me when people think because it's commercial, it's bad,' she told *Rolling Stone*. 'It's completely opposite. If people like it, that's what it's supposed to be." [23]

In this lane, she has survived that horrible fate in the industry of ageing out. She has survived cancel culture, and she has survived being classified as a past generational.

'The history of soft rock has been told mostly by men, and that's why its queens have mostly been marginalised. Olivia Newton-John was one of the biggest. RIP to a master of delicacy.' [24]

She was, and is, a singer for all ages; her 50-year career has hits from all decades, and as she battled her health problems from 1992 until she died in 2022, she flexed her considerable power for good and positivity. Olivia performed for charity and wrote and produced music to help heal others and comfort herself. She wrapped the clock of her global superstardom modestly around her slender frame and stood tall on any world stage.

'As for the industry, it has certainly changed. I think with all of these television shows and YouTube and the Internet, you have so much less time to develop as an artist and perfect your craft. So many things today are 'instant' and that's not always a good thing.' [25]

Australia is proud to have this woman call Oz home. Proud that Melbourne played a part in preparing her for her chosen life, turned the studio spotlights on her and helped her pack her adventurous bags and head out into the world. Australia is proud we offered her a haven from the noise as well. Proud to be the ground on which she planted her Healing spa in Bryon Bay and her Wellness Foundation for Cancer Research.

Her music is of happy times, disco and '80s flamboyance and experimentation. The beauty of ballads will break your heart and declarations of love no matter the cost. She took the LGBTQ community into her arms and demanded equality. She really was quite simply a cultural ambassador for all things good. A woman whose strength and influence will not pale over the years but continue to impress generations.

Olivia's ethereal voice is part of people's lives – she was the sound of Australian music at a pivotal time in history, five decades' strong. What a talent and what an incredible body of work. 'A gorgeous woman and fabulous singer … and pretty good bloody actor too!' [26]

She made fame her friend, and she used it well. She was a charming authentic megastar – those who met her never forgot that feeling.

'I don't know if wanting to be a performer was a conscious thing, but [as a child] I was always dressing up, and doing shows, and singing and writing songs and poetry all the time … I loved to sing.' [27]

Rest in 'Magic'
Olivia Newton-John. [28]

Chapter 11
Legacy

Guess mine is not the first heartbroken,
My eyes are not the first to cry
I'm not the first to know, there's just no gettin' over you.
'*Hopelessly Devoted to You*' lyrics

If you Google Olivia Newton-John's legacy, this question pops up: Why is Olivia Newton-John important?

The answer is: 'Olivia Newton-John was one of the biggest Australian stars ever to make a successful international career. Whether it was in music, movies, as an entrepreneur or as an advocate for breast cancer research, she left an indelible mark on the world around her.' [1]

There it is in a nutshell. She was an extraordinary person.

'Olivia Newton-John was that rare thing: an unproblematic icon whose light and star quality never seemed to dim.' [2a]

The Dame was one of Australia's greatest publicists, performers and philanthropists. 'She is one of the world's most successful recording artists, having sold an estimated 100 million records worldwide. In a six-decade career, she has earned a legion of fans as a teen pop star, Eurovision finalist, country music star, screen idol, music video pioneer, and environmental activist.' [2b]

Iconic music magazine *NME* said, 'Olivia Newton-John was the girl-next-door who lived her best life to the end.' [3] She is so many things to so many people, which is why Melbourne hosted Olivia's grieving family and fans a state memorial-held at Hamer Hall on February 26th, 4pm 2023.

Premier of Victoria Dan Andrews said, 'I think giving Melburnians and Victorians and people who travel from other parts of the country and even the world a chance to celebrate such an important, rich and generous life — that was the right thing to do.' Importantly to 'take her cancer journey and to turn that into more research, better treatment, better care and this focus on wellness, is such an amazing legacy.' [4]

This 90-minute event celebrated what Olivia loved doing and what she believed in. A memorial for all to feel her 'Love and Light' legacy with Delta Goodrem (who played Olivia in her biopic) singing a six-minute medley of her greatest hits to an audience filled with celebrities, friends and fans. The memorable event was live streamed with many international celebrities sending video messages and tickets for the public were free. Her grateful husband John said of Olivia, 'She had an uncommon ability to care – I mean genuinely and authentically care'. [5]

When she passed, Olivia's legion of Aussie fans pushed her *Greatest Hits* album and the *Grease* movie soundtrack back into the top of the ARIA Albums chart.

Olivia's family reportedly held a private memorial service one month after the actress and singer lost her battle with breast cancer. Her loved ones, including husband John Easterling and daughter Chloe Lattanzi, gathered to remember the life and times of the Aussie star. [6]

Tottie Goldsmith, whose mother Rona was Olivia's sister, has now revealed that the family had anticipated her aunt's death. 'Fighting back the tears, Tottie said the family would accept the offer of a state funeral on behalf of not just our family but also Australia. She's so loved, and I think our country needs it, so we're going to accept it.' [7]

November 24 2022, the ARIA Music Awards featured a moving tribute by Australian-born, now UK resident Natalie Imbruglia. In 1999 Olivia received an ARIA Award for Highest Selling Album (*Highlights from The Main Event*), and in 2002 she was inducted into the Hall of Fame.

In the USA, 'Superstar P!nk paid tribute to Olivia Newton-John at the Nov 2022 American Music Awards, performing a rendition of the *Grease* classic tune, '*Hopelessly Devoted To You*', to an audience that sang along and clapped their hands. While she sang, a montage of images of Newton-John played on a screen … P!nk's performance was met with a standing ovation.' [8]

Olivia received 10 AMAs throughout her career and co-hosted the show with Glen Campbell and Aretha Franklin in 1976.

P!nk was introduced by singing star Melissa Etheridge – who also underwent surgery and chemotherapy following her breast cancer diagnosis and who praised Olivia's 'sweetness' and star power: 'As her tens of millions of fans will attest, to hear her sing – whether live at a theatre or up on the silver screen – was to feel the power of art to transform the feelings we all have of love, of elation, and disappointment into something sublime.' [9]

Around the world, the unforgettable Olivia was endearingly known by the media as The Goddess, Livvy, Olivia Neutron-Bomb, and Lovely Livvy. But who was Olivia?

On paper, she was a Libran, her eyes were a lovely mix of blue/grey, and her hair was glorious silky blonde. Her clothes size was 6, her shoe size 8, and she loved playing golf (10). She was lauded across many musical categories, including Pop, Country, Adult Contemporary, Soft Rock, New Age, Dance-Pop, and Country Pop and was the Queen of it all from 1963 to 2022.

She never struck back at the press and was never struck by them. Olivia Neutron-Bomb could also play the guitar and piano – 'I've written songs on the piano and guitar, but I've never been game enough to play them publicly.' [11] She always filled her house with lilies and orchids and loved cosmetics, often doing her own makeup for photo sessions. Her $85m empire extended beyond singing and acting – into property, fashion and medical marijuana. [12]

The most treasured item in her wardrobe was a beautiful opal and diamond ring that her mother left her, and in 2012 The National Trust of Australia designated her a National Living Treasure.

Where did this certified National Treasure think she would go after death? Olivia said she meditated with her Buddhist friends, prayed with her Christian friends, and in her heart, she had a 'spirituality of her own'. She reflected further that Matt Lattanzi once said 'nature was his church', 'and I thought that was a beautiful description'. [13a]

The definition of 'Legacy' is something that is passed on – something gone but not forgotten.

'The humanity and humanitarianism of pop's first female chameleon ensures that her personal legacy will be as all-encompassing as her musical one.' [13b]

Olivia put Australia on the music, film, and cancer research international map. She left behind a myriad of legacies as an entertainer, in wellness, a literary legacy, an environmental legacy, even a legal legacy.

Her environmental legacy was built over her whole life; nature was her safe place. She continuously gave back to the community and was 'acknowledged by charitable and environmental organisations for her ongoing efforts, among them: the American Red Cross, the Environmental Media Association, the Women's Guild of Cedars-Sinai Medical Centre, and the Rainforest Alliance and Concept Cure.' [14]

In 1996 she created National Tree Day, responsible for planting more than 20 million trees in Australia. She co-founded One Tree Per Child, an international school initiative to have every child under ten plant at least one tree.

Olivia even had a beautiful rose named after her in 2008, the Hedging rose (Floribunda) Olivia Newton-John. 'Fully double peachy-apricot-coloured blooms, complemented by a delicate tea rose fragrance. Part proceeds of every sale are donated to the Olivia Newton-John Cancer Centre Appeal.' [15]

Olivia's love of animals is well documented. She always had a pet, no matter how busy she became during her career. 'She advocated for adopting from shelters rather than buying from breeders, and her 'animal rights activism extended to awareness of wildlife toxicology and the dangers of global warming. In an interview, she said, 'the loss of a pet can be as powerful as any family member. I know this from going through it myself and watching friends who have lost animals who can't function for a long time.' [16]

Olivia's Wellness Legacy has been laid out in the previous chapter. This charity, this legacy, was created to find 'kinder options for treating cancer', a genuinely accurate reflection of this woman who radiated kindness throughout her career. She firmly believed, 'Once you face your fear, nothing is ever as hard as you think.' [17] This fighter pulled on her public battle armour – her positive and prominent advocacy for cancer research, with the result being her foundation.

Olivia and partners left the world the Gaia – the 'spirit of mother earth' – Retreat & Spa in Byron Bay, New South Wales, Australia, as an ideal place to renew, refresh and restore. This Spa will continue to heal and help those needing to recover, even though it was sold in 2021, for a rumoured $30 million, to West Australian mining magnate and philanthropist Andrew Forrest.

Gaia has received numerous awards since it opened, including the Best Health Retreat award at the Gourmet Traveller Travel Awards and the World Travel Award for Australia's Leading Spa Resort and Australia's Leading Boutique Hotel. Trip Advisor named Gaia #3 of the 'Top 10 Celebrity-Owned Hotels in the World', putting Olivia in the company of fellow hotel owners Robert Redford, Bono and Robert De Niro. [18]

Olivia's Music Legacy will play on for as long as people listen to music. She modestly said, 'I've been so blessed throughout my career to have worked with some of the greatest songwriters and producers who have helped me achieve my musical successes through the years.' [19a]

Her music brand is in safe hands with Primary Wave Music Publishing, a leading independent publisher of iconic and legendary music worldwide. They announced a partnership with Olivia in 2020 (which we hope now extends to her family). The Primary Wave team promised her brand would expand to wider audiences. 'The icon will now have access to Primary Wave's entire marketing, branding, Broadway, Film/TV, and digital strategy teams, as well as their licensing and synch departments. This includes working with her catalogue of masters and publishing assets encompassing hits such as '*Physical*', '*I Honestly Love You*', '*A Little More Love*', '*Please Mr Please*' and '*Have You Never Been Mellow*', as well as some of her biggest hits from *Grease* and *Xanadu*, including the Oscar-nominated '*Hopelessly Devoted to You*' and the #1 smash '*Magic*'.' [19b]

Lawrence Mestel, CEO & Founder of Primary Wave, added: 'I have admired Olivia for many decades, her artistry, philanthropy, and grace as a human being are second to none. She is the definition of an iconic artist.' [19c]

The Australian Performing Arts Collection at Arts Centre Melbourne has Olivia's personal collection of career treasures, including two gowns, design sketches, scripts, tour music and a prestigious award. 'It will also provide the ability to tell stories from several different phases of Newton-John's career and will ensure her legacy is accessible for generations to come.' [20]

Olivia left a trail of glitter and light in every creative orbit she entered. If she worked with someone, they were friends for life. Her incredible list of duets is a musical legacy testament to this.

Her duet list reads like a 'who's who' of famous singers, from all around the world. Her song collaborators included Peter Allen, Elton John, Cliff Richard, John Travolta, Electric Light Orchestra, John Farrar, Helen Reddy, Bruce Welch, John Farnham, Anthony Warlow,

Billy Thorpe, Jimmy Barnes, Barry Gibb, Andy Gibb, Kenny Loggins, Kelly Lang, Human Nature, David Campbell, Delta Goodrem, Barbra Streisand, Tina Arena, Johnny O'Keefe, Darren Hayes, Richard Marx, Keith Urban, Barry Manilow, Gene Kelly and Dionne Warwick.

Unforgettable moments become the stuff of legends; the stories fans tell become the bricks of immortality for an artist.

One such moment for Olivia fans was a 1998 February night in Melbourne. 'It's not every day you get two of the world's greatest female singers on stage together, but that's exactly what happened when Mariah Carey and Olivia Newton-John joined forces in Australia.' [21] Mariah Carey was on the Melbourne leg of her *Butterfly* tour. She launched into a version of '*Hopelessly Devoted To You*'. Unbeknown to the fans, Olivia was there and walked on stage to sing the famous hit with Mariah, 'coming together at the end to hold their hands high in the air, met with screams of delight from the Australian audience'. [10]

Another mythical moment was in January 1979 NYC, at the televised fundraising concert *The Music for UNICEF Concert*, a gig held to raise money for world hunger programs. This was the day ABBA, the Bee Gees, Olivia Newton-John, Rod Stewart and Andy Gibb sang a staggering medley. This momentous coming-together of talent was joined by Donna Summer, Kris Kristofferson, Earth, Wind & Fire, Henry Fonda and The Fonz (Henry Winkler). A 'line-up of an era's legends all on one stage'. [23]

Sony Music's 2017 music video of a special version of The Beatles' '*With A Little Help From My Friends*', featuring the vast line-up of 29 musicians, including John Farnham, Olivia Newton-John, Jessica Mauboy and Guy Sebastian, to support Australia's most vulnerable young people shows the world the power of a song to raise awareness and money and Olivia was there front and centre.

Olivia also left a Legal Legacy by fighting for what she believed was right. 'Whether it was support for the LGBTIQ+ community or medicinal cannabis before it became 'mainstream' – Newton-John showed time and time again that she was on the right side of history by doing what she knew as the right thing, even if it wasn't popular, or even legal at the time.' [25a]

Neil Pharaoh is a government engagement and campaigning agent. He has spent most of his voluntary and professional life in and around social purpose organisations and advocacy for Pro Bono Australia. He posted these accolades for the behind-the-scenes legal work Olivia had been part of. 'I had the tremendous privilege and honour of working for Olivia Newton-John for a decade on her government engagement, advocacy and campaigns. Newton-John was passionate about cancer wellness, cancer research and medicinal cannabis. Over the decade working with her and the government, we had many tens of millions of dollars wins from both state and federal government.' [24b]

He went on to say that he learnt five valuable lessons from Olivia, which apply to any ambassador or patron:

1. Always find time for people.
2. Live your values, speak from the heart.
3. Follow the advice, but then do it your way.
4. Build effective teams, and, most importantly …
5. Stick to the right beliefs and values before they become 'popular'. [24c]

As a result of her 1975 lawsuit against MCA Records, 'record companies changed their contracts to be based on a set number of albums recorded by a musician and not a specific number of years'. [25]

Olivia also left us a stunning Literary Legacy, with four books under her belt. Her 2018 magnum opus autobiography, *Don't Stop Believin'*, debuted at No.12 on the *New York Times* Bestseller list and gave the world her mantra – Don't stop believin'!

In 2011, as a proud foodie she released in Australia (through Murdoch Books), *LivWise: Easy Recipes For A Healthy, Happy Life* being a huge believer in the importance of eating a healthy diet to maintain wellness and balance.

There was also *Surrender - The Story of Gaia Retreat & Spa Book*, written by friends and original co-founders: Gregg Cave, Ruth Kalnin, Olivia Newton-John and Warwick Evans (G.R.O.W). With, of course, proceeds from all three going to the Olivia Newton-John Cancer and Wellness Centre.

And then there was her co-written children's book, *A Pig Tale*, which had an environmental theme. 'Ziggy's a piggy, and Iggy's his pop. And Iggy collects and saves just about everything.'

Lastly, Olivia left behind a Family Legacy.

Her daughter Chloe Rose was her greatest legacy. She acted with her, sang with her, and her daughter was her reason for being.

In 2021, Olivia Newton-John, at the age of 72 and perhaps thinking about musically retiring, shared a brand-new hopeful piano ballad featuring her daughter.

'There is always something special about singing with my daughter,' she said. 'She not only has a gorgeous voice, she's an amazing musician with tremendous instincts as a singer.' [26]

It's time to heal (it's time to heal)
To turn the page (to turn the page)
Too much to lose, so much to save
We have to change
Looking for a window in the wall
Maybe we can see the other side
'*Window In The Wall*' (with Chloe Lattanzi) (2021)

This dynamic duo previously released '*You Have to Believe*' in 2015, a cover of Olivia's hit single '*Magic*' from *Xanadu*. It went to #1 on the US Dance charts.

Chloe's grief at her mother's passing is overwhelming, and as she works through it, she has been releasing little memories, photos, and plans on her social media. The 36-year-old 'has revealed she wrote a special song for her late mother, admitting in a video that she was 'terrified' when putting pen to paper to honour her legendary mum. 'Oh shit, I'm scared,' Lattanzi said in a voiceover as she prepared to sing in a studio. "This is a scary place right now because there is so much inside, and I don't know how to put it into words." [27] She also revealed to the world that her mother secretly officiated at her beach wedding to long-term fiancé James.

Like her cousin Tottie, Chloe has taken up the task of keeping Olivia's Walk for Wellness in the public eye. 'I want to carry the torch for my mama. My mum's dream was for kinder treatments for cancer. So I feel the torch has been passed, and this is my mission, my passion, and I'm so grateful to be doing this with my beautiful cousin, for my mother.' Tottie Goldsmith praised her younger cousin for 'taking over the shining light of her mum'.

'What a beautiful way to celebrate Liv's birthday today in Oz by announcing @chloelattanziofficial jumping in with us to continue her mama's dream, her legacy.' [28]

Tottie added, 'I know it's very important to me that this place survives and her legacy lives on.' [29]

With these two working together, the future looks bright for the Olivia Newton-John Cancer Wellness Centre.

Olivia was a spiritual seeker throughout her life. She once ascribed her restlessness partly to her grandfather Max Born who had a famous quote: 'The belief that there is only one truth, and that oneself is in possession of it, seems to me the deepest root of all that is evil in the world.'

'My whole life, I searched for one thing I could believe in, but I couldn't find just one because I believe in possibilities and respect all people's different faiths. I have a real problem with people killing each other for what they believe, so my grandfather's words put it all into perspective for me. I agree with him.'

To ensure Olivia's memory, it has been proposed that Olivia Newton-John should replace the Queen on the Australian $5 note. [31] And a laneway in her honour in the Melbourne suburbs of Joilmont or Parkville or even the Melbourne University gardens would be a perfect tribute. Make it one with lots of trees.

Finally, and peacefully, Olivia said that she wasn't afraid about the end of her life, 'because I've had the icing on the cake and the candles on top of that and the icing on top of that and more candles and hundreds and thousands on top of that. I've had the most wonderful career and the most wonderful life.' [32]

Olivia and her mother Irene at the celebration of her film *Xanadu* at the Underground disco, 1980.

Singing duo Pat Carroll with Olivia in London, England, circa 1966.

Singer Johnny O'Keefe and Olivia Newton-John, 1970.

Olivia and John Farnham during the concert
The Main Event at Brisbane Entertainment Centre, 1988.

Olivia with Sir Cliff Richard promoting their anniversary tour of Australia and New Zealand, 1998.

Olivia Newton-John attends the 32nd Annual Academy of Country Music Awards at the Universal Amphitheatre in Universal City, California, 1993.

Olivia with daughter Chloe and then husband Matt Lattanzi, 1993.

Olivia dancing with Michael Beck, Gene Kelly in a scene for *Xanadu*.

Olivia and Molly Meldrum at the Koala Foundation Million Dollar Lunch, 2007.

Olivia with singer Barry Gibb at a live performance charity appeal in Sydney, 2009.

Olivia along with Nicole Kidman, Keith Urban, Hugh Jackman and Russell Crowe on stage during the taping of the *Oprah Winfrey Show* at the Sydney Opera House in Sydney, 2010.

Olivia and MC Richard Wilkins at her fundraising gala event at the State Theatre Sydney, 2009.

Olivia and co-star John Travolta attend the premiere of the film *Grease*, 1978.

Olivia at the opening of her new Cancer and Wellness Centre at the Austin Hospital, Heidelberg in Melbourne, 2012.

(L-R) John Easterling, Tottie Goldsmith and Olivia during the annual Wellness Walk and Research Run in Melbourne, 2018.

Part Two

Olivia Newton-John and Her Place Amongst Women In Music

'Newton-John's legacy endures as one of the earliest women in pop to embrace different eras, genres, sounds and even self-presentation, she lives on in the DNA of every female pop star's self-reinvention.' [1]

Part Two will explore Olivia Newton-John's personal legacy and her public footprint, which encompass her Wellness Research Centre and Foundation, both based in Melbourne Australia.

This Olivia tribute will look at this legend's place and sphere of influence amongst women in music. ONJ was a woman who stayed her course in the music business – now an icon and always determined entertainer who proudly said of her career: 'I always went with my instincts.' [2]

These instincts were clearly gold. The controversy her single '*Physical*' caused in the '80s blew the lid off video charts and the notion women should stay in their own 'sweet little lane'.

Olivia hit every target she aimed for and later in her career she did it all while battling three bouts of breast cancer, falling in and out of love, getting married and having her greatest life achievement – her daughter Chloe.

When Olivia became an advocate for breast cancer, she chose to use her music and her profile for healing. She explored herself and her strengths and her song writing ability. She explored a woman's place and power in music and woman's ability to heal through song – an ancient art made modern by her determination.

Her innate graceful nature and charm was regal in its sincerity and a character trait in her, from a young girl to her last breath.

The gratitude she constantly expressed to those around her who helped her privately and on stage was legendary. She never took anything or anyone's hard work for granted, and she believed in good karma – spreading positivity wherever she went. This was a woman who was forever thinking about others, about how to help and how to get attention for those who needed it.

She really was the Queen as John Farnham crowned her one night before 70,000 fans gathered at Sydney's ANZ Stadium. 'Would you please do me a favour and welcome to the stage my friend Dame Olivia Newton-John?' Then he asked, 'Where are you, Your Highness?' [3]

We will look at ONJ's unbreakable ties to Australia and how that shaped her life. Then through two delicious and beautifully written thought pieces by Melbourne thought leaders in the musicologist field – Melbourne University's Dr Frederic Kiernan and RMIT's Dr Kat Nelligan. They explore Olivia's place within women in music and her impact on the LGBTQIA+ community by delving into the intense memories and emotions her music creates in the listener. How a music memory can generate layers of discussion about legacy, achievement and, importantly, how her music made people feel. This is so interesting: the legacy of Olivia is that she made people feel good! How lucky is Melbourne to have such passionate and clever people to record, study and interpret and spread the love of music?

Part two will also look at how Olivia belonged to Australia because even though she sported a well-stamped passport and lived happily in the US for many years, Australia always remained her home in both heart and mind. In 1980, during a *Countdown* interview with Ian 'Molly' Meldrum, she said, 'An Australian upbringing is a really good leveller, a good balance in life.' [4] Her place in Australian music history, and mirrored in the international scene, is a usual one – she doesn't fit into one genre, she invented a few genres along the way.

This section will shine a light on her favourite people and projects and peek into the private side of this woman through her life with the men she chose to partner with over the years. And we follow her journey as a mother of daughter Chloe.

In 2020 when Chloe performed on the *Dancing With The Stars* reality show in Australia, Olivia came to cheer her on. 'I encouraged her to just be herself. She's in her own dancing shoes and they're beautiful – she'll do great.'

Through the memories of her dear friends and people in the Australian music industry we see that her golden image was as true off stage as it was on. People who have met and worked with her over the years try to define what it was about Olivia that gave her such career longevity. It's all praise and no haze when it comes to 'Our Livvy'as Ian 'Molly' Meldrum, Richard Wilkins, Tony Espie (one of Australia's best mixing engineers) and James Young (Melbourne Night Mayor and Cherry Bar owner) will attest.

Lastly, let's wade through the glorious words of fans and friends alike – the tributes and accolades – like millions of facets of the one diamond that all came together in the days after her death. Like Kira the muse in *Xanadu*, she had now taken up residency in immortality. The tribute chapter tries to capture just some of the phenomenal wave of grief that flooded social media at her passing; social media was like a constantly graphitized upon wall of love for Olivia. 'By paying tribute, we can remember and celebrate those who shifted the boundaries before us, rather than take for granted the position we're in now. As Kurt Cobain once said, 'the future of rock belongs to women'. [6]

Chapter 12

Her Place Amongst Women In Music

Episode 2 of the music documentary television series *Love Is In The Air*, narrated by Toni Collette, was called 'She's leaving home'. It initially focused on Helen Reddy, as one of the talented and influential women who paved the way for other Australian women to make it big in the international pop scene. It went on to say, 'Reddy was able to weather the tall-poppy critics in Australia to pursue her career and that women have been Australia's most consistently successful musical export', including Marcia Hines, Patsy Ann Noble, Renée Geyer, Olivia Newton-John, Pat Carroll and Debra Byrne. [1]

Helen Reddy was Olivia's mentor and Olivia, in turn, was a guiding light to many other up-and-coming female musicians.

Olivia built a support group around her that included family, lifelong friends and industry supporters. This network got her safely though the six decades of her career and with her credibility and sense of self-intact. Olivia set up a community of trust and relied on it constantly. She relied on Australia, as it was her adopted heritage, and proudly took it with her wherever she went. She never apologised for her accent, for the distance it took to fly here, for the slang or larrikin sense of humour.

'That voice … That face … and that accent, which she kept, and which showed girls in suburban Australia – always at least six months behind the rest of the world in everything back then – that one of us could make it over there.' [2]

Like Helen Reddy, Olivia's first lesson in her school of rock was that Aussie girls were just as good as all the other contenders worldwide.

Growing up in Melbourne in the '80s, I knew who Olivia was … who the hell didn't? She was a hero to girls everywhere and a crush to boys alike. I knew she looked like a surfer chick, sang like a bird and lived overseas, because that's where you became a star, but l also knew she came home a lot.

She was queen of the radio waves and we all know a teenager's best friend is the radio. Moving to Melbourne from a country town for school and university, I fell in love with the Melb Uni Union live band nights. The bands were elite, such as Hunters and Collectors, Models and Flowers (now Icehouse). I started working for street press magazine *Inpress* and then for Mushroom Records, moving on to become a research/writer for Ian 'Molly' Meldrum. Now as one of the owners of Cherry Bar and other live music venues around Melbourne, music is like oxygen in our house and watching musicians' careers a lifetime habit.

Olivia Newton-John was a path-maker, a pioneer for women in music, and her influence on singers past, present and emerging is massive.

Australia claimed her whenever we could, she was an 'Aussie Battler' and 'her infectious smile, angelic voice and humble nature made her a beloved cultural emblem'. [3]

In Australia, before the ARIA Awards and the *Countdown* Awards, in the late '60s, and '70s had the King of Pop Awards. Early on, the women weren't even acknowledged with an award until 1972. When John Farnham won for the fourth year in a row, he suddenly had a Queen and that year it was Colleen Hewett. [4]

Debbie Byrne was crowned in 1974, then the US-born stunner Marcia Hines took over. Marcia has been a trailblazer for more than five decades, dominating the mid-'70s to early '80s with a record-breaking run of hits. She was a regular on *Countdown*, hosted her own TV show and was crowned Queen of Pop three years running. [5] Livvy (although not living in Australia at the time) got a special mention in 1976 for 'Best Australian International Performer'.

'Telling the history of Australian female musicians is a tricky mission. Women are – and always have been – musically innovative in Australia, often at the forefront of new musical formats ... Women have shown great musical versatility in their ability to straddle rock and pop, punk and new wave, stage musicals and comedy, jazz, blues, soul and folk.' [6]

Australia female's musicians influenced by Olivia come from all genres: Jessica Mauboy, Delta Goodrem, Dannii and Kylie Minogue, Sia, Tina Arena and more. Not just singers, let's not forget the acting girls that owe Olivia a nod. Rebel Wilson, who played Olivia's daughter in the film *A Few Best Men*, revealed on her Instagram page it was Olivia who inspired her to pursue acting while embracing her Aussie accent.

'Seeing you star in the huge Hollywood blockbuster *Grease* with your natural accent was so instrumental to me as a little girl, helping me to believe that it was possible for an Aussie girl to star in huge international musicals. You were the reason I auditioned for my high school production of *Grease* at 15 – I was only in the chorus, but it was a start!' [7]

Kylie Ann Minogue, an Australian superstar singer and actress, has lived most of her career in London, recently returning home to live in Melbourne. Kylie starred in the Australian soap opera *Neighbours* at a young age, playing mechanic Charlene Robinson, and went on to become a worldwide pop princess. Kylie admitted she 'wanted to be all Newton-John', as Olivia was one of her biggest inspirations (along with Prince, David Bowie, Michael Jackson & Madonna). [8] Kylie has often talked about growing up watching *Grease* and idolising Olivia, and it's obvious that there are many parallels between the two women. Each began their careers with an innocent, girl-next-door image, which they went on to change publicly, in Kylie's case, the gold hot pants clip is a timeless sexy disco diva moment. Both are gay icons, both have shown the world their excellent business acumen and both have fought cancer. [9a]

'Kylie gave so many Australian kids the green light to dream. To morph from pop to Impossible Princess, stun us with extraordinary visual concepts in video and on stage, take risks at a time when few dared to, and (just quietly) slay for more than three decades across trends, generations, and geography.' [9b]

In 2021 Double J radio released a list of 50 game-changing women in the Australian music scene, in celebration of International Women's Day as curated by Zan Rowe. The list includes Amy Taylor from Amyl and the Sniffers, Courtney Barnett, Jessica Mauboy, Kylie Minogue, Marcia Hines, Sampa The Great and Tiddas, as well as late musicians Helen Reddy and Chrissy Amphlett and, of course, Dame Olivia because: 'Without her, Australian music would sound very different.' [11]

ONJ and the other ladies on this list were artists who 'shifted the needle in our local scene. To be a game-changer is to leave the world a different place than how you found it. And, in doing so, to show those in your wake that they can too.' [12]

Tina Arena is a singer who is a 'beacon of femininity, strength and power ... standing up for women in music, showing long careers that include motherhood are possible, and that no one can define your career except you.' [13a] Tina recorded with Olivia Newton-John in 2002 – the tune '*I'll Come Runnin*'' for Olivia's first-ever duets album, simply entitled '*2*' and released in Australia.

She was once described as a singer who 'comes on strong with a voice that is a diva hybrid of Celine Dion, Mariah Carey and Olivia Newton-John.' [13b]

Sia is another Australian artist making serious international impact. She is hard to pigeonhole: eccentric and brilliant would be a start. Both songwriter and singer, she famously said in 2015: 'I don't care about [playing live] so I'll throw the most ludicrous idea out and say, 'I'll do a live show if you can get Olivia Newton-John to perform with me', because that's my childhood dream.' [14]

Dame Olivia Newton-John said she was willing to get up on stage and sing with Sia and make this dream a reality; she also said she would love to write some new music with her. They met up and hugged it out in Vegas and Olivia sympathized with Sia's reluctance to perform live. 'I can relate, and I was like that for years … She's very fortunate in this time, because of social media, she doesn't have to perform live if she doesn't want to.' [15]

Australian singer Vanessa Amorosi was overcome with emotion and had to bow out of her live interview on *Sunrise* morning TV the day of Olivia Newton-John's death. She said she had looked up to her since she was a kid and that 'I don't think I've really processed it yet … I'm actually very sad about Olivia, to be honest.' [16]

Jessica Mauboy is another supremely talented Australian singer and actress. 'With her big, blistering voice, she's effortlessly hopped from music to film to TV and back again. She has performed at *Eurovision* twice and made history as the first Indigenous woman to top the ARIA charts three weeks in a row.' [17]

Commenting on her latest Eurovision entry, she said, 'Following in the footsteps of Olivia Newton-John (1974) and Gina G (1996) feels so crazy. I got to make this performance really good!' [18]

'Mauboy has been described as an exotic Olivia Newton-John. Both caught international attention with musical films, but that is not all they have in common. Mauboy has the same fresh, girlish innocence with which Newton-John won over Americans in *Grease*, and, like Newton-John, acts as well as she sings, a powerful double as Hollywood rediscovers the musical.' [19]

Delta Goodrem idolised Olivia since childhood and is one of Australia's most well-known singers. 'Olivia influenced my earliest years as an evolving artist and became the backbone of influence to living my life and heart as a proud Australian artist. I aspired to have her grace, humility and talent from the time I started singing.' [20]

Delta was the girl picked to play her idol in the *Olivia: Hopelessly Devoted to You* biopic. 'She was always such a wonderful mentor, a guiding light.' [21] Delta has had her own illness battle – beating Hodgkin's lymphoma a few years ago. 'I grew up with Olivia's energy and beautiful voice in my world through her music, and then from an early age I was truly blessed to find friendship and mentorship from Olivia. She is an icon.' [22]

Dannii Minogue, the dynamite younger sister to pop star Kylie, participated in Olivia's 21-day charity walk appeal in Beijing, China and was proud to be personally invited by Olivia to be an ambassador for the Olivia Newton-John Cancer and Wellness Centre Appeal. Other Australian celebrity ambassadors include Eddie McGuire, Sigrid Thornton and Deb Hutton.

Minogue said she was inspired by Olivia to become an actress and that it was the Olivia's role as Sandy in *Grease* that spurred her on to take up singing and dancing as a child. 'The former *Australia's Got Talent* judge told Sophie Ellis-Bextor on her podcast *Spinning Plates*: 'The thing that really got me into it was I saw Olivia Newton-John in *Grease*. I was like, 'Yeah that's what I want to do'.' [23]

Olivia's mentorship was naturally not just confined to Australian girls. *Juliana Hatfield Sings Olivia Newton-John*, was a stunning 2018 tribute from this American indie-rock singer. 'This tribute was a salute to her first musical heroine and illustrates the broad appeal of Newton-John. Punk rockers and pop idols were both drawn to the slightly ethereal, eternally sweet hits she had at her peak, soft rock so dreamy that it can still sound as if it's floating in the air.' [24]

In an interview back in 1994, Olivia was asked: 'It occurs to me when I listen to '*Physical*' that it's very much a statement being sung by a woman, for if not feminism, certainly a woman's choice to take the lead, whether sexually or emotionally.'

Olivia replied: 'I knew it was a very commercial song, and I knew it was risqué and risky, and I think *Grease* had taken me to a point where I was able to do those things.'

Every step Olivia took emboldened her and showed those to come that it was all doable. She was a woman who was 'constantly stretching both her sound and her vision, maybe not to extent of David Bowie, but more than any female artist who came before her.' [26]

In every genre she landed in, she made friends and influenced so many other young singers and actresses: Country Olivia. Pop Star. Movie star Olivia, Adult Contemporary Olivia, all the way to Healing Earth Mother. 'The humanity and humanitarianism of pop's first female chameleon ensures that her personal legacy will be as all-encompassing as her musical one.'

The role of women in music today is thankfully more than just looking pretty, it's to be whomever you want. To be unfettered by judgement and to feel able to explore the full gamut of their own supported creativity.

Olivia took on the labels of fashionista, role model, game changer, healer, mother, and charity advocate and delivered all with her natural brand of grace and gratitude.

For all genders, the music industry is hard, hard work. The access the public demands, the touring, the trolls and the trying to maintain healthy relationships. The fickle nature of trends and the need to feel safe all swirl around our creatives like a tornado.

Olivia broke ground, so perhaps the path she followed is now a little better lit and those coming up behind her can see the potholes.

'The impact of Olivia Newton-John on contemporary pop goes far beyond her breakout role in *Grease*, especially in Australia. From her earlier, country-oriented artistry to bright pop rock and '80s dance beats, the singer and actress has had profound influence on so many, including Kylie Minogue, Sia and Sophie Ellis-Bextor.' [28]

A great friend and a career mentor for Olivia was Australian singer Helen Reddy.

In 1972, Reddy co-wrote, with Australian musician Ray Burton, the song '*I Am Woman*', which became a worldwide feminist anthem, Reddy is quoted as saying that 'she was looking for songs to record which reflected the positive self-image she had gained from joining the women's movement, but couldn't find any, so I realised that the song I was looking for didn't exist, and I was going to have to write it myself.' [29]

This song was in Olivia's blood as well – it was an anthem for her. She couldn't find what she was looking for, so she invented it herself as did these ladies below.

Stevie Nicks, of Fleetwood Mac, said of women in the business: 'My generation fought very hard for feminism, and we fought very hard to not be labelled as you had to have a husband or you had to be in a relationship, or you were somehow not a cool chick.' Taylor Swift said, 'My hope for the future, not just in the music industry, but in every young girl I meet, is that they all realise their worth and ask for it.' The singer and incredible actress Lady Gaga said, 'Some women choose to follow men, and some women choose to follow their dreams. If you're wondering which way to go, remember that your career will never wake up and tell you that it doesn't love you anymore.' [30]

Everything adds up to her simple life plan: 'follow your instincts'. For Olivia these instincts were clearly gold. They saw her navigate the entertainment world and put paid to the notion women should stay in their own 'sweet lane'. The lyrics for '*Sisters Are Doin' It for Themselves*' by the Eurythmics sum up the Olivia vibe well.

'Sisters are doin' it for themselves
Standin' on their own two feet
And ringin' on their own bells, we say'

Olivia kept hitting every goal she aimed for, and later in her career she did it all while battling three bouts of breast cancer, falling in and out of love, getting married and having her greatest life achievement – her daughter Chloe.

After Chloe's birth and her first health battle she chose to use her music and her profile for healing. She turned inwards and explored herself though her music and focused on her strengths and her song writing ability.

Her place in music at this time, as a woman, was to heal others and herself. She cleverly tapped into the ability of a song to give strength – an ancient art made modern by her determination.

Her positive energy – and a tonne of hard fundraising – created her Wellness Centre and Foundation, which is a concrete legacy that will shine on as brightly as her timeless songs.

In 2007 Olivia was asked the million-dollar question: 'Longevity in any career is difficult, particularly as a performer. What advice would you give to a young woman embarking on her career today?'

Her answer: 'Do what you love. Be yourself and don't try and emulate another artist. There is already one of those!' [31]

CNN Entertainment, on hearing the news Olivia had passed, announced 'Olivia Newton-John was an icon who opened so many doors for women in music. She was the epitome of grace and style.' [32]

This simple accolade is so true, like a big sister who sneaks out at night to live her life or has the argument with her parents about what she wants to wear and who she is. She has these battles for herself and the sister to follow. The kids who come behind her thank her for her battles won and for the easier path they can now walk. ONJ was a hero and a steering light to so many Australian and global singers – she was loyal and knew she needed a team to succeed and took everyone with her as she conquered the world stage. She was a hero in many ways.

Professor Jim Bright of Career Education also commented on Olivia's legacy. 'Heroes are important in fostering career ambitions. What struck me in the tributes that followed their passing was that [Judith] Durham and Newton-John were true heroes. Newspapers and social media were full of personal accounts of how these singers had influenced people's lives.' [33]

The pioneers are music heroes and torchbearers. Judith Durham, lead singer of The Seekers, was such a lady and sadly she and Olivia passed within a week of each other – what a loss but what a body of work they gleefully left behind. Thankfully, the global music industry is changing and listening to women more. Our governments need to invest more in this vibrant industry to discoverand help who will become our next Olivia Newton-John.

A recent *Forbes* survey showed that 'a whopping 64% of respondents named sexual harassment and objectification as a major challenge women face in the industry'. This roadblock needs to be removed so it's a level playing field and one that promotes creativity and all the joys that come with performing. [34]

Mentoring women already in the field is a fantastic way to move forward and Olivia was an early adopter of the mentor strategy – preaching individuality, inclusiveness and ambition.

Way back in 1994, Olivia was asked: did you have any long-term aims about your career? She replied, 'When I was young, ambition was a dirty word for a woman to have. It was that symbol of if you were ambitious you were grasping to do anything to get places. That was the kind of image that word had in those days if you were a woman, especially from this country. So that kind of freaked me out that someone would think that. And now I think it's a great thing to be.' [35]

Olivia was ambitious and she had the tools to make that ambition a reality. She was inducted into the Australian Women In Music Awards (AWMAs) Honour Roll in 2021, just before she passed away.

'The AWMA Honour Roll acknowledges outstanding women in the Australian Music Industry who have made significant and lasting contributions in their chosen field. It provides a platform for recognition and appreciation of political activists & exceptional creative pioneers in our sector. 'The seemingly timeless singer', Olivia joined the inaugural AWMA inductee Helen Reddy, and Judith Durham AO.' [36] These awards were started in 2018 and are credited with 'driving a major cultural shift across the entire sector, highlighting the achievements of women'.

I can think of so many women who work in the music and entertainment industry that love their jobs, are elite at their jobs and will always strive for a better industry. Women who work in the TV and recording arena, the publishing companies, the writers, the DJs, the touring agents, who are all so welcoming, clever, adventurous, gracious and kind, like Pam Barnes, Linda Bosidis, Eleanor McKay, Jo Wilson, Janet Dawes, Rebecca Batties, Katrinia Hall, Kathy McCabe, Fifa Riccobono, Mermaid, Mary M, Kate Bentley, Janey Rainey, Denise D'Sylva, Clea Freeland, Lisa Thurbon, Sue and Kate Gudinski, Mel Varga and so many more. This is not discounting the boys – but it's all about the girls here.

AWMA Founding Executive Producer Vicki Gordon said, 'Olivia's success as a recording artist secures her place, globally, as one of the all-time legends of contemporary music – a voice with a clarity and beauty that is deeply emotional … Olivia's achievements as a musician and singer, combined with her humanitarian work, determination and resilience, make us so proud.' [37]

Awarded during Covid times, Olivia accepted from her home in the US. 'I am so grateful to be presented with this wonderful honour from Australian Women in Music Awards. I have been blessed to have had such a wonderful career with so many women who inspired me – from Helen Reddy to Nina Simone and Dionne Warwick. Today, more than ever, it's a joy to see so many talented female producers, songwriters and singers bringing their music and voices to today's generation.' [38]

On the concert night, held a year later, after Covid restrictions had lifted in May 2022, Tina Arena performed a beautiful rendition of Olivia's 1974 hit '*I Honestly Love You*' to rapturous applause.

Dame Olivia added: 'It's exciting to see the wonderful work that the AWMA is doing to bring visibility to so many talented women – from First Nations and multicultural artists to producers, engineers, singers and musicians across all genres of music … I'm honoured to be in the company of these amazing women.'

A fitting honour for her highness Dame Olivia. A coronation that honours her valued and living legacy among women in music.

Chapter 13

Chloe: Family Love Is Why We Are Here

Olivia Newton-John was asked years ago to describe her daughter Chloe as a child: 'She's beautiful... She's very bright and she's very concerned about the planet and the animals... and she has a great sense of humour, she's very witty and she's great company, she's only eight, but she's great fun to be around.' [1]

In the world's eye, Olivia was a superstar singer and actress. She was a force of nature: impressive, perhaps even daunting – try putting that on your dating resume and see who swipes left. This is her public profile; what was her private one? Who was this woman when the spotlight was turned off? At home she was a mother and someone who wanted to be surrounded by love. She earnestly believed 'love is what makes the world go 'round. No matter how old or young, love is why we are here. It is the very essence of one's being.'

Due to her natural beauty and vivacious personality, Olivia always attracted a lot of attention, a lot of suitors as my mum would say. Many good men and a few stalkers. Thankfully, most of the attention Olivia received was positive. She had boyfriends from the age of 16 and was married twice. She had her only child, Chloe Rose Lattanzi, with her first husband, Matt Lattanzi. Highlighting another rare aspect of this woman's nature, she remained friends with all her past lovers – not many people can manage that feat.

There was the mysterious vanishing of her second husband, Patrick McDermott, on a fishing trip and the media rumours that surrounded his departure made her life hell for years. But like a Walt Disney movie, Olivia found her true love at 59 when she married businessman John Easterling, who cared for and loved her through her most trying years.

Olivia was a romantic; her ballads attest to this. Perhaps she got this from her dad, as she remembered when her mother Irene turned seventy, her father – who had been married twice more since their divorce – sent her seven bunches of violets, one for each decade. 'They were her favourite flower.' [3]

Olivia's loves included family, friends, animals, nature and the few lucky men who partnered her in life.

Let's start with her biggest love: Chloe Rose Lattanzi. This girl came into the world a few weeks early, on January 17, 1986 at Cedars-Sinai Medical Centre in Los Angeles, California. Her proud mama recalled her first vision of her daughter, 'Chloe was the most beautiful angel, with bright blue eyes and fair hair.' [4]

Olivia and actor Matt Lattanzi married in 1984 and were together for 11 years, divorcing amicably in 1995. Despite this split, the family unit maintained a close friendship and they and their respective spouses celebrated Christmas and birthdays together – all for Chloe's sake.

'Olivia Newton-John's memoir is dedicated to 'my darling daughter Chloe, so that you may know more about my life before you were in it! You are my world and I love you bigger than the universe. Signed Mama ❤ [5]

Olivia's *Warm And Tender* album, released in 1989, was not really aimed for the mainstream market; it was almost a private indulgence from mother to child, an album of children's songs and lullabies, just meant for Chloe.

Chloe revealed in an interview that her parents regarded her as their 'lucky egg'. Matt and Olivia wanted more children, but after several miscarriages, Olivia was diagnosed with breast cancer in 1992 and split with Lattanzi three years later. Little Chloe was only 6 when her mother was first diagnosed and has dealt with the shadow of disease over her mother her whole life.

'I have had somewhat wonderful things happen to me during my career and lifetime. Of course, personally, the birth of my daughter is the highlight of my life.' [6]

When Chloe was born, her mother has told of a pact she made with God to save her, as the Australian superstar suffered complications during her pregnancy. 'I was close to losing her … I went to bed and asked God to save her and if he did, I would say the Lord's Prayer every night for the rest of my life and so I have,' she said. [7]

These two had an unbreakable bond. They could not be apart for long and, although their relationship had its ups and downs, Chloe and her mum always circled back to each other; their tight union never frayed for long. Over the years, Chloe has been very open about her serious battles with anorexia, substance abuse, depression, anxiety and body dysmorphia. She has shared in the past that the divorce, her mother's illness and also her fame contributed to her mental health difficulties over the years.

Chloe admitted, 'I had body dysmorphia, so I couldn't see myself clearly.' She said at one stage she weighed just 37 kilos. [7] In her struggle with her image she had a breast augmentation, lip fillers and Botox, but had fillers removed from her face because, in her own words, she looked 'bizarre'.

Chloe has often spoken about growing up in Hollywood, in the public eye as the daughter of a famous singer and what a toll it took on her. Her mother travelled a lot – that was the lifestyle and the work necessity. 'I've spent a lot of time alone in big houses. That was hard.' [8a]

Chloe, too, had aspirations of singing, and began performing when she was just seven years old. Asked if Chloe had showbiz ambitions as a child, Olivia answered: 'She goes back and forth, you know, a teacher, an actress. She has the ability, she's great, but I'm not forcing it, She's only eight, she's a baby, but she's a born actress.' [8b]

At age 15, Chloe landed her first record deal. Sadly, it was later that year her eating disorder would begin. Chloe buckled under the pressures of fame as a teenager and turned to drugs and alcohol abuse to manage her depression. Olivia spoke publicly about Chloe's battle as early as 2007 in an interview with *Entertainment Tonight*, admitting she feared for her daughter. 'You don't want to think anything could be wrong … There was a time I was in denial about it, I have to admit that.' [9]

In 2013 Chloe was starting to deal with what was happening to her by checking into rehab. 'Fame totally messes you up. I don't blame my mother for my problems, but I would never want to be famous or raise a child of my own around the cult of celebrity. It ruins lives.' [10] Olivia saw why Chloe was having troubles. It broke her heart that Chloe was being judged and photographed by media, but together they dealt with it by getting professional help. In 2016, during an interview with *60 Minutes*, Olivia spoke of her daughter's struggles. 'I think it's hard to be the child of a person in the limelight, I really understand that. There's privilege but there's also other things that come along with that.' [11]

Then, publicly, things started to turn around. Chloe became a contestant in the Australian reality series *Dancing With The Stars* in 2020, in a serious effort to put her earlier problems behind her.

Chloe bravely pointed out, 'People forget that I'm a legitimate singer and musician because my depression and anxiety have overshadowed that part of me. I want people to see me for who I am, not an illness I overcame … It feels really good to be able to be my own person – to be Chloe Lattanzi and not Olivia Newton-John's daughter … I'm my mum's biggest fan, but she's ready for me to be me, too.' [12a]

Olivia came to Australia to see Chloe on *Dancing With The Stars* and said, 'I encouraged her to just be herself … she's in her own dancing shoes and they're beautiful – she'll do great.' [12b]

Chloe knew her mother felt helpless during her darkest hours, and also knew that she did everything she could by sending her to every specialist she thought might be able to help. Chloe knew she had to learn to be stronger and deal with her own demons in order to be there for her cancer-stricken mother.

In 2020, Olivia – in full mother mode – broke down in tears during an emotional TV interview when Chloe said she had found her 'self-worth' again. 'I'm so happy that she's happy, and just shining, and has so much power and strength and bravery.' [13]

Mother and child shared many passions: marijuana farming, music, acting and, yes, a belief in alien life. Both shared a lifelong fascination with extra-terrestrials, which began when a 15-year-old Olivia Newton-John claims to have seen a UFO streaking across the Australian sky. They have always considered the potential of life on another planet.

Chloe, like her mother, has always had an important relationship with music. Singing and writing songs is part of her DNA. They both share the philosophy of using music to spread positivity.

Starting back in In 2002, Chloe was Chrissy in a Melbourne stage production of the 1960s musical *Hair* and then went on to write the song '*Can I Trust Your Arms*' on her mum's 2005 hallmark album *Stronger Than Before*. Singing on reality TV beckoned with an appearance in 2008 on *Rock the Cradle*, finishing a respectable third. In 2010, Chloe's debut single, '*Wings and a Gun*', was released digitally in Japan.

The '*Play With Me*' single came out in 2011 with a controversial video clip and then the hit single '*You Have to Believe*', with Dave Audé and Olivia, hit the airwaves in 2015.

Her *No Pain* album came out in 2016 with two singles, '*Delicious*' and '*Lonely Nights*' and another hit single with her mother, '*Window In The Wall*', was released in 2021. [14]

Olivia, as a proud mother, announced to the world that Chloe had 'written most of her own songs, and I started out singing other people's songs, so Chloe is more aligned with her own music.' [15]

Acting is also in Chloe's blood, with a cameo in *Paradise Beach* (1993) to a voice over in *The Enchanted Billabong* (1999) to being a part of TV and big screen movies such as *The Wilde Girls* (2001), *Dead 7* (2016) *Sharknado 5: Global Swarming* (2017) with her mum, as well as *Dancing with the Stars* in Australia.

In 2017, she moved with her fiancé James Driskill to Oregon, where they bought a farm and started a marijuana business. Like her mother, Chloe is an advocate of medicinal marijuana and was farming her own crop in Portland, Oregon (near where her father Matt lives). When Covid hit, the pair bunkered down together ather Mum's Santa Barbara farm, where her husband John Easterling also grew strains of the plant to help treat Olivia.

'My fantasy is for all of us to live on the same property. Life's so short. I want to spend every minute with the people I love,' Olivia said. [16]

After her mum passed, Chloe, perhaps as a way of dealing with her grief, has been sharing through social media, memories and moments with her mother that made her happy.

Life advice Olivia gave her: 'Be yourself because everybody else is taken.' And then Olivia added: 'She doesn't really need my advice; she gives me advice.' [17]

Chloe revealed her mother secretly officiated her wedding to James Driskill, a martial arts expert, many years ago. In the posted video clip, you could see the couple holding hands on the beach. 'This is one of the most precious moments of my life … Years ago in the Bahamas I asked my gorgeous mama to marry me to this incredible man. Thank you, mama. For everything. I miss you every moment.' [18]

She also revealed that one of Olivia's little-known skills was photography (like her mother Irene) and Chloe shared three perfectly framed photos of herself on Instagram, which looked like they had been taken by a professional, but Olivia had shot them. 'Through mama's lens. She always got the best and realest out of me … Helped me with my shyness.' [19]

Chloe's beautiful words echoed around the world when the news of Olivia's death spread in 2022. 'You are my lighthouse mama. My safe place. My heart space. It has been my honour and continues to be my honour to be your baby and best friend. You are an angel on earth and everyone touched by you has been blessed. I love you forever, my life giver, my teacher, my mama.' [20]

Importantly, Chloe has taken on the task of ambassador and champion for her mother's work – the Wellness and Research Centre in Melbourne and will support the yearly fundraising Walk every year.

The first one without Olivia front and centre was October 2022. Olivia's niece Tottie and her half brother Toby led the charge in Australia, and John and Chloe and her husband James did the virtual walk for wellness around Olivia's property in the US.

Chloe posted a tearful thank you online: 'This is her dream, her life's work and her heart.' [21a]

Once asked if she's her daughter's favourite singer, Olivia laughed. 'I'm just Mom to her.' [21b] She also said of her daughter: 'She seems so fragile, but she has an iron core, which the world can now see.' In return, Chloe said these elegant about her mother, 'She is a warrior. She chooses to be positive.' [22]

Olivia's extended family was her touchstone and her anchor in life. From her parents Brinley and Irene to daughter Chloe and her husband James, as well as Olivia's ex-husband Matt and current spouse John Easterling.

Rona Newton-John was born 1 February 1941 in Cambridge, Cambridgeshire, England. Rona, like Olivia, worked as an actress, model and writer during the '70s and '80s.

Her first acting role was in the movie *Homicide* released in 1965. She had several small acting roles, notably on *The Benny Hill Show* (1969), the British television series *UFO* (1970) and the film *The Same Skin* (UK) (also known as *Country Dance*). She also recorded a song, '*Just Us Two*', with Olivia in 1972.

She was a guest on *The Mike Douglas Show* in the US in 1979. The cooking segment of the show also featured Rona and Olivia preparing their English soup recipe.

Actress Jane Seymour's father, a doctor, delivered one of Rona's babies and Rona had four children from three marriages. She married Melbourne restaurateur and nightclub owner Brian Goldsmith in 1961, with whom she had three children before divorcing in 1968. The children are Fiona Goldsmith (Edelstein), Brett Goldsmith and Tottie Goldsmith (a singer and member of the Chantoozies pop group in Australia).

She married Graeme Anthony Fifield-Hall in 1969. They had one child before they divorced, Emerson Newton-John, who was born in the US (1974) and became a racing car driver.

She married American actor Jeff Conaway (a *Grease* co-star of Olivia, as Kenickie) in January 1980 and divorced in 1985. They had no children. Her grandchildren are Emerson's son and daughter, Brin and Valerie, and Tottie Goldsmith's daughter, Layla Lee-Curtis. Rona sadly passed on 24 May 2013, in Los Angeles, of brain cancer. She was 72. After her death, she was cremated and her ashes were scattered at Cape Byron, NSW, Australia.

Olivia often praised her dear sister as her biggest supporter.

'My late sister Rona was an inspiration in her own right. Later in her life I began to recognise that she too had a lot of Mum's values deep inside her. As a young girl, Rona was a successful model in London, working with people like Helmut Newton. I used to look up to Rona because she was so funny, beautiful and elegant. Many of my fond memories of living in London include going over to Rona's to learn what the counterculture was doing, exposing me to different experiences.' [23]

Big brother Hugh Francis Newton-John was born 3rd July 1939 in North Bucks, Buckinghamshire, England. Hugh graduated from university with the dual degrees Bachelor of Medicine (MB) and Bachelor of Surgery (BS) and became a practicing doctor in the early 1960s. He later specialised in infectious diseases, and in the 1970s and 1980s worked at the Fairfield Infectious Diseases Hospital (formerly Queens Memorial Infectious Diseases Hospital), The hospital, the last specific infectious diseases hospital in Australia, closed in 1996.

Hugh led several research projects, particularly among patients in the hospital's intensive care unit, including means of managing tetanus, helping identify the link between Campylobacter gastroenteritis and the subsequent development of Guillain-Barre syndrome and improving the ventilation methods for polio patients, as well as developing new approaches to preventing airway obstruction among patients with chronic upper airway weakness.

Hugh died on 7 May 2019, aged 79, in Ringwood, Victoria, Australia, after a long battle with debility and decline. Olivia's tribute to her brother: 'My dear, sweet, gentle, clever, brother Hugh passed away in Melbourne, Australia after many years of decline. I love him so and will miss him terribly… Hugh was also a talented musician and artist who shared his gifts with many friends, colleagues and associates throughout his entire life.' [24]

Caroline Tottie Goldsmith OAM, Olivia's beloved niece, has been front and centre in the media with cousin Chloe since ONJ's passing. Both have seen Olivia remembered the way she would have wanted, with Tottie proudly saying: 'Olivia is a healer at core, and we are going to keep her legacy alive if it's the last thing I do.' [25]

Tottie was extraordinarily close to her Aunty Liv and is a multitalented entertainer in her own right. She founded the fantastic band the Chantoozies, who have toured Australia and sold more than 200,000 records. Tottie has also had a rich solo career and travelled overseas to work and study, incorporating singing and acting – just like her famous Aunty Olivia had done.

She has hosted many successful Australian TV shows, breakfast radio, and starred in various musical theatre roles and telemovies, as well as singing for our troops in Kuwait and Baghdad. Tottie is also an amazing MC and motivational speaker and an incredible host and patron of many charity events including Clown Doctors, RVIB Ball, TLC for Kids and, of course, Olivia's Wellness Foundation and Fund. A healer like her Aunt Olivia, Tottie released a meditation CD *Unwind Your Mind* and has also teamed up with sleep scientist Chris Bunney, to research, validate and produce *Falling Asleep with Tottie Goldsmith*, her next CD in the series, to help people with sleep problems. In the 2020 Queen's Birthday Honours, Tottie was awarded the Medal of the Order of Australia (OAM) for 'service to the community, and to the performing arts'.

When news of Olivia's death filtered though, Tottie released the statement: 'My heart is broken, like so many of us. Today marks the passing of our family matriarch and one of the world's truly divine and magical human beings. She is irreplaceable.' [26]

Toby Newton-John, Olivia's half-brother, is now the Professor of Clinical Psychology at the University of Technology Sydney, but was only 11 when Olivia shocked the world with her *Grease* makeover. He said, 'Our surname is unusual … people do recognise it. I'm very grateful people have a universally positive connotation with the name.' [27]

He is also another family member proud to continue Olivia's work with the Wellness Centre and after his sister's death said, 'The best way to acknowledge her legacy is to emulate the values she lived by, which is to be kind, thoughtful and generous. She was Miss Goody Two Shoes, but she was also a fun-loving person, who could laugh at herself, and have fun with others as well.' [28]

He stood beside Tottie and her brother Brett Goldsmith at the 2022 Wellness Walk, saying: 'All the family that are on the ground here, and all the people that loved her... It's going to be really powerful and really beautiful.' [29]

Chapter 14

Boys Boys Boys ...

'Loving Arms'
If I could hold you now
Just for a moment if I could make you mine
Just for a while turn back the hands of time
If I could only hold you now
Lyrics by Olivia Newton-John

We will never know all the crushes, all the possible affairs and every boyfriend that appeared in Olivia Newton-John's love life. 'Our Livvy' was the sweetheart of millions and a romantic at heart. She understood you get the good days with the bad, but never wavered in her belief in love.

As she cheekily remembered in her autobiography one such unnamed suitor: 'He was a Hollywood bad-boy legend with a long list of girlfriends ... He called up one night ... and asked me out again ... His name? I'll never tell!' [1]

Olivia was a wholesome girl, not a gossiper. She didn't kiss and tell and certainly wasn't a love 'em and leave 'em type. She followed her heart and, like most people, was looking for long-lasting love and a partner to trust. ONJ certainly knew how to have fun and laugh and enjoy the world and the trappings her stardom afforded her. Upon reflection, perhaps due to her career or her youth, she was time poor with some loves, and the tyranny of travel and distance also took its toll on some people in her life. But like the promises of every love story every written, she prevailed and found her Prince – her second husband, John Easterling, when she turned 59 years old.

Way back when Olivia was a blonde, blue-eyed teenage girl, the first record of a high school crush was Graeme Holdsworth – a fellow classmate at University High in Melbourne. According to school whispers, Holdsworth was 'more interested in football' than Olly – as some classmates called the rising star – and was the 'one that got away'. [2]

During an iconic 1983 interview with Joan Rivers and John Travolta, Olivia confessed her crush on Graeme. 'He didn't want to know about me,' she told Rivers. Years later, a tenacious journalist tracked Holdsworth down, reporting that the 'tall, blond, surfer-type schoolboy' was now a retired architect'. He revealed that he and Liv knew each other well, and he walked her home many afternoons … but said that they were just good mates and part of a large friendship group. 'We were all keen on her!' he joked. 'She was one of the cutest girls in the school.' But he didn't know she liked him. [3]

This is pure Shakespearian stuff: the young potential lovers who didn't fess up to liking each other. Who knows what could have been? But you snooze you lose, Graeme, and up stepped Ian Turpie, a handsome, ambitious, Australian entertainer who was doing what Olivia knew she wanted to do – Sing!

Olivia dated Ian for one year (1964-65) and he was her first real love. Olivia was just 16 when she met Ian, then 19, on the set of Australian variety show *Time For Terry* in 1964. When Turpie was recruited to present *The Go!! Show* on ATV 0 in Melbourne, Olivia also became a regular guest, miming to pre-recorded covers of British and US pop hits.

Ian, was a talented singer and actor, and would later go on to host the long-running Australian game show *The Price Is Right* in the 1980s. In 1965, the young sweethearts also starred together in Olivia's first movie, *Funny Things Happen Down Under.*

Their chemistry was obvious, they were inseparable, singing together, going to the football, concerts, dances … they allegedly vowed to each other they wouldn't break up.

But Olivia's mother thought it was all too serious and packed her baby girl off to London. Ian spoke of his heartbreak back in 1981, saying '[Olivia] was away for more than three months. She'd phone me every month with reports of how she was going, and of her big hopes of landing a recording contract.' [4] Olivia's career took off and they knew they had to break up. 'By the time [Olivia] came back [from England], things had changed with her and I'd found Jan.' Ian ended up finding love with Jan Hamilton, a stunning blonde model. The pair married in 1968 and had three children. [5] Sadly, Ian passed away at age 68, in 2012, but the pair was in touch at the time.

Olivia is now living in the UK, where she met Bruce Welch, the guitarist and songwriter and founding member of the British rock group The Shadows who were the backing band for Cliff Richard from 1958 to 1968. They were massive and had 69 UK chart singles from the 1950s to the 2000s. 34. Olivia was with her new sweetheart for five years, 1968-1972. They met the night she was booked as the support act for his band. 'She was absolutely stunning, she was 17 and was the support act when we did a week in Bournemouth,' Bruce recalled. [6]

They never got married – she was 21 when they got engaged, which created a stir, since he was separated at the time but not quite divorced. And in her autobiography Olivia said, 'I was abruptly fired from a TV show in Australia because of my boyfriend's 'entanglements'. I was mortified.' [7]

In 1971 Olivia released her debut album, *If Not For You*, at only 23 years old. 'It was exciting to have an album out and the next months went by in a blur of getting-to-know-you promotional appearances on television shows across Europe, the UK, and Australia, along with a stage tour … Perhaps I was too young to handle it all, but I went down a path that I would later regret, which led to Bruce and me breaking off our engagement.' [8]

Olivia broke off the engagement in 1972, amid rumours she was seeing someone else, and moved to Los Angeles for a career in Hollywood. Sadly, Bruce didn't deal with the breakup well.

The musician reportedly attempted suicide and was lucky to survive, saying in an interview in 2004: 'I told everyone that I was going away for the weekend and not to bother calling me, but I forgot about the window cleaner … He found me on the Tuesday … I had taken the pills on the Sunday.' [9]

But time has made him see it all in a clearer light and he fondly remembers his time with Olivia, congratulating her on becoming a Dame. 'She'll always be Livvy to me. I'm thrilled for her.' [10]

Single Olivia went on holiday to the South of France in 1974. She was sitting on the beach in Monte Carlo when out of the water swam a very tall, blond, very handsome man. Her friend (and then London roommate) Chantal from Australia invited Olivia to meet her fiancé's cousin, Lee Kramer. 'The next day I was going back to England. Who was sitting next to me on the flight? Lee Kramer. He actually paid someone off to get that seat by my side.' [11]

Olivia and Lee Kramer dated for about five years, 1974-1979, with a year spilt in 1976 but reunited in '77. At the time they met, Lee was working for a business with his brother that imported and exported cowboy boots to and from London, but after he met Olivia, he was happy to follow her to the US, and become her manager.

Kramer was a good manager and helped Olivia through her country phase to mega-star actress and singer, during her hugely successful period with the musicals *Grease* and *Xanadu*. The partnership ended for good in 1981, after the making of *Xanadu*, where Olivia met her future husband, dancer Matt Lattanzi. After ending his relationship with Olivia, Kramer decided to pass on his role as manager. He offered the job to Roger Davies, who was another great manager, guiding her through the next phase of her career in the1980s. [12a]

Lee Kramer was an entrepreneurial manager-boyfriend who was by Olivia's side for seven platinum albums, eight gold singles, three Grammys and a sackful of other awards during their six bumpy years together. They separated just before Livvy rebounded with Lattanzi. 'Lee is a very articulate man ... But we finally broke it off because of personal differences.' With Matt she was careful not to mix too much business with pleasure, since she counted that as part of the cause of her split with Kramer. [12b]

The two always remained friends. 'We still spoke, and she called me for counselling on her life, and me the same way.' [12c]

Enter stage left her dear first husband, Matt Lattanzi. They were together for 16 years, 1979-1995. Blue-eyed, dark-haired Matt Vincent Lattanzi was born on February 1, 1959 in Portland, Oregon. His paternal grandparents were Italian immigrants. His mother had Polish ancestry. Matt loved being outdoors, swimming, camping, fishing and hiking.

One of 10 kids, Matt had dropped out of a local community college (he was a dance major) to head for LA, where he landed the *Xanadu* role just a few weeks after his arrival. Olivia was 31 years young when she met Matt, a dancer on the *Xanadu* set in 1979; he was just 20. 'The first time I saw Matt he was roller-skating,' she recalled. 'When he finally asked me out three months later, it wasn't like I was a star but just a woman he wanted to be with.' [13]

They married in 1984 and had a daughter, Chloe Rose, in 1986. Olivia said of having a child and meeting Matt, 'The songs of the film – '*Xanadu*' and '*Magic*', both No. 1s – were not the only gift it gave me ... He was ten years younger than me but smart, sweet and very handsome.' [14]

During the filming of *Xanadu*, in an effort to keep this new love private and just for them, when hair and make-up arrived in the morning at Olivia's hotel, Matt would 'hide in the cupboard with a blanket and pillow, without anyone knowing he was there ... Enough of my life was out in the world for public consumption. I was keeping this for myself.' [15]

She dedicated her biggest album ever, 1981's *Physical*, to her then-boyfriend Matt.

Married at her California ranch, the couple enjoyed a fairy-tale honeymoon in Paris. Olivia said about marriage: 'I certainly don't need to marry for security, and it's not a decision I take lightly.

'When I marry,' she continued, 'it will be a man with whom I expect to spend the rest of my life and have children.' [16]

During the wedding she was hiding the fact she had been pregnant and had sadly lost the baby. At 37, in 1985, she fell pregnant again, and Chloe arrived a few weeks early. After her birth, Olivia and Lattanzi were apparently keen on adopting a child from Romania. 'I think it was my gut instinct that this was something I needed to do ... However, in a tragic twist of fate, her passion to bring another child home was overshadowed by the death of her goddaughter and Olivia never made the trip.' [17]

In 1992 Olivia and Matt faced her first cancer battle together and survived intact. Olivia suggested that Matt represented a new genre of mister in her life. 'I used to gravitate toward men who were strong, self-assured and almost arrogant,' she said. 'Matt is more relaxed.' [18a]

Then, Matt and Olivia made a decision that changed their lives, moving from the US to a beautiful farm in Australia in 1993. The decision was made so Lattanzi could audition for the Channel Nine soap opera *Paradise Beach*. He landed the gig and starred in the series as fashion photographer Cooper Hart. Sadly, just a few years later, things had changed between them and devastated that their marriage was over, he and Olivia divorced, finalising their split in 1995.

Two years later, Matt (40 by this stage) moved on romantically with the family's previous babysitter Cindy Jessup, then 23. Olivia had hired Cindy in 1993 to help look after Chloe while Matt was working on *Paradise Beach*. Matt and Cindy did not last, splitting after 10 years of marriage in 2007. And then he married third wife Michelle and they now run a medicinal cannabis farm, like his and Olivia's daughter Chloe.

Despite their split, Olivia and Matt always remained friendly and shared a supportive relationship as they co-parented Chloe.

Then Korean-born Patrick McDermott came on the scene in 1996. This nine-year relationship would end in a shocking and traumatic way for Olivia. Olivia and Patrick (a Hollywood cameraman and lighting technician) were very on-again, off-again and never married.

'Indeed, Newton-John became Australia's first big silver screen export, paving the way for many Australian performers to follow suit. Yet despite her stratospheric superstardom, she led a humble, quiet life, all the while navigating extraordinary challenges, including the mysterious disappearance of her long-term partner in 2005, with steely grace.' [18b]

A beautiful moment between the pair that was shared with the public was in 2004 while appearing on *This Is Your Life* in Australia. Patrick showered his partner with praise, telling Olivia that she was an 'incredible' and 'special' human being, and added that if people could be 'a little bit like [you], the world would be a better place'. [19]

They had broken up (again) the last time she saw him at her house in Malibu. In 2005 McDermott boarded a fishing boat named *Freedom*. Olivia was in Australia for a holiday and heard he had gone fishing on a charter boat off San Pedro in Los Angeles. News filtered through to her that he had not picked up his son Chance as promised and did not turn up for a family event that weekend. His ex-wife Yvette Nipar set off the alarm bells – both she and Olivia strongly believed Patrick would never leave his son. He was missing! 'I had been through cancer and divorce, but the idea of someone in my life suddenly being gone without a trace left me with an emptiness I hadn't known before.' [20]

Four months later, US Coast Guard officially said Patrick 'most likely' drowned. Media sources had many different theories, all based around him disappearing due to financial problems.

'In 2009 *Dateline* NBC investigators say he was found in a Mexican beach town, living under the name of Pat Kim and working on a tourist yacht. This remains unconfirmed.' [21a]

Questions remain, with the release of new podcast *Pseudocide*, which has reignited interest in this strange night. PI Philip Klein was hired by *Dateline* after another alleged sighting went down in South America and later released a book titled *Lost at Sea: The Hunt for Patrick McDermott* in 2012. Olivia stated: 'I don't think I will ever really be at peace with it. I think there will always be a question mark.' [21b]

The final result is no one really knows what happened to Patrick McDermott.

In 2007 Olivia spoke to an interviewer about her *Grace and Gratitude* album, which combined music and religious chants from diverse spiritual influences, such as Tibetan and Japanese Buddhism, Islamic and Hebrew prayers and a Latin Benediction. She confirmed that writing the songs on this album helped her confront the pain of losing Patrick McDermott. 'It helped me greatly because I found that when I write music – when you write lyrics, like keeping a diary, writing poetry or a song – you take yourself out of your emotional body into more of an analytical body and it takes your mind out of grief. It kind of takes you into the healing.' [22]

After all this sadness, Olivia still remained receptive to a new love and she met 'The One', John Easterling, in 2007. They married a year later and he remained her loving partner for 15 years, right up to her death.

Olivia once said, 'To be love[d] is the most basic of human needs. Like a flower, it waters the human soul. But to love is a true blessing.' [23]

Like a movie script, they met in the Amazon Rainforest. Olivia was on a trip to Peru and saw John, whom she had met before, years ago at an environmental show where he was displaying his botanicals.

John founded the Amazon Herb Company and he had been visiting this country for more than 30 years. He offered the then 59-year-old Olivia a taste of ayahuasca, a potent Amazonian hallucinogenic believed to have healing properties as part of an ancient Peruvian ritual. The potion had a strong effect on the *Grease* star, who recalled hallucinating and having visions, and she said it changed her life. She dreamed of herself and Easterling in a past life during the ancient period of the native Inca people, claiming that it recalibrates your brain'. [24]

The couple started dating after the Amazon trip and returned to Peru to privately tie the knot on 21 June 2008 in an Incan spiritual ceremony, followed by a legal ceremony nine days later on Jupiter Island, Florida. Olivia had only love talk for John. 'He says yes to everything, he says yes to life! l always tell my friends you're never too old to find love. I found the love of my life at 59 going on 60. I'm grateful.' [25a]

Throughout their marriage, Olivia had to struggle through more health battles. Together they launched the Olivia Newton-John Foundation and their mission statement was to 'support research for kinder and more effective ways of preventing, treating and curing all cancers, including plant medicine and other therapies'. [25b]

When COVID-19 closed down the world, Olivia said, 'I'm so grateful I'm able to be in the countryside. I have my animals and my husband ... This has actually been one of the rare times in my life where I have been in one place for more than three weeks.' [26]

She and John shared matching tattoos on their left ankles – a spiral pattern they designed when they were in Australia on their fifth anniversary and John's favourite song of hers was '*If Not For You*', her first hit and written by the great man Bob Dylan

When she passed away, her dear husband posted a moving tribute via social media: 'Olivia has been a symbol of triumphs and hope for over 30 years sharing her journey with breast cancer. Her healing inspiration and pioneering experience with plant medicine continues with the Olivia Newton-John Foundation Fund, dedicated to researching plant medicine and cancer.' [27]

John and Chloe and her husband James and Olivia's niece Tottie Goldsmith and all her family have gladly shouldered Olivia's charity work and will make sure her legacy in the field of research and wellness will continue to flourish.

We cannot talk of all Olivia's loves without mentioning animals and nature. 'I feel very passionately that we need to take care of the planet and everything on it. Whether it's saving the Amazon or just being kind to those around you, we need to take care of each other and Mother Earth.' [28]

Olivia first became aware of her love of animals in Cambridge, England, and when she married first husband Matt, she filled their Malibu farm with dogs and horses. 'Animals are my biggest expense and my biggest joy,' she enthused. Every month she had two tons of hay delivered to feed four Quarter Horses and a Thoroughbred. An entire refrigerator was stocked with special food for her eight dogs: two Great Danes, two-part coyotes, three setters and one 'cute' mutt. 'They're all so loving and all they expect from me is a cookie and a stroke.' [29]

Olivia championed animal welfare whenever she could, privately and professionally, such as when she refused to go to Japan until they amended tuna fishing practices to reduce the needless waste. Which they did and in 1990 she served as the first Goodwill Ambassador to the United Nations Environment Programme.

Her friend of over 30 years, fellow nature lover and issues campaigner Jon Dee posted an incredible tribute to Olivia on Twitter, praising her dedication as a campaigner for the natural environment. In 1988 Jon founded the charity Rock Aid Armenia, then with his friend, tennis champ Pat Cash, co-founded the environmental organisation Planet Ark. With Olivia they co-founded National Tree Day in 1996 and were also behind the One Tree Per Child campaign. In his last letter to Olivia, he thanked her for the great things she'd done for the environment, to which she replied: 'I am so very proud of what we have achieved.'

'During her long career Newton-John used her fame to draw attention to matters close to her heart – no matter whether it was endangered wildlife or rescue dogs at a shelter. As far back as 1977 she flew to Namibia in southwest Africa with conservationist Dr Laurie Marker to film a segment about the plight of the cheetah.

'Since then, she has urged people to stop trafficking animals; helped establish thousands of trees on her north coast NSW property; and in recent years has helped campaign for the release of bears held in captivity in Asia.' [30a]

Olivia and John Easterling teamed up with ACEER to help educate the children of the Amazon about the importance of maintaining the rainforests – they live in it; they don't realise that not everybody has a rainforest in their backyard. 'So we provide them with boats, food, clothes, but the main focus of the ACEER affiliation is education. We also want to educate the outside world too. There is so much to learn from the rainforests, and we are losing them at such an incredible rate.' [30b]

Australia's greatest animal loving and campaigning family has to be the mighty Irwins, and Bindi Irwin, daughter of icon and hero Steve Irwin, posted a touching tribute to Olivia on Instagram: 'One of the kindest and most wonderful souls the world has ever known.' [31]

Olivia loved her friends with the same passion she loved her family. Her friends were so integral to her personal and public life, and she held them very dear for many years. It's impossible to mention them all as

Olivia had a lot of them, but a few words from her mates she left behind show how loved she was.

Sir Cliff Richard, now 81, had a close friendship with the late *Grease* star, which spanned more than 50 years, being her mentor and singing partner since the '60s in UK. He said when the news of her death reached him: 'We hit it off straight away. She was the sort of soul mate that you meet and you know is a friend for life.

When I and many of us were in love with Olivia she was engaged to someone else. I'm afraid I lost the chance. I'm just one of an army of lucky people who knew and loved her. How could we not love her? She was gorgeous, gifted and had a heart of Gold.' [32a]

John Farrar, who produced a string of hits for Olivia, was a lifelong friend, as was Olivia's girlfriend and life-journey partner Pat Carroll. His resume with her is so impressive, it deserves to be listed. He was Olivia's music producer, arranger, singer, and guitarist. He is a former member of several rock and roll groups including The Mustangs (1963–64), The Strangers (1964–70), Marvin, Welch & Farrar (1970–73), and The Shadows (1973–76). He worked with Olivia Newton-John from 1971 to 1989.

He wrote her American number-one hit singles: '*Have You Never Been Mellow*' (1975), '*You're the One That I Want*' (1978 duet with John Travolta), '*Hopelessly Devoted to You*' (1978), and '*Magic*' (1980). Farrar also produced most of Olivia's recorded material during that time, including her number-one albums. He was a co-producer of the soundtrack for the film *Grease* (1978). And he produced Olivia's first American number-one hit single, '*I Honestly Love You*'. [32b]

John Farnham and Olivia met in London in their early 20s as aspiring pop stars. They instantly hit it off and always 'looked to each other for love and support in one of show businesses' most remarkable friendships'. 'I love pretty much everything about her,' said John. 'She's one of my closest friends. I love her with my soul, and to have a musical relationship is even better.' [33] They had fun together and when they teamed up on stage, their chemistry, the melding of their voices was magical and moving. They really were breathtaking in tandem as their timeless Christmas albums and The *Two Strong Hearts*, Main Event and Fire Fight live concerts attest.

Then there was John Travolta – her *Grease* movie man.

The film's two main stars went on to have wildly successful careers, but also maintained a friendship spanning more than four decades. [34]

He said 'Danny and Sandy forever' and she said in her autobiography 'he was a triple threat – acting, dancing and singing – plus all that charisma and incredible sexy movie-star looks.'

Despite numerous rumours to the contrary – and some steamy pictures of the pair kissing at a party in 1978 – there had been no romance between the two stars. Olivia, then 28, revealed why she couldn't date John Travolta, then 23, during filming and why it helped the chemistry on screen. 'I think it was good because I think it kept the tension there and the chemistry. It might have been a real disaster had we decided to date, or we had a falling out or something.'

Long-time friend and Bond girl Jane Seymour 'realised that Olivia was a unique friend. She recalled, 'I have friends, but not like her in my life. I just remember so clearly our conversations and the smile on her face. And then the fact that she wasn't afraid, I don't think, to pass. She just didn't want to miss out on life.' [36]

Seymour's father, a doctor who delivered Olivia's sister Rona's baby, first introduced her to the Newton-Johns when Seymour moved to the United States to pursue an acting career.

'We trusted one another implicitly, and we were very similar kind of people,' she said. 'We both liked to work hard, but we also knew family was everything. We had a lot in common.' [37]

Actress Susan George was another best friend to Olivia. They met as teenagers and grew up in Hollywood, but away from the camera they created a lasting friendship and bonded over their love of nature and horses. Detailing their last phone call, Susan said, 'We spoke a few weeks ago and had the longest talk about times past and present, laughed a lot and I worried that it might have been too tiring, but she insisted not.' [38]

Chapter 15

Musicologists and the LGBTQIA+ Love

'Olivia could hop from genre to genre, but she threw herself into every style with the same effervescent hyper-glitz enthusiasm, which is why she never sounded the least bit phony.' [1]

Dame Olivia's authenticity was an integral part of her success. When she sang a song – be it her own or a cover – you believed every word. She never phoned a song in – it was always delivered with heart.

Olivia's place in music history involves the support she gave to women, spotlighting our Australian girls, and her unwavering support for the LGBTQIA community.

'Whether it be support for the LGBTIQ+ community before it became mainstream, Newton-John showed time and time again that she was on the right side of history, by doing what she knew as the right thing, even if it wasn't popular, or even legal at the time.' [2]

Olivia's life was always suffused with music and the study of music due to the influence of her academic family. Brought up in universities for the early part of her life, it's only fitting we touch base with two Melbourne musicologists to get their view of Olivia Newton-John and her place in music history. Musicology is the scholarly analysis and research-based study of music and the Musicological Society of Australia exists to foster greater understanding and valuing of music, musical thinking and musical life.

There is even a Prince album called *Musicology* – his twenty-eighth studio album released in 2004. The point of this album was Prince's desire to bring musical education to people, The song '*Musicology*', which is featured on the album, quotes pieces of his earlier music, such as '*Little Red Corvette*', '*Sign O' the Times*' and '*Kiss*', as a reference to his own musical history. [3]

The musicologist insight is not a lecture but a memory from both that leads to discussion, which, like their writing, is accessible, intelligent, layered and lovely.

Music lovers are lucky to live in Melbourne – we have live music venues all over our fair city pumping out new musicians and future superstars. Covid gave us a smashing, but the old saying 'rock and roll never dies' is actually true.

In amongst all this music, at our institutions of higher learning RMIT and Melbourne University we have two resident musicologists who have dedicated their lives to the sweet study of music. They are young and curious and bristling with ideas. I love their studied and emotional perspectives and Melbourne is lucky to have these academic talents as sources of information. Musicology helps us to appreciate music; it's useful to performers, and the history of music is connected with the history of everything else. [4]

Dr Frederic Kiernan is an early career Research Fellow at the University of Melbourne whose work examines the relationship between music, creativity, emotion and wellbeing, both presently and in the past.

Dr Fred gave us an honest and beautiful free-forming think piece on Olivia titled '*It Felt Like Love*'.

One of his focus points is to study how music makes you feel, how it makes you act and think and be. How it connects you with others and perhaps combats loneliness and gives people a way to interact socially with others in this overwhelming city. Dr Fred is a specialist on the music of Bohemian composer Jan Dismas Zelenka (1679–1745) and his PhD thesis (2019), titled '*The Figure of Jan Dismas Zelenka (1679–1745) in the History of Emotions*' won the University of Melbourne's Chancellor's Prize for Excellence in the PhD Thesis (2020). He has also focused on the area of creativity and wellbeing, and is currently a Research Fellow and Academic Convenor of the Creativity and Wellbeing Hallmark Research Initiative.

Interestingly, over the period 2022–2025 he will be working on a Melbourne Postdoctoral Fellowship project titled '*Musical Value in a Loneliness Epidemic*', which will use an interdisciplinary approach to examine how notions of musical value may mediate and enhance experiences of social connection.[5] He is also a co-host with Myf Warhurst of the podcast *We Are Lonely* on Spotify and Apple Music.

Dr Fred titled his piece on Olivia:
'It Felt Like Love'– Olivia Newton-John

In 2008 I went to Mardi Gras in Sydney, as a young gay man in my mid-20s looking for fun and a bit of an adventure. I hadn't started researching music yet. I did that a few years later, completing a masters and then a PhD in musicology, because I knew that I was fascinated by music in all its forms. Mainly, I was interested in what music does for people, and all the different things we use music for. But in my mid-20s I had too many other things to work out about my life, many of which had to do with my sexuality and finding a sense of belonging. I was a bit of a mess, and I was partying all the time.

At some point during Mardi Gras, Olivia came on stage at goodness knows what time (I think it was 4am, but don't ask me) and performed 'Xanadu'. I was in the crowd somewhere, shirtless, bopping around and dancing with every person that walked past me. I later found a recording of Olivia's performance on YouTube which noted that the 'Xanadu' remix that night was by Steve Anderson. It was a peppy electronic dance remix and I remember the atmosphere of the pavilion during her performance being absolutely electric.

Years of researching music since that time have given me a way of understanding why I loved that performance so much. From some perspectives, music is like an object with particular properties that can be described. For example, a song can be in a specific key, it can have fast or slow rhythms, ascending and descending melodies, and so on. In this sense, music is a 'thing' with features that are discernible through hearing or reading a score. From other perspectives, though, music is more like an 'event' than an object, something that occurs over time and across space, and it is something that we are a part of.

Musical sound can physically take up time and space in a room, a hall, or a concert venue, but more than this, it can create its own internal or parallel sense of time and space through the manipulation of elements like rhythm, melody, timbre, form and harmony. This 'musical space' somehow supervenes on reality and can even alter our sense of perceived reality. In these imaginative musical spaces, or musical events, we feel like we are somewhere/sometime else, and, in a way, we become somebody else, even just for a few minutes. We might get our bearings back, by thinking about the things that brought us to this moment, or all the possibilities for our 'selves' that lie ahead.

Olivia Newton-John was a long-time queer ally, and the fact that she came to Mardi Gras, to be there, at 4am or whatever time it was, to sing for us so joyfully, mattered a lot. Of course, she was absolutely professional, the moves rehearsed and the smile very practised. But she also seemed relaxed and comfortable, fluid, and she seemed to enjoy the silliness and the queerness of just throwing on a sparkly top and dancing around with a group of all sorts. Her song created both a physical space for being together, as well as an imagined, fantasy space for belonging, for being whatever you wanted to be, scaffolded by the thumping electronic pop beats and her perfect vocal melodies. In that space, I let it all go, I just danced, and turned into the person I was trying to become for a few minutes. It felt like love. Is 'Xanadu' a 'good' song? I'm not sure; I guess it depends on the criteria you use. But did it do something good? In that moment, yes, it sure did.

– Dr Fred Kiernan

Dr Kat Nelligan (RMIT) gave us a deeply layered instinct piece on Olivia's place within women in music and how she instinctively remembered her. Dr Kat is a lecturer at the School of Media and Communication at RMIT University, Melbourne. Kat's research focuses on marketing and branding narratives in pop music and her forthcoming book, *Brand Lady Gaga*, will be published in 2023 (Bloomsbury). Her current research interests focus on the mental health and wellbeing of music industry workers. She is a songwriter, music producer, and performer who composes music under the artist name of Zaffiri (zaffirimusic.com)

Dr Kat titled her piece:

'When I heard the news of Olivia Newton-John's death'

When I heard the news of Olivia Newton-John's death, childhood memories of my time watching Grease in grandmother's living room came flooding back. My sister, my cousin and I would recite every line and sing every lyric with enthusiasm. And when we weren't watching the film, we were acting it out, notably the final sequence: you know the one (that I want). I always felt disappointed with our game because my sister and cousin would claim the roles of Sandy and Danny before I could get a word in. 'You can be Kenickie!', they would say in unison. As the youngest I had to accept my fate, but how I longed for my moment to say: 'Tell me about it, Stud.'

Olivia Newton-John has positively impacted the lives of many. Her collaborators speak of her as family; they describe her as an inspiration and a true icon. Her fans connect with the warmth of her smile and the richness and intimacy of her voice. Her desire to help others can be seen in her unwavering support of breast-cancer research. Here in Australia (where I was born and raised) her legacy has unique significance. Her international success as a singer and actress in the 1970s and '80s helped to place Australia musically on a global stage, and as such her public image has become a marker of our cultural heritage and national identity (Strong 2022).

Notably, her rise to fame came at a time when mainstream music in Australia was shaped by the sounds of Oz Rock. Bands such as AC/DC, Cold Chisel, Rose Tattoo (to name a few) were crucial to the formation of this style, which was largely white and male-dominated, given the hyper-masculine pub environment in which it was often performed (Homan 2008). Newton-John's success during this time was significant because, along with luminaries Judith Duhram (who also sadly passed away only days before Newton-John) and Helen Reddy, she showed the world that Australian music could extend beyond the Oz Rock sound. The trifecta of Newton-John, Durham and Reddy paved the way for the next generation of women in pop: Kylie Minogue, Delta Goodrem, Natalia Imbruglia and many more.

Writing in the early 1990s about Australian music, popular music scholar Graeme Turner contended: 'To look for 'the Australian' element is to look for a local inflection, the distinctive modification of an already established musical style' (Turner 1992:13). Such local inflections include: an Australian accent; Indigenous languages and/or instruments (didgeridoo or clapping sticks, for instance); lyrics that contain Aussie vernacular or slang; references to Australian places, landscapes, landmarks, or cultural events. While listening to Newton-John's hit songs, 'Hopelessly Devoted to You', 'Physical', and 'Xanadu', we hear no such local inflections. Her sound is global, reflecting the international pop-music trends of the time.

Yet, many Australians view her (and her music) as a representation of who Australia is as a nation. What makes Newton-John a true Aussie icon is not so much the fact that she was raised in Melbourne, (although this carries significance), nor is it inherent in the musical sounds of her songs. Rather, it's embedded in the memories and the collective imagination of the Australian people.

Her iconic 'Aussie-ness' is brought to life in their stories and recollections about the ways in which her music and films shaped their childhood. As Catherine Strong shows in her recent tribute to the star: 'Like many Australians, ONJ has been part of the soundtrack to my life, from arranging my own little performances to Xanadu in kindergarten, to singing along to the 'Grease' mega mix at school discos' (Strong 2022). For John Encarnacao (2022), it was 'her voice, her way with song' that connected with him personally. Olivia Newton-John is an Aussie icon because we describe her as such in our stories. Her iconic Aussie status is thus brought to life by the populace – the Australian people – who will remember her, as Encarnacao (2022) so eloquently puts it, for the 'lessons… [she] taught me about music – and life'.

It has often been said that 'Sandy's journey in *Grease* in a way mirrored many a young queer person's path of personal transformation and being comfortable with yourself, even if that self changes or is seen as wrong by people who don't understand.' [6]

Olivia commented on her gay fans saying, 'With *Grease* and *Xanadu*, how lucky am I that I've been in two films that are still loved! I find it so much fun that it's still going on. My publicist will tell me that both films are shown in gay bars, and I get such a kick out of that.' [7]

Olivia's ties to the gay community have always been strong and open and she will be missed worldwide. Her role in the 1996 film *It's My Party*, where she played Lina Bingham, is 'based on the actual events of the death of Harry Stein, architect and designer and previous partner of director Randal Kleiser. [8] It was one of the first feature flms to address the controversial topic of AIDS patients dying with dignity.

'*Xanadu*' and '*Physical*' are both enduring LGBTQiA+ anthems and Olivia remembered in 2018, 'This week I sang on the Atlantis gay cruise aboard the stunning '*Harmony of the Seas*' – the biggest ship in the world! It was amongst the most memorable of nights in my whole career! Fun, warm, loving people who shared those feelings with me! Thank you.' [9]

In a fantastic article about Olivia and her impact, the author Alison Stine wrote: 'It would be years before I recognised Newton-John's full impact, particularly as a queer icon before it was cool, and a gay ally beginning at a time well before it was popular, accepted or even safe to do so.' [10]

Olivia Newton-John was a singer who could perform ballads for the masses as well as anthems for gay clubs. *Grease* cemented her place as one of the great icons of her day and '*Physical*' solidified her position as a legend. 'The '*Physical*' video is predominantly played for laughs, but it's the end that really cemented her position as a gay icon. She proved that it was possible to own her sexuality, to change her image, and to move with the times.

'Olivia Newton-John leaves behind a legacy of LGBTQiA+ friendship and a glittering career that makes her an eternal gay icon.' [11]

She was a tireless supporter of same-sex marriage and spoke to the press about what it was like to perform at New York Pride the night after the state introduced same-sex marriage. 'The air was electric, and there was so much excitement in the air from the couples. People who have had long relationships and care about each other and take care of each other should have the right to be married.' [12]

Olivia was an advocate of the life motto 'Stick to the right beliefs before they become popular'. When the '*Physical*' clip aired around Australia and went to No. 1, sadly being gay was still illegal in most states and territories here. 'So here was Australia's number one 'gal' openly supportive of LGBTIQ+ rights in a movie clip, when it was still illegal.' [13]

In October 1973 the Australian Parliament passed a motion in favour of the decriminalization of homosexual acts between consenting adults in private. While at the same time, the Australian Medical Association removed homosexuality from its list of illnesses and disorders, two months before the American Psychiatric Association did the same. Five hundred people marched to and rallied in Martin Place in Sydney on 24 June 1978. Organisers said the March and rally were part of 'international homosexual solidarity day' to demonstrate against sexual repression in Australia and other countries. Police attacked a late-night street party or Mardi Gras that night and arrested 53 people. This response, coupled with the publication of the names of the activists arrested in the local press over the next few days, attracted considerable public sympathy and led to this event becoming an annual community event, the Sydney Gay and Lesbian Mardi Gras.

In 1994, the Commonwealth passed the Human Rights (Sexual Conduct) Act 1994 – Section 4, legalising sexual activity between consenting adults (in private) throughout Australia. Same-sex marriage legislation would fail 22 times in the Federal Parliament. On 9 December 2017, the right to marry in Australia was no longer determined by sex or gender. In 2017, the Federal Parliament passed a law amending the Marriage Act 1961 to allow same-sex couples to marry in December 2017. [14] Australian Marriage Equality National Convener Alex Greenwich said at the time: 'Australians admire celebrities like Olivia Newton-John and Hugh Jackman because they reflect our values of tolerance and a fair go for all, values which they are reminding us apply just as much to same sex couples as to other Australians.' [15] Olivia was so happy for the Gay Community victory after years of pledging her support for gay marriage.

'With respect to marriage equality, I believe that no-one has the right to judge and deny couples who love each other the ability to make a marriage commitment: 'Love is love." [16a]

Newton-John was a dear and strong LGBTQI ally, saying, 'The gay fans have always been very loyal, there are a really great audience and have always been there for me.' [16b]

Australian singer Darren Hayes (Savage Garden) tweeted, 'Oh dear, sweet, magical, eternal Olivia. You gave so much to this world and to this little boy who saw acceptance in your twinkling eyes and glittering world. You made us all feel held by the sweetness of your voice and the capacity of your heart. I hope you are in *Xanadu*.'

American Star Trek actor and LGBTQI activist George Takei tweeted, 'We have lost a great, iconic artist in Olivia Newton John, gone too soon from us at age 73. I trust she is now in the great *Xanadu* beyond. Know that we are forever hopelessly devoted to you, Olivia. Rest in song and mirth.'

@RuPaulsDragRace posted:

'Rest in peace, Olivia Newton-John. Thank you for sharing your talent and inspiring us all.'

Chapter 16

Australia – Olivia's 'Heart Home'

Olivia Newton-John, receiving the Order of Australia in 2019 and with tears in her eyes, said she 'was really grateful for Australia and would continue to do my best for a country I love'. [1]

The honour was presented by Australian Ambassador Joe Hockey in Los Angeles, who said, 'You are being recognised by your nation not just because we are proud of you but because you have changed the world. It is not just because of your singing, song writing, acting – that's the stuff that has lit up so many faces … but you are doing it now from a philanthropy perspective, simply by illustrating to the world you never give up. You never walk away from any challenge. You are the most optimistic person I have ever met.' [2a]

Bono once did a sweeping bow in front of her. 'You are the queen of Australia,' [2b] he said. How right he was. This career-diverse woman was the Queen. Everyone knew she was Australian and she identified as Australian, which gave her a place to lay her head and Australia a once-in-a-lifetime role model.

Olivia Newton-John brought Australia to the world. 'When the American public saw *Grease* for the first time they heard that wonderfully flat Australian accent turning up at Rydell High … and they heard Australian name drop lines in the *Grease* script such as:

Sandy: What if they dance differently than we do back home?
Rizzo: Hey don't worry, maybe you'll invent the kangaroo bop.' [2c]

She was publicly proud of being an Australian. The notion of belonging was important for Olivia, and even though she had a British birth certificate and a long-term home in Malibu, Australia stayed as her home in heart and mind. Another gift of character Olivia Newton-John had was that she could 'navigate seamlessly between the three countries she had been born in, raised in and resided in'. [3]

This said she chose to become an Australian citizen and when the world was too much and when she was ill she came back to Melbourne and Byron Bay to regroup. Olivia Newton-John left Melbourne to chase the dream of a recording career, but always kept the city as her heart home.

Dame Olivia 'was a woman who took her identity – Aussie accent and all – to the world stage and platformed it for all of us.' [4a]

Olivia was a global and cultural icon – hopelessly devoted to Australia. A cultural icon is something or someone that is an internationally recognised symbol used to identify cultural property – property being something of importance to the country.

Art, music and food definitely shape our cultural identity, as do Australian symbols like Golden Wattle, Koalas and the First Nations spiritual wonder Uluru. Hopes and values are part of the iconic Australian makeup, such as the idea of the Aussie battler and 'One of the highest accolades that can be attributed to an Australian that has fought hard and come out on top is that of a 'real Aussie battler'. Today, I can think of nobody more deserving of that moniker than Olivia Newton-John'. [4b]

She achieved so many things for Australia that ONJ became a cultural Aussie. 'My education was in Australia, and I always felt I was Australian.' [5] She adopted Australia and all its beliefs and mannerisms. In turn, we gave her a safe haven and a sense of belonging. She fitted in here – always.

Peter Allen, Olivia's dear friend and fellow musician and writer and singer of '*I Still Call Australia Home*' (which Qantas still plays to this day as you fly into Sydney) said, 'My duty is to be a nice Australian, which is basically to stay out of jail and keep saying I'm an Australian.' [6] Olivia was also a nice Australian – she stayed out of jail and introduced

Australia to the world. 'Newton-John absolutely set the bar and standard for any ambassador or patron in a social purpose organisation in Australia.' [7]

Former Australian Foreign Minister Julie Bishop proudly said, 'She was not only a global ambassador for the music industry, but she was also an ambassador for Australia. In 2018, we honoured Olivia at the G'Day USA awards.' [8a] Former Foreign Minister Alexander Downer added, 'Olivia Newton-John … was a proud Australian. Having her involvement made a big difference in the Australian effort in the United States … She was very loyal to Australia and very patriotic about Australia and proud of her Australian heritage.' [8b]

She effortlessly achieved so many things for Australia. In 2021 *Rolling Stone* Australia put together a list of the 50 Greatest Australian Artists of All Time – with Dame Olivia sitting pretty at number 20.

At the LA 1984 Olympic Australia gala, she hosted the team and performed '*I Still Call Australia Home*' – which is always popular amongst homesick Australians.

In 1987 she participated in the 'Invites Americans to 'Say G'day to Melbourne'' campaign – a $3 million pitch to the world by Victoria Tourism launched in the States, which she graciously waived her fee for.

You know you have made it Down Under when you make it onto our postage stamps. Olivia has done this twice, the second time was 26 June 2012, when the Australian government issued a postage stamp to help raise funds for the Olivia Newton-John Cancer & Wellness Centre Appeal.

Her Koala Blue fashion chain was devised to take a corner of Australia to the world and inspired by homesick times while she lived in LA. She stocked it with chocolate, biscuits and treats from her Aussie childhood. Olivia could also take some credit for the Australian Capital Territory's 2019 decision to legalise cannabis – she had been a firm proponent of medicinal marijuana, to which she was introduced after her breast cancer returned.

When asked in 2017 whether she considered herself to be a British, Australian or American citizen, she said, 'I am still Australian.' [9]

Reviewers for her bestseller *Don't Stop Believin'* stated 'don't dare to miss this memoir if you're Australian. Because, let's face it, Olivia is nothing short of a national treasure.'[10] *Better Reading Australia* captured Olivia perfectly: 'Australia is known for our great beaches, sunny weather, and general laid-back disposition, but few things are more quintessentially Australian than our very own golden-haired sweetheart, Olivia Newton-John.' [11]

Reflecting on her love of Melbourne, Olivia said, no matter what, she would always be a Melbourne girl at heart. Asked about her connection to Melbourne she reminisced, 'We lived at Jolimont next to the MCG. I used to hear the roar of the footy crowd coming through every weekend. We also lived in Parkville next to the animals, so I'd hear the lions roaring every morning. I've savoured all the fun parts of Melbourne and kept them with me.' [12]

Her Olivia Newton-John Cancer and Wellness Centre was built and expanded on in Melbourne, which made coming home more of a regular thing than before, both publicly and secretly. Attending her regular charity Galas and Wellness walks were vital to her. 'I make a point of visiting the patients at the ONJ Centre whenever I'm in Australia. I want to see everyone is being cared for.' [13]

Showing up for what she believed was important, and the fact her family lived here, kept Melbourne as her home in heart and deed. Her niece Tottie said, 'Family was so important to her and she brought everyone together, here in Melbourne.' [14]

Olivia grew up in Melbourne, but Australia held a fascination for her. 'Byron Bay has been dubbed ‹Aussiewood' thanks to its stunning beaches, thriving food scene and popularity with A-listers – but it was Olivia Newton-John who put the small New South Wales town on the map.' [15]

Olivia owned a 187-acre Australian farm for nearly 40 years near Byron Bay in New South Wales, which she sold in 2019, and her Gaia Spa, founded in 2005 in Byron Bay, was her spiritual home. Asked once what her favourite places in Australia were, she answered: 'Gaia Retreat and Spa; Coober Pedy, as it is a unique and quirky place with many colourful characters, that are hard to forget; the Sydney Bondi to Bronte Walk – it is simply stunning. I feel like a world away there.' As she did at Tallow Beach – Byron Bay and 'my old hometown, Melbourne, still holds many fond memories for me especially as my mum lived there and most of my family still live there. I stay at the gorgeous Lyall Hotel … Last but not least is the tranquil Lizard Island in north Queensland right on the Great Barrier Reef. It is one of my most cherished little Aussie islands.' [16]

Recently selling her farm, which was 76 hectares of land – located in Dalwood, New South Wales and originally bought in the 1980s. She planted 5000 trees here and created a wildlife habitat. The compound has its own robust rainforest with a natural waterfall, two dams, a creek and large bird populations, 'The *Grease* star then decided to spend her remaining days in the California home.' [17]

In a never-before-seen interview aired after her death in Australia, it was revealed Olivia wanted part of her to come home after she died. She explained that when she had passed, she wanted some of her ashes scattered in Byron Bay, some at her property in California and 'in other places I love'. Her late mother and sister were also scattered in Byron. 'I'd like to be with them, I'd like to be with them … that would be nice.' [18]

A constant theme in the discussion of Olivia's incredible international career is the concept of a Gum Leaf Mafia in LA and the world, really. Journalist Michael Dwyer wrote a fascinating article about the Australians that surrounded Olivia and aided her in world domination. How did a girl from the suburbs of Melbourne become one of the biggest singers on the planet?

'History does record the fingerprints of a secret society of managers, songwriters, producers and other backroom players that paved our Olivia's way from Melbourne TV talent quest at just 16 all the way to the Grammy Awards for Record of the Year.' [19]

Olivia mentioned this group of supporters during a 1994 Australian interview saying, 'there is a whole network that still goes on'. [20] Her network involved Peter Allen, who Olivia crossed paths with when he was one half of The Allen Brothers on Australian television and wrote her signature song for a time, '*I Honestly Love You*'. The Gum Nut posse members also included songwriter and producer and best friend John Farrar, Pat Carroll, and songwriter Steve Kipner, Roger Davies, Helen Reddy, Andy Gibb, Australian couple, singer Darryl Cotton (Zoot) and costume designer Fleur Thiemeyer.

The Gum Nut Mafia was a 'group of creative expat Australians that all helped a fellow Australian out was an indispensible asset to Olivia and opened many varied doors for her she could never have dreamed to go through'. [21]

The term 'gumnut mafia' was defined by music historian Clinton Walker, as 'a crafty league of Australian entrepreneurs in 1960s London, most prominently represented by Adelaide expat Robert Stigwood, whose record label RSO Records hit its straps when the Bee Gees sailed from Sydney into his open arms in 1967'. [22]

Walker then went on to identify in his 2021 book *Suburban Songbook*, another key player of that era the 'late Peter Gormley … who managed pop king Cliff Richard and his band The Shadows. Soon enough, his Savile Artists stable would include Judith Durham and Newton-John.' [23]

This is huge! It links Olivia's whole circle of massively talented friends together, and how they shared their talent and supported each other is quite phenomenal. Connections can only do so much, however – luckily, Olivia had the bones to hang all these connections on. She is the one who took the chances, changed things up and did the hard yards in Melbourne and London and then the US.

'Melbourne helped shape me for success because I got my first training in show business here. There are not many places in the world where you can get all that experience. It gave me good stead when I went overseas.' [24] Clinton Walker doubled down on this, saying, 'Still, great business connections can only explain so much in the rise of a fair dinkum global superstar ... I suppose it's just that incredible breath of fresh air that she was.' [25]

This Gum Nut Mafia is traceable all the way though Olivia's career. I would put Ian 'Molly' Meldrum in the mix as the Gum Nut Godfather as his influence was international even though he chose to base himself in Melbourne. These connections continued for Olivia's whole life. She met Australian country superstar and husband of Nicole Kidman, Keith Urban, at a 2002 song writing retreat in a castle owned by Police manager Miles Copeland. They both discovered they were reading the same book, *A Sunburned Country* and penned the classic song '*Sunburned Countr*' together. Both their schedules were so hectic that they ended up hooking up again in Nashville between concert tours to finish writing and recording it in one day.

Sunburned Country
by Olivia Newton-John and Keith Urban

She taught me to be strong
She taught me to fight
And I am who I am today
Because she raised me right

In a sunburned country

Her magic and her mystery
In a sunburned country
Forever will be home to me
Oh that's where my heart is truly free

Glenn A. Baker, one of Australia's greatest rock historians, also wrote an insightful article titled '*The Australians who helped Olivia*'. 'In every stage of her recording span, Olivia Newton-John drew upon Australians – as songwriters, producers, singers, musicians, mentors, partners and friends … Australian music makers were never that far from her.'

Then he added the important line: 'But there is no doubt that her formative years in Melbourne would have an immense impact on her; in ways interwoven with almost all aspects of her long career.' [26] Clearly her impact on Australia through music was immense. Olivia gave back to her homeland through song, hard-fought charity work and representing the best of OZ overseas whenever she could.

The 1988 Bicentenary celebrations in Australia inspired Olivia's first solo single in nearly three years. She released 'I*t's Always Australia For Me*', co-written with John Capek. This sweet autobiographical love letter to her adopted homeland is pure and personal sentiment. [27a] To promote this nation's celebration of 200 years, she travelled around the whole country, touring her *Rumour* album and saw it as a thank you to Australia for welcoming her. The video for this song is a classic and filled with iconic Australian imagery, even a Melbourne tram! [27b]

'It's Always Australia For Me'

By Olivia Newton-John and John Capek

As a young girl I came here by the sea
To a new home for my family
It welcomed us with open arms
A chance to live my dream
And there's no place that I'd rather be
Yes, it's always Australia for me

Live, love knowing that we're all free
Know that we are blessed in our country
And realise how lucky we are
Safe beneath our southern star
And there's no place that I'd rather be
Yes, it's always Australia for me

In her later years, Olivia and husband John Easterling divided their time between California, Florida and Australia. She always missed being away from her chosen country. She always came when it called for bushfire benefits and events that celebrated her homeland. ONJ was one of our greatest emissaries and part of her now lies here in perpetuity.

In 2021 during the pandemic, Olivia was locked down at her home near LA. She told the media that she pined for her 'heart home' – Melbourne. 'I miss the sounds of the birds in the morning,' she said. 'Those years from 5 to 16, that I spent in Australia, they're the very formative years – that's a very important period in your life.' [28]

What does it mean to acknowledge that Olivia was proudly Australian when she was such an international superstar?

Vicki Gordon, founding AWMA Executive Producer and Program

Director, said it perfectly when Olivia was being inducted into the Australian Women in Music Honour roll: 'It is an acknowledgement that genius of that brilliance can grow in this soil, on this land and in this culture. That we lift up in value and esteem the Australian women singers, songwriters and cultural leaders who gift us so much beauty and creativity by using their talent to create music.'

'Brilliance can grow in this soil' – that is what a country can pride itself on, that gives future creatives hope that it can happen to them as well. Olivia will always be in the 'upper echelon of acts who began their careers in Australia – the Bee Gees (220 million records sold), AC/DC (200 million) and Air Supply (100 million). She personified pop culture in the '80s and had three number ones in Australia: '*Banks Of The Ohio*' (1971), '*You're The One That I Want*' (1978) from *Grease*, and '*Physical*' (1981). [29]

What an absolute bonus that this little girl landed on our shores way back in 1954. She has set the world on fire with her talent and stamina and all with our flag draped around her shoulders.

'Olivia Newton-John's Aussie roots were never broken. Her ties to Australia bent but never severed … She loved Australia dearly, but even more than that Australia loved her back.' [30]

Chapter 17

Molly and Livvy

August 8th 2022, the world's media bowed their heads and spread the word that Australia's Sweetheart had died.

'Tributes are flowing in for Olivia Newton-John in the wake of her tragic death, with celebrities remembering the iconic Aussie actress. Newton-John died, aged 73, at her ranch in California following a long battle with breast cancer.' *Sky News*

Amongst all the media noise one voice was silent for a few days. Ian 'Molly' Meldrum – music industry legend and Australia's rock guru – was a long-time close friend of Livvy's as he called her. Devastated by her death, he took some hushed time to mourn her and then released the statement below.

Official Statement from Molly Meldrum on Dame Olivia Newton-John

Tonight, the start will shine a little brighter and I am heartbroken!

Livvy, as I call her, was one of those rare people who had a profound effect on the world and the people in it. Her purity was real, her passion for life was unwavering.

A Grammy Award winning record artist, and extraordinary wife, mother and humanitarian, Liv's tireless work has changed millions of lives and her legacy will live on forever.

To me, Liv is family. My heart is broken. There simply will never be another like her.

As Molly said so succinctly, Olivia did have a profound effect on the world and her purity was real.

Remembering his dear friend and her connection to Melbourne he said, 'She would bring her huge smile, her giggle, her playfulness, and, as she went through these last horrible years, she brought her steel. I will never forget how strong she was. But she loved Australia and she loved Melbourne. If it wasn't for her career, I believe she would have lived here always. She loved coming here, and we loved having her here. It was family, it was home.' [1]

Sitting down with Molly and his beloved dog Ziggy at his Richmond home (Tuesday 6th Sept 2022), he agreed to a quick chat about Olivia, obviously still very upset at her passing and ready to do anything the family needed for her future State Funeral.

I asked where he thought Olivia was placed in the Australian Women in Music Hall of Fame.

He smiled and said he had been thinking about this question for the last few days. 'You know that song by Tina Turner – '*(Simply) The Best*', well that's how l feel. She was simply the best and great at everything she did. Every time l think of her, my dear mate, l will say, Olivia is simply the best.'

He had a flashback to when he used to (laughingly, not in the real sense) stalk her at Sportsgirl in Collins St, Melbourne many years ago when she helped out there. He went on to reminisce a bit as I brought up some of the many *Countdown* interviews he had filmed with Olivia and the many times she had come to his house and he had travelled to the UK and US to see her.

He said he actually worked with Olivia and Pat Carroll on the 1983 Koala Blue store concept. Her unique Australian-themed boutique, for which she picked up major business awards in the US. This US-based fashion empire had more than 60 stores operating worldwide, selling casual clothing and iconic Australian accessories.

Sadly, the worldwide recession claimed the stores in 1993, but taking a taste of Australia to the world was something Olivia did proudly and something Molly Meldrum has also done his whole life.

He laughed at this fond memory of being in LA: 'Possibly 1976, it was a long time ago,' he smiled. 'But it had to be before the film *Grease* came out as Olivia wanted me to see *Grease* the Musical stage show with her and her long-time Australian-born manager Roger Davies – also a great friend of mine.'

Olivia told Molly she wanted his opinion as she was in talks to do the film *Grease.*

After the show he remembers shaking his head and saying, 'That's not going to work, translating this musical to a film, I just can't see it.'

He then confessed he said the same thing about Abba and the Mamma Mia movie being filmed on an island.

Shaking his head, Molly then sat up to his full height and said to me: 'It doesn't happen often, but both these times I was totally wrong. Could not be more wrong and it was clearly the other way around. They could not be better movies!

Thank goodness they did not take that crap advice.'

Molly had many fond mentions of Olivia in his published autobiographies. *The Never, Um, Ever Ending Story, Life, Countdown and Everything In Between* with Jeff Jenkins in 2014 and *Ah Well, Nobody's Perfect, The Untold Stories* with Jeff Jenkins in 2016 was one of them.

Both of Molly's fantastic books are crammed with stories and recollections over his jam-packed years in the music industry. Written with Jeff Jenkins, Molly's mate, fellow sports lover and a great rock historian for his clever and gentle way of recording lives and checking facts.

From *The Never, Um Ever Ending Story* there was a classic tale from Billy Miller of The Ferrets about loving Olivia from afar.

Molly asked Billy to put a band together for the *Xanadu Countdown* film night and knowing that Olivia would be there, Billy 'had this great idea I was going to meet Olivia and we would get together that night. I had it all worked out. I think I got to say hello to her at sound check and that was that.' He ended up spending the night in jail – but you will have to read Molly's book to find out why. [2]

In the same book, Molly remembered in 1978, 'I was certainly on my best behaviour when I spent a night with Olivia Newton-John and John Travolta at Studio 54, the world's hippest disco.' [3] I found myself (two decades later, Nov 1998) 'sitting in a Melbourne cinema watching the Studio 54 movie. In the opening scene, someone yells, 'We've got to get down there because Olivia Newton-John's there!'

Everyone on the planet wants to know the history of Molly's signature hat. He revealed in his book that 'Olivia gave me a hat, a Stetson, in the early '80s and I wore it a few times on *Countdown*. When I stopped wearing it, people wrote into the show asking, 'Why doesn't he wear the hat again?' Then my friend Lindsay Fox, the trucking magnate, brought me a hat back from America – a 'Billy The Kid Stetson'. In his kitchen, I remember folding it and tying it because I didn't like the strap hanging around my chin. And THE HAT was born!'

So, can we make a massive leap here and say perhaps historically Olivia Newton-John is responsible for giving Molly a taste for the hat and then Lindsay gave him the right hat!

Molly was, of course, invited to Elton John's famous Australian wedding on 14 Feb 1984, Valentine's Day, at St Mark's Anglican Church in Darling Point Sydney to Renate Blauel. He spent the day with fellow guests including Olivia Newton-John, Michael Parkinson and Barry Humphries.

Molly has publicly said before that he doesn't consider himself to be an icon despite the success of his popular music program *Countdown*. The 76-year-old explained to *Stellar* Magazine that the title of an icon makes him cringe. 'I just feel I don't deserve that title. Others do, but I don't.'

Molly listed names such as Barry Humphries, Sir Donald Bradman, Michael Hutchence, Kylie Minogue, Paul Hogan and Olivia Newton-John, as being worthy of the title of an 'icon'.

'These are all people I really admire for what they've achieved.' [4]

I discovered the original review of the *Grease* opening night ball, held in Sydney in August 1978, to mark the film's release down under – written by none other than Molly Meldrum and Christine Richter.

'Bobby sox, sneakers, flared skirts and slicked-down hair were the order of the night when TV stars and celebrities turned out for the Sydney launching of the movie *Grease*. With the star of the film, Australia's own Olivia Newton-John, in town for the premiere, fans went wild.

'More than 5000 people gathered outside the theatre from early afternoon to welcome her in true Hollywood style. By the time the real star of the show was due to arrive, the crowd had reached fever pitch. Police and security men stood against the barricades as Olivia arrived, but the 29-year-old blonde singer was jostled as crowds swarmed in to get a closer look.

'After the film, guests were transported to the Paddington Town Hall for the *Grease* Ball where Chiko Rolls, hot dogs and soft drinks were available. Olivia mingled with local radio and TV people in a function room off the dance area.' [5]

Here's a snippet of Molly's parts of his *TV Week* review of the actual film.

> 'Last week the much-publicised, much-talked about film of the '50s *Grease*, starring our own Olivia Newton-John and superstar John Travolta burst onto the Oz screen … Olivia flew in from Hawaii to attend the Sydney premiere, and although utterly exhausted from the trip she delighted the hundreds of people who crammed the footpaths outside the cinema in George Street to catch a glimpse of the

celebrities arriving. Johnny Cougar, who'd flown in from England for a short promotional trip, caused excitement when he stopped outside the cinema to sign autographs…

'And now the big question: What was the film like? Personally, I don't think it matches up to Saturday Night Fever, although both John and Olivia's performances are solid – good light entertainment.

'Perhaps I'm crazy criticising a film that recouped its investment in 60 hours in America … in fact, when I think of it, I AM crazy.

'But the one of many things that shines out in Olivia is that she's a true lady of the rock scene and has somehow retained her niceness throughout the years of becoming a superstar. She's one Australian artist of which we can be really and truly proud.' [6]

As always, Molly tells the truth how he sees it, even to Olivia. And their friendship was one of mutual respect, with lots of love and humour thrown in on top.

The *Countdown* film archives are a rare record of Australian music – in all its chaotic, rough-and-ready brilliant glory. Molly travelled the world and brought all the new music home and hand delivered Australian music to the globe. There was never any way of telling what might happen at any moment on this show, but everyone watched it, learnt from it, and loved it.

Olivia frequently appeared on *Countdown* and looking back over the years here are a few classic Lovey (one of Molly's nicknames) and Livvy interview moments.

1978 *Countdown*

Shortly after the release of *Grease*, ONJ sat down with Molly Meldrum for a chat. He asked about her rise to stardom, and Livvy — then about 30 years old — laughed that she never thought she'd 'get all of this attention'.

'It's a strange feeling because when I lived here [Melbourne], I did a lot of local TV and such. I'd see other people come through and get all this attention, but I never thought I'd get all this attention,' she quipped.

'It's a really lovely feeling, it's the way to come home.' [7]

1979 Dec 16 *Countdown*

Molly leads with the comment that in music charts the 'ladies are getting into the act' and Olivia says during the interview that she 'tries to get braver and braver' and grow a bit each time she made a new recording and that the whole *Grease* experience gave her confidence. [8]

1980 July *Countdown*

Olivia discusses chart positions with Molly. At the time '*Xanadu*' is number 1 in England and Europe whilst '*Magic*' is number 1 in America. In Australia, '*Magic*' is going up charts along with '*Don't Cry For Me Argentina*' (having recently performed her 1977 recording for the Queen in Australia). Olivia mentions that she doesn't think she's ever had a solo number 1 in England and that '*Xanadu*' made it there within 4 weeks. (In the UK, Olivia previously had two number one duets with John Travolta from the *Grease* soundtrack but '*Xanadu*' is not a solo record because it's a collaboration with ELO.)

Molly asks why Olivia turned down the movie *Can't Stop The Music*. She replies that her instinct, after reading the script, was that it wasn't right for her. The producer Allan Carr wasn't too happy with her for a while, but they are 'friends again now'. [9]

1980 24th August *Countdown*

Olivia was guest presenter at the Grand Final of the *Countdown Xanadu* National Dance contest held at Chasers Disco in Melbourne with Molly 'who was clearly overjoyed at having Olivia there. There's such a lot of kissing and hugging.' [10a]

A satellite link was set up with John Travolta, also in Australia to promote his film *Urban Cowboy.*

They were meeting the next day to see the Melbourne sights and to meet Olivia's mum. Olivia talked about meeting Michael Jackson and how nice he was and 'very cute' and that Michael told her that he loved '*Magic*' and John Farrar's work. Olivia mimed '*Magic*' and '*Xanadu*' in gorgeous sparkling outfits. 10b

1982 Jan 17 *Countdown*

Classic satellite interview with Molly, set in a gym with Olivia on an exercise machine. The big news was how she changed her hair from long to short for the iconic film clip '*Physical*'.

The critics were all talking about her change of image, which she thinks is all fun. She said her hair was the 'punk version of Lady Di's hair'.

She just decided she was bored with how she looked and cut it all off in NY. The '*Physical*' film clip was the director's idea – and she claimed she didn't see a lot of it until it was done. And there was also another ending that no one saw.

Olivia talked about how it's hard to keep up with trends and images, and the challenge is to come up with something new – and she is the happiest she has ever been 'with no urge to tour'. [11]

1983 Aug 28 *Countdown*

Molly is talking to ONJ about Two of a Kind, her new movie with John Travolta. Both stars had been looking for a film to do together since *Grease* and 'thought this might be it'.

Olivia touches on a stalker incident that she did not really want to talk about, saying that '99 per cent of being a celebrity is fantastic, 1 per cent can be bad, invasive'. [12]

1985 *Countdown* (reprinted for a CD release in2006 and contains an 11-minute Olivia interview with Molly).

'Olivia didn't do much media for the *Soul Kiss* album due to being pregnant at the time. She even admits in the interview that she isn't doing as much publicity as the record company would probably like her to do. When Molly asks Olivia to describe the image of *Soul Kiss*, she laughs, slightly embarrassed, describing it as 'kind of erotic. Sensual.' The album is more up-tempo than her other albums; Olivia had said that about the *Totally Hot* and *Physical* albums, so there's a increasing curve here. Molly asks her about the current hot female artists of the time: Cyndi Lauper and Madonna, who she of course admires and likes, describing their individuality and strength. [13] Tina Turner, who's also managed by Roger Davies, her manager at the time, also comes in for praise due to her energy and hectic tour schedule. Molly asks about her favourite songs and Olivia mentions '*Suspended in Time*' and '*Don't Cry For Me Argentina*'.

Another anarchic and much loved Australian TV show that showcased music was *Hey Hey It's Saturday.*

Long-time host and TV legend Daryl Somers spoke about the loss of Olivia on the *Hey Hey It's Saturday* facebook page.

Dame Olivia Newton-John

We all suffered a dagger to the heart earlier today with the news that our national treasure, Olivia Newton-John had finally succumbed to the cancer she fought for so long.

Apart from her beautifully mellifluous voice and worldwide hits, what sets Olivia apart is that throughout her long and illustrious career she retained that 'girl next door' appeal. She was still Olivia; warm, natural, wholesome, caring, giving and, dare I say, a musical version of Audrey Hepburn with her beauty, grace and compassion for others.

She was an inspiration to so many artists and still will be for a long time to come. Rest in peace Olivia. [14]

1985 *Hey Hey It's Saturday* Charity Appeal fundraiser

Featured a live cross to LA where Olivia Newton-John and Matt Lattanzi and Molly were all together not long after her Dec 1984 wedding. Actor Christopher Atkins was also on set and gushed that their wedding was great. Olivia is clearly so in love and Matt sweetly admits he would love to come fishing in Australia.

March 27 1999 *Hey Hey It's Saturday*

Olivia was interviewed by Molly Meldrum at the newly built Stadium Australia (sometimes referred to as Sydney or Homebush Stadium).

Olivia was to introduce the Bee Gees who were the first act to ever perform there. Olivia jokes that she is a mascot for the Bee Gees as she also appeared in their 1997 Las Vegas concert video.

2009 *Hey Hey It's Saturday* showed iconic footage of Olivia passionately singing '*I Still Call Australia Home*'.

Chapter 18

Behind The Scenes 'Our Livvy' Recollections

People who knew Olivia Newton-John and worked with her behind the scenes have many rare stories to tell. You can scour the world's press and you will not find anything negative about Olivia, which is almost unheard of. No one had a bad word to say, because there wasn't one to say. An American singer in the '70s had a crack, saying: 'It's nothing but the blonde singing the bland.' [1a] But we all know that was just jealously!

Jamie Donnelly, who played Pink Lady Jan in *Grease*, wrote: 'Olivia's heart was as pure as her voice. Her goodness and grace will shine through the ages in her work. I have known her for over 40 years and never heard her say a negative word of anyone or anyone say a negative word of her. What a glorious soloist for the heavenly choir!' [1b]

More memories of Olivia come from her close friend Richard Wilkins:

'I worked with Olivia once and, yes, she is as nice as they say…'

One of the most recognisable names in Australian entertainment, and known for his sense of humour and honesty is Richard Wilkins. He has a stellar career of 30+ years since launching MTV Australia in 1987 and shows no signs of slowing down. His book *Black Ties Red Carpets and Green Rooms* was a best seller and his attitude to life and work seems very much like his dear friend Olivia's – work hard and enjoy life. He said in a radio interview that in his line of work, 'every day is different … I work hard, I have fun, and love being part of a terrific team on and off camera. I've been blessed to work with such talented, smart, professional people who bring out the best in me. Most of whom have become lifetime friends. I guess I am lucky after all!' [2]

New Zealand-born, Richard Wilkins' name will be familiar to anyone who has switched on a TV, picked up a magazine or listened to the radio. Over the past two decades, Richard has interviewed the greatest stars in the world, including Olivia Newton-John, Britney Spears, Leonardo DiCaprio, Pink, Barbra Streisand, Barry Humphries, Neil Diamond, Justin Bieber, One Direction and Lady Gaga, to name a few. In demand as a professional MC and speaker, he has hosted countless events across Australia and internationally. Richard has been Master of Ceremonies for the G'Day LA and G'Day USA Gala events in Los Angeles and New York, to honour Australia's most talented and well-known actors and singers and to celebrate the ties between America and Australia. He has graced the red carpets of the Oscars, Grammys, Brit Awards and ARIA Awards.

Fantastically in 1980, he brought his band Wilde And Reckless to Australia and released some singles and a six-track EP, then toured with the legendary Grace Jones. He left the music industry to work behind the scenes in radio and interestingly in 2006, he returned to the stage for his role as Vince Fontaine in the mega-production *Grease: The Arena Spectacular.* In the 2014 Queen's Birthday Honours List, Wilkins was appointed a Member of the Order of Australia (AM), for 'significant service to the community through a range of charities, and to the entertainment industry'. He is currently, amongst many other duties, the Network Nine's Entertainment Editor.

When Richard delivered the sad news about Olivia's passing, on the *Today Show*, always a professional he visibly held back his tears, but on-air moments later it was too much, he was too close to the story and broke down in tears in a later segment remembering his friendship with 'Liv' and how her long-term battle with breast cancer had come to an end.

'Dickie, I'm so sorry for your loss,' co-host Karl Stefanovic said, and was quickly followed by a warm embrace. Richard responded, 'It's our loss. The world has lost a beautiful human being today. We kind of knew this day was coming but hoped it would be a long way away.' [3]

Richard had heard the news of Olivia's sad death in the early hours of that August 8 morning and had to admit to his co-hosts: 'I'm still numb – I've got nothing more I can say.'

After seeing Richard's on-air grief, Olivia's daughter Chloe sent him this lovely and comforting message just two days later:

'Hi Richard, this is Chloe, I just saw your beautiful tribute to my mummy. I just wanted to hold you. I saw how much you loved her and I just want you to know she's free now and out of pain and all the family is here together.'

Chloe continued, reassuring the *Today* host that Olivia was in a better place. 'She's making the sunshine and the dogs are running around and smiling and the horses are galloping.' She continued to comfort the emotional host. 'I just want you to know that she's free from pain now and she fought so hard and I was with her every step of the way. [Our Family] felt your love, mummy and I both care about you, care about you so much. I love you, my friend, thank you for doing that.' [4a]

Due to Covid travel restrictions, the last time Richard had seen Olivia was in 2020 when his son Christian Wilkins and Chloe appeared in *Dancing With The Stars* together. 'She was never flashy. She was never a show-off. You never see her on the social pages … she just was so dignified,' he said. 'Everybody lucky enough to come on her radar, she left with an impression. She was just so generous, she had time for everybody.'

As Richard said on *Today*, Olivia was just 'pure goodness', noting you would 'never hear a bad word said about her'.

Stories of Olivia's fantastic sense of humour have come out from so many people who knew her and clearly the Dame and Richard shared this bond. Talking to Richard after Olivia's passing, it is clear why they were mates. The warmth in Richard's voice when he was talking about Olivia brought her to life. Olivia used to sign her autograph 'Love and Light' and it's important to bring her to life in the way she would have liked with happy stories and memories that make people smile.

Reflecting on his history with Olivia in October 2022, Richard said, 'For a while, I was dating her niece Tottie and … I got to know her well during that period. It was a really lovely relationship.

'I used to MC her events in Melbourne anytime she called me when she was raising money for the hospital and her foundation. I had a few charity events, and she would always sing at those. For 12 years I also hosted the fantastic G'Day USA events.'

Julie Bishop, the former Foreign Minister, described the importance of the G'Day USA events: 'This is a platform that we use to showcase Australian talent and industries, goods and services – whether it's food, wine, tourism, the defence industries, innovation – across the vast audiences in the United States. This is one of the most lucrative consumer markets in the world. The US is one of our closest economic partners, and so this is an opportunity for us to show Australian ideas, innovation and talent to the United States.' [4b]

In 2006 the G'Day guests included John Travolta, Kelly Preston, Steve Irwin, Chloe Lattanzi, Eric Bana, Hugh Jackman, Rupert Murdoch, Sophie Monk and INXS. And Olivia received the Lifetime Achievement award. She proudly said, 'I'm just thrilled to be here and I'm thrilled! I'm going to enjoy every moment. Instead of being nervous, I'm gonna just enjoy every second, because life is short and fleeting, and the good moments aren't always there, so I'm very happy.' [5]

All the stars on the night commented on how lovely Livvy was. 'Yes, Olivia knows, as I've confessed this a long time ago to having plenty of posters of her in my bedroom as a child,' Eric Bana said. 'So, yeah, I've embarrassed myself before. I've embarrassed myself before in front of Olivia. So, that's OK.' [6]

'I had a crush on her, too,' confessed Hugh Jackman's wife Deborra-Lee

Furness. 'I wanted to get physical,' she continued, laughing. [7]

Hugh said, 'Well, I grew up absolutely in love with Olivia, like every boy or man in Australia, and woman. I mean, she's universally loved there. And she's a singer, she's an actor. She can do everything. She is a great Australian. And she's done amazing things on a charitable basis.' [8]

Presenting Olivia's award was her *Grease* co-star John Travolta, who attended the gala with actress-wife Kelly Preston. 'Well, Olivia has one of the more important careers of our generation,' Travolta said. 'She put Australia on the map in America for entertainers. And she opened the door for all of the great gifts we've gotten from Australia. So, she deserves it more than anybody.' [9] As he handed the award over to Olivia, he said, 'Even today, when she walks in the room, 'I GET CHILLS, THEY'RE MULTIPLYIN', and I'm losing control, cause the power you're supplyin', it's ELECTRIFYIN'!' [10]

Olivia spoke very eloquently, thanking the Farrars, Steve Kipner and John, and added that her greatest lifetime achievement was Chloe.

Richard Wilkins has a great story from the past with Olivia:

When I introduced Olivia Newton-John on stage for the G'day USA events in LA I always used to say, 'the last time I introduced Olivia on stage I always used to describe her as the most popular Australian on the planet and that nothing much in the last 12 months has changed my opinion on that. Ladies and Gentlemen, please welcome the wonderful Olivia Newton-John!

There was one time when we were waiting on the side of the stage to go on and she said 'How are you going to introduce me?', and I said, 'Oh I don't really think you need an introduction Liv – I thought I would say 'Ladies and Gentlemen Olivia Newton-John.'

She looks at me and goes, 'Oh yeah, OK, (pause). You don't think, umm, you know the Grammys or something like that?

I said, 'Oh OK, I will mention Grammy Winner Olivia Newton-John.

'Olivia comes back with: Hmmm, the OBE potentially?'

I came back with, 'Yeah, yeah, whatever you need, right, Grammy winner, Olivia OBE.

Olivia, trying not to laugh said, '*Grease* maybe?'

Me (now softly laughing) replied, 'Well, gee whiz, you're umm very demanding today.'

Then someone pushed me onto the stage to go and do my intro and l gave her my all with this long 60-sec intro:

'Ladies and gentlemen, the last time I interviewed this person on stage I described her as the most popular Australian on the planet and nothing has happened to change that opinion. She has won Grammys, made a Dame by the Queen, she starred in one of the most loved musicals of all time and has hit records, inspiration to millions a bastion of blah blah blah – I went on and on and on – Ladies and gentlemen, be upstanding and welcome Olivia Newton-John!'

The whole audience rose as one and as I walked off and she walked on, she looked at me and smiled and said, 'There you go.'

I got off stage and laughed and laughed.

Another time, she asked, 'Could you come and walk on the Great Wall of China with me?' and I replied, 'What are you talking about?

She said, 'I would really love you to come, everyone is coming – all friends and family.'

And l said, 'Bloody hell, I would but I am so busy. l was in LA, doing something with Will Smith out on the Valley in his house and I flew from there to Hong Kong to Beijing but I got there and I arrived just in time for the after-party. And [Olivia] saw my arrival when she came off the walk and said, 'Typical, you get here just in time for the party … Perfect timing."

'Funny and sweet, and the most popular Australian on the planet and nothing will ever change my opinion on that.'

Brett Goldsmith remembers his dear Aunty Olivia

Her nephew Brett Goldsmith was a big part of Olivia's life and the son of her sister Rona Newton-John and Melbourne nightclub owner Brian Goldsmith. He remembered that 'Olivia bought my first guitar for me and encouraged me to become a musician. She told me, "you're a great songwriter."' [1]

Singer/actress Tottie Goldsmith is Brett's younger sister, and race car driver Emerson Newton-John his younger half-brother and in the mid-1980s Brett programmed and played bass guitar and keyboards for the Chantoozies (which went top ten for Mushroom Records).

Brett co-wrote the singles '*Wanna Be Up*' (No.8 on the ARIA charts) and '*Kiss n Tell*' with fellow band member Eve von Bibra. Then he toured with Australian Crawl legend James Reyne as his bass guitarist. In 2013 Brett released a solo album, *Ordinary Life*. The title track was covered by Olivia Newton-John in 2014 on her *EP Hotel Sessions*, also co-written and produced by Goldsmith.

As a fellow iconic bar owner, he understands the Melbourne music and nightclub scene, having run the legendary Saratoga Bar years ago. Now he travels between Melbourne and Byron Bay, shooting as a professional photographer.

Roaming the world at a young age, he learned that life is about living the moment and when asked in October 2022 about Olivia and her place in Australian music history he kindly remembered the time when he was 'lucky enough to record her on some of [his] songs. The most memorable for both of [them] was her version of [his] some '*Ordinary Life*', a song [he] wrote for [his] mother Rona after she passed.

'I recorded it myself and she covered it,' Brett said. 'We did the vocal on a hotel bedroom one day in Melbourne and I remember so clearly her willingness to seek direction and ask if I liked what she was doing. Her tone was amazing and her pitch was uncanny. Not often do you get to record a voice that can soar with such a huge vocal range, ability and control but be so humble and unsure at the same time.

She trusted me with her voice and that was a massive compliment. She will be classed among many artists as one of the purest singers, with incredible technical ability and of course her contribution to humanity. As an Australian singer, she is the pinnacle of success.'

In a fantastic unearthed interview from 2014 [2] titled *Olivia Newton-John, Hotel Sessions* about Brett's collection of previously unreleased demo tracks that he made with his famous aunt between 2002 and 2011 at various Melbourne hotels, Brett said,'My mother was a fan of Olivia's. She was a big fan of Olivia's voice… Like most artists, Olivia knows exactly what she wants. She left me alone – she respects me as a photographer and as a musician – to work. I know she has an incredible ear. When you're cutting vocals with Olivia Newton-John, you'd better be on your best behaviour. She's a serious singer.'

When news of Olivia's death spread, her family all remembered her in their own way. Brett said, 'I was lucky to be in her family, and I was proud that she recorded some of my songs and we wrote together. I also got to photograph her, and we always had a blast together. She is a rare human that can never be replaced nor forgotten.' [3]

He also recalled a funny time when he joined the singer on a tour in Paris in 1978. *Grease* frenzy had taken over the world and in an attempt to not be seen by the paparazzi, his aunt spent hours working on a disguise to become unrecognisable. She thought it would fool everyone.

'She had a makeup artist and costume designer come to the hotel and chose a Cleopatra wig and makeup and some crazy coat. It took hours to do, and when she was finally ready to leave, we walked out of the hotel thinking we had fooled everyone.'

He confessed that 'nobody was fooled' since people recognized Olivia within 'seconds' and recalled how they 'spent the next hour racing in the car from the photographers and fans'. [4]

Grace & Gratitude Remembering 'Our Livvy' by James Young

James Young is affectionately referred to as the Night Mayor of Melbourne. Today he owns and books five late-night live music venues in Melbourne, including the iconic Cherry Bar in the city and Yah Yah's in Fitzroy.

Formerly a lawyer, a journalist, a radio and TV presenter, RRR's Program Manager and the Managing Director of an advertising agency, it is fair to say that James has been intimately connected to all aspects of the Australian music scene for more than 30 years.

'In 2006, some 16 years ago, I had a creative agency called SEE Life Differently and we were working for the then Festival Mushroom Group. One of the up-and-coming artists we were helping was Olivia Newton-John's daughter Chloe Lattanzi. I had the privilege of meeting Olivia when she joined her daughter at a full day's collaborative strategic session in Port Melbourne.

'Olivia was truly an enigma. Such a superstar, full of such grace and poise. And such a humble girl-next-door type, happy to meet and get photos with all the excited staff.

'I remember thinking when I was upstairs and Olivia was downstairs that you could just tell she was in the building from the positive energy filling the air...

Now, in 2022, remembering this positive meeting with Olivia and thinking about the great women in Australian music's past and present and the ones who are already smashing their way into the future, James wrote this little piece about Olivia's place in Australian music history.

Graceful Olivia always showed gratitude to her female Australian singing inspirations, and in turn she inspired singers who followed her lead...

Olivia Newton-John left a musical legacy Australians will never forget; yet she always acknowledged she was standing on the shoulders of giants. The lineage of Australian female singers who have taken the world by storm starts with Dame Nellie Melba who was the first Australian to appear on the cover of Time magazine in 1927 (the operatic soprano remains relevant via the fact that her face appears on the current Australian $100 note). Another soprano, Dame Joan Sutherland, was Australia's first winner of a Grammy Award in 1961 (for Best Solo Vocal Classical Performance). Like her predecessor, Sutherland wowed audiences in major opera houses internationally.

As lead singer of The Seekers, Judith Durham's wonderful voice topped the charts in the UK and Australia on numerous occasions. In 1967 '*Georgy Girl*' (from the film of the same name) reached No. 2 on the US *Billboard* Hot 100 (at No. 1 was no less than '*I'm A Believer*' by The Monkees). In the same year it was nominated for Best Original Song at the Academy Awards (beaten by '*Born Free*').

Helen Reddy then broke the glass ceiling in 1972, when she wrote and performed the first US No. 1 hit by an Australian artist, with her iconic feminist anthem '*I Am Woman*'.

Born in England, Olivia Newton-John's family migrated to Australia when she was five. Olivia won a TV talent quest in 1965, hosted by wild rocker Johnny O'Keefe, the prize for which was a return ticket to the UK. Olivia was initially hesitant to use the prize but her mum encouraged her to expand her horizons, and so in 1966, Our Livvy, as she'd affectionately become known, spread her wings.

It took seven years of hard slog, with barely any tangible progress taking place, before Olivia struck gold in 1973 when she released '*Let Me Be There*' in 1973. The US country music scene embraced the song and within months she'd scored herself a Grammy Award for Best Country Female. Olivia's golden blonde hair and sunbeam of a smile, combined with the purity and raw emotion of her vocals, proved her to be one of the most magnetic new talents on the planet.

It was her next single release in 1974 that cemented her in the hearts and minds of music lovers worldwide. Co-written by a fellow Australian, Peter Allen, Olivia's studio take of '*I Honestly Love You*', its gentle cat's purr delivery disguising a passionate dispatch of pain the likes of which not many songs have been capable of conveying since, captivated record buyers and Grammy judges alike. The song was her second US No. 1 in as many years, winning two Grammy Awards, for Record Of The Year and Best Pop Vocal Performance.

Her third US No. 1 in three years landed with '*Have You Never Been Mellow*' in 1975. Above and beyond the chart positions and awards was a definable Australian-ness which the whole world warmed to. In the eyes of Australians themselves, Olivia Newton-John defined how we wanted to be, how we hoped we were seen by other nations. Before Paul Hogan's popular tourism commercials, Olivia's friendly, honest, funny and accessible personality was alerting anyone interested in our culture to what they might expect if ever they were to make a trip 'down under'. She was a glowing, glorious, gregarious girl, open to opportunity and willing to warmly embrace all-comers. When promoting her latest material she was incredibly at ease in the company of polished intercontinental tonight show hosts such as Bob Hope, Johnny Carson and Michael Parkinson. Audiences adored her, other musicians admired her, and all this was before she co-starred in the most commercially successful movie musical in history, *Grease*, in 1978.

Can you immediately think of a more perfect virtuoso vocal than what Olivia delivered on '*Hopelessly Devoted To You*'?

'But now there's nowhere to hide
Since you pushed my love aside
I'm out of my head

Hopelessly devoted to you...'

Her phrasing of these lyrics is seared into our collective consciousness, whether we like it or not. The plaintive, passionate hurt we hear coming from deep inside the song's protagonist is palpable. How could you, how could I, how could everyone on earth not fall completely in love with this woman?

The surprise switch of Olivia's character Sandy in *Grease*, from nice to naughty, via her new leather-clad duet with John Travolta's character Danny in '*You're The One That I Want*', was later mirrored by her own personal transformation when she sprung the song '*Physical*' on an unsuspecting fan base.

'*Physical*' had a subtle underlying message which was more risqué than we'd known Olivia to toy with before, and despite the fluorescent work-out gear she wore in the promo video, it didn't take a great leap of the imagination to understand there was another meaning under the surface.

Another Aussie music star, Divinyls lead singer Chrissy Amphlett, dispensed with innuendo and got straight to the point in 1990 with '*I Touch Myself*', but who can say whether her fellow Aussie Olivia didn't inspire and/or ease the path of acceptance for such a blunt lyrical statement when she ushered music purists into a new era by imploring listeners to 'let me hear your body talk'?

Kylie Minogue and Sia have publicly named Olivia as a major influence on their own respective output, while Olivia's original barrage of international chart toppers broke down barriers for the likes of Tones & I to walk through years later with the brilliant mainstream classic '*Dance Monkey*' in 2019.

As the likes of Courtney Barnett, Iggy Azalea and Amy Taylor from Amyl and The Sniffers sell out their overseas tours, they'd gratefully concede that they owe a debt to their fabulous musical forebear, for her pioneering pop impeccability. Olivia Newton-John's professional and private courageousness is unquestionable and unparalleled. Long may we say, hooray for Olivia, who became a giant on whose shoulders her successors now stand.

Tony Espie: The Malibu Mansion

Tony Espie is a NZ-born, Australian freelance engineer and widely recognised as one of Australia's top mixing engineers. He mixed the #1 album on JJJ's 100 Greatest Australian Albums Of All Time – The Avalanches *Since I Left You* LP.

Tony is a five-time ARIA Awards nominee (Best Engineer) and based in Melbourne at TUFFTONES music. His vast studio experience spans over 35 years, having worked with some of the finest artists and producers from this country and around the world, crossing genres from pop to hip hop; indie rock to soul; electronica to jazz and film soundtracks.

Tony has worked with artists like Paul Kelly, The Avalanches, Kate Miller-Heidke, Kav Temperley, Yothu Yindi, Missy Higgins, and Guy Sebastian, just to name a few.

But it is his Olivia story that is a treat of an insight into this woman's life away from the public eye. Stories that confirm Olivia was as lovely and generous and encouraging as her public persona portrayed her.

Chloe Lattanzi, Olivia's only child from her first marriage to Matt Lattanzi, announced she was going into the music business in the early '00s.

Chloe signed with Warner Australia and started working on demos for the project, which was then called '*Lonely Nights In Paradise*', way back in 2003. The album was promoted but sadly delayed when Chloe's battle with body dysmorphia came to light. Chloe told the press that after overcoming anorexia – which she underwent treatment for when she was 18 – she developed obsessive-compulsive disorder (OCD) and depression. [2] Her important life decisions delayed this album for more than a decade which she later released in 2016 with a new title *No Pain*!

Happily, in later years she has worked so hard to heal herself and said, 'I look back at myself as a teenager and I'm like, 'What a beautiful young woman, what was I thinking, why was I so insecure?'' [3] Tony Espie was there for the start of this project and said that Chloe, who released her LP in 2016, had changed a lot, been through a lot and grown as all people do since she wrote the album and worked with him.

'I first met Olivia in 2006 – I was working at the iconic recording studios in Richmond, Sing Sing with producer Jarrad Rogers, mixing Chloe's debut album. Olivia popped in for a listen one day:

'It was nerve-racking before she came in, but she was so approachable and you could see that both she and her daughter were a team and that she was very supportive of her.

'Olivia was super friendly and encouraging, down-to-earth, approachable and just really super cool to be honest.

'Chloe and her mum had to go back to California and the record was unfinished, so it was decided that they would fly me over.

'It was decided that the album could be finished up in Malibu and so l was flown over to work with them in March and May of 2007 for ten days at a time.

'What a dream those trips were. On the second trip, I didn't know that Olivia had bumped up my Qantas flight to business class! To this day it's still one of the best statements anyone ever said to me:

"To the left please, Mr Espie, you are in business, not economy."

'I assumed I would be staying at a hotel but the car took me straight to Olivia's gated community and amazing Malibu mansion. Chloe had a granny flat (as big as a house) at the back and the James Cameron Compound was across the road and (as next door as it can be when talking about massive land properties), was Britney Spears' house. I had to pinch myself regularly.

'I remembered when Olivia threw a pool party to say congratulations to her girl for finishing the album – Olivia grabbed me by the hand and said, 'Let's nick next door and press Britney's buzzer and see if she wants to come.' 'So, we did. Sadly, she was not home but her designer tracksuit-wearing partner Kevin answered the door and was so lovely to Olivia as well.

'The whole gated area had this invisible security. There was no security in the house or that travelled with her when she went out, say, to the supermarket. She did have a housekeeper, but sometimes liked to go herself, which I did with her a few times and the staff all knew her to say hello and other people there would be doing a double take – with the 'is that really her?' expression on their faces.

'My room was beautiful and filled with serious Olivia Newton-John memorabilia from her films *Grease* and *Xanadu*. I actually slept next to famous rollerskates that she used as Kira the muse in *Xanadu* – and spent a few nights debating with myself: 'Should I try them on, just for a second or not?' I chose not. The studio that Chloe and I worked in was only 20 minutes away and Olivia loved hanging out there. She would turn the lights down and dance around to the music, singing along to the songs. She just loved being around music.

'She was so proud and encouraging of her daughter, even though there was a history of some issues Chloe and Olivia were dealing with. Some of the tracks were called '*Pushed*', '*Never Really Mattered*', '*Make it Stop*', '*Me and You*', and '*Lonely Nights*', with the lyrics clearly highlighting the soul searching going on in this young girl's mind. A healing journey her mother took with her.

'A lot of the lyrics Chloe wrote were very deep and cathartic. They were heartfelt and great to work with words. She wrote about Olivia being away so much and the mental issues she was battling inside. They had forgiven each other and Olivia was there for her. I feel that Olivia was never intentionally neglectful, that's how life was to be a star.

'When we were back in the house, we had heaps of long funny chats, drinking wine and sitting in the sun or the stunning gardens. She made me feel so comfortable, she was not formal and encouraged me to be myself.

'It was lovely, she just seemed to be laughing a lot of the day.

'Olivia said one night that she actually loved having Australians around her. They had the same sense of humour as her, left field and a bit bawdy and fun. While I stayed in her Malibu mansion, Olivia was so generous to me, opening her home, the long and funny chats and the fantastic meals out.

'We all went to Nobu for dinner one night and lunch once at the famous Ivy restaurant in Beverly Hills. We walk into the garden area where we were sitting and hear this gorgeous female voice say, 'Hi Olivia'. I turn and it's Priscilla Presley. 'Hi Priscilla,' says Olivia and they have a chat – I am just standing there, taking it all in. She says, have whatever you want and we stayed for hours, with Chloe showing up a bit later.

'Olivia was never flashy or used her celebrity to shine a light on herself. She was natural and funny in the company of all.

'I also remember her lovely housekeeper who Olivia treated as one of the family. She was so dear to Olivia, she would help cook amazing dinners and then go home to her family. I believe Olivia helped pay for her kid's education and to go to college. They were all in the journey together.

'I also remember towards the end of my trip, she called me into her room to ask me to help her with the Netflix connection. I was like, 'What is Netflix?' She was all over it and it hadn't come to Australia yet. Time for me to go home.'

Chapter 19
Tributes

'I love commercial music,' John Lennon said in 1980, right before his death. 'I like Olivia Newton-John singing 'Magic,' and Donna Summer singing whatever the hell it is she'll be singing. I like the ELO singing 'All Over the World.' I can dissect it and criticise it with any critic in the business."

– Rolling Stone [1]

The sails of the Sydney Opera House glowed pink on the night Dame Olivia Newton-John passed, in honour of her magnificent life.

'Olivia Newton-John touched the hearts of so many people around the world with her music as well as her compassion and kindness – particularly toward people living with cancer. She radiated with positivity in her lifetime and now our most famous performance space will shine in her honour.' NSW Premier Dominic Perrottet. [2]

Olivia Newton-John was an Australian arts icon who inspired generations of Australians with her talent and resilience.

For decades Olivia inspired Australians with her artistic ability and unrelenting courage. 'It is a touching tribute that the Sydney Opera House, a venue she performed at many times, will tonight be cloaked pink in her honour.' Minister for the Arts Ben Franklin. [3]

Famous buildings all over Australia lit up to guide Olivia to her home among the stars, including Melbourne's heritage Flinders Street Station, the iconic Melbourne Cricket Ground, and a black and white picture of the star was also projected on Federation Square, with a message that read: 'Fed Square is lit up pink in memory of Olivia Newton-John and to recognise her inspiring life.'

Even a church tucked away in the Groningen, Netherlands rang its bells in a sweet tribute to the tune of '*Hopelessly Devoted to You*', played on the famous 62-bell Carillion in the Martinitoren church steeple.

Words and deeds of tribute for the passing of Olivia Newton-John spread and fired up the world like lava. All avenues of social media bowed their heads and filled their pages with kind words as shocked souls tried to deal with the news.

Across the film world, the political arena, the music industry, and of course the public fan base, the accolades flooded in. Tweets, Instagram, Facebook, all chorused the same sad loss.

Stars like Hugh Jackman, Delta, Rebel Wilson, Kylie, Goldie Hawn, John Farnham, John Travolta, Bindi Irwin, Nicole Kidman, Barbra Streisand, Kate Hudson, Antonio Banderas, Brian Wilson, Melissa Etheridge, Mariah Carey, Dolly Parton, Dionne Warwick and so many more shared a memory and a kind word in her memory.

Journalists reminisced about their favourite singer and her impact on their lives: 'Farewell and thank you to the queen of Australia, the angel of our childhoods, and the voice of a generation.' *SMH.* [4]

Coldplay and Natalie Imbruglia paid tribute to Olivia at London's Wembley Stadium on the Tuesday evening after her passing. Imbruglia sang Olivia's part of the hit song '*Summer Nights*' from *Grease*, while Chris Martin sang John Travolta's part with Jacob Collier joining him during the chorus.

Pink sang her heart out for Olivia at the American Music Awards, as did three Australian artists at the ARIA awards in November 2022. And in the UK, *Grease The Musical* London's cast dedicated its current show run to Olivia.

During the Chicks' concert at The Gorge in Washington, singer Natalie

Maines told the audience: 'We lost a worldwide sweetheart last week, Olivia Newton-John … I thought I was Olivia Newton-John from like [ages] 4 to 12, and then I just wished I was Olivia Newton-John.'

The celebration of the life of Olivia Newton-John spread over all Australian, and worldwide television stations. With Channel 7 showing *Olivia – A Magical Life*, which paid tribute to the extraordinary life force of Dame Olivia Newton-John, with the Bee Gees' Barry Gibb, UK music veteran Cliff Richard and pop star Delta Goodrem all sharing their memories. Channel 9 played *A Celebration of Olivia Newton-John* and featured a story on *60 Minutes*.

Harry Styles, actor and singer and handsome fashion icon, dressed as Danny from *Grease* on stage during an Oct 2022 Halloween concert in LA and sang '*Hopelessly Devoted to You*' along with Olivia's voice and image behind him, with an adoring crowd singing along. Olivia is even being honoured with a comic biography this year from Tidal Wave Comics, whom she had worked with before.

If Olivia was the Queen, then we have to mention her brush with the King, Elvis Presley, and the tribute he paid to her. Olivia was lucky enough to see Elvis in concert at least twice but just missed out on meeting him. The first time was in 1974 at the Hilton in Las Vegas. It was a celebrity-packed row, with Tim Rice and Andrew Lloyd Webber sitting next to Olivia. Sadly, Elvis had to leave and she didn't get to meet him. Interviewed about the King, she said, 'Elvis always, still. Still the King. He's got a magic on stage.' [7]

In 1976 Olivia again saw Elvis in concert, and while she did not get a second chance to meet him, she said, 'During the show, Elvis shocked me and sang my song... It blew me away to hear him say my name because I was such a big fan.' The King had noted the presence of Olivia and the Eagles at his April 1976 Long Beach concert and performed '*If You Love Me (Let Me Know)*' that glorious night. [8]

Our Livvy spoke on the *A Life of Greatness* podcast in 2021, saying she wasn't afraid of dying, because she believed there was some form of afterlife. 'We all know we're going to die, but I think we spend our lives in denial. It's extremely personal, so it's hard to put into words. I feel that we are all one thing, and I've had experiences with spirits and spirit life.'

She continued: 'I hope the energies of the people you love will be there … I think all the love will be there. I'm sort of looking forward to that … It's almost like we are parts of the same computer and we go back to the main battery.' [6]

What a great way to think of life after death: we can see her sitting with her family and blushing at the deserved accolades she received from earth.

Tributes to Olivia Newton-John as they appeared in the world media on the day she passed on 8 August 2022:

FILM /TV

John Travolta, ***Grease*** **co-star**

'My dearest Olivia, you made all of our lives so much better,' the actor wrote on Instagram.

'Your impact was incredible. I love you so much. We will see you down the road and we will all be together again. Yours from the first moment I saw you and forever! Your Danny, your John!'

Jane Seymour, actress and Olivia's friend for 40 years

'She was always a great friend and confidant to me. Olivia inspired everyone with her positive attitude to life and unfailing desire to help others.

'She was not only a brilliant musician, actress, and singer but a wonderful mother, wife, and sister. The world has lost one of its brightest lights. I will never forget you Livvy. Love always, Jane.'

Kathy Griffin, comedian

'Olivia Newton-John rolled with EVERYTHING.'

Michelle Pfeiffer, actress

'Thank you for the care and talent you gifted us all so graciously with.'

Nigella Lawson, celebrity chef.

'Her memory is already a blessing.'

Stockard Channing, bad girl Rizzo in *Grease*

'I don't know if I've known a lovelier human being. Olivia was the essence of summer – her sunniness, her warmth and her grace are what always come to mind when I think of her. I will miss her enormously.'

Randal Kleiser, *Grease* director and friends with Olivia for 40 years

'She never changed, she was always exactly the way everyone imagines her. She was charming, lovely, warm... There are so many clichés you can say about her, but in her case it was all true.'

Didi Conn, Frenchy in *Grease*

'She was such a humungous, big, big pop star and her persona was of this beauty... pure and sweet. In the movie we would call her Miss Goody Two Shoes, you know, but simmering under that façade of innocence was a hot mama ready to come out.'

Lynda Carter, *Wonder Woman*

'I am crushed to hear that my friend @olivianj has died. She was a true light in this world and I loved all the times we worked together. My love goes out to her family and her friends. What a beautiful human.'

Kate Hudson, actress and daughter of Goldie Hawn

'There are a handful of people in my life who inspired me to lock myself in my bedroom and sing from the top of my lungs in the mirror. May we all today sing for Olivia and celebrate her courageous years of fighting.

'Mimicking every move she made, wishing I could hit those clean high notes and striving to try with my little rasp. What a lovely light of a human. She was an inspiration to me as I dreamed of what my performer's life ahead may be.'

Robert Greenwald, director of *Xanadu*

'A bright light who lit up a room and the world would remember Newton-John's sense of hope, possibilities and positivity. And her voice was as full of joyousness and the sense of genuine love.'

Brooke Shields, actress

'A true class act whose light shined everywhere she went… she inspired us all ❤ A wonderful mother and wife, who was grace and strength personified. Sending all of my love to Olivia's family and friends. She'll never be forgotten.'

Goldie Hawn

'A light landed on this planet 73 years ago. Her voice brought us to such joyous heights, nothing held her back, nothing. Her mind was strong and heroic. Olivia's light will continue to shine and will never flicker. Never. Rest sweetheart. Rest peacefully, you are Love.'

Viola Davis, actress

'Oh man!!! You were my childhood!! Your talent, poise, beauty!! Rest in glorious peace. God bless your family ... and thank you for creating eternal memories.'

Mia Farrow, actress

'Very sad that lovely, talented, brave Olivia Newton-John has died. I never got to meet her, but everyone says she was wonderful – always kind.'

Rita Wilson, actress/singer, Tom Hanks' wife

'Her tenderness, joy, love and light live on. No one does this one better than Olivia Newton-John. *I Honestly Love You*. Written by #JeffBarry and #PeterAllen. God Speed, brave Olivia. Love to Chloe and John. #olivianewtonjohn'

MUSIC

Barry Gibb, Bee Gees legend

'A diamond and in this world there's only a few diamonds.'

P!nk

'I met her maybe three times – and she was an absolute angel. One of the loveliest, kindest, light from within human beings I have ever met. Kindness personified. May she Rest In Peace and may her family be held in love and light during this difficult time.'

Sir Rod Stewart

'My great friend Olivia Newton John has passed away. She was the perfect Lady, gorgeous, with great poise and with a certain Aussie sophistication. Her spandex trousers in *Grease* were my inspiration for my '*Da Ya Think I'm Sexy*' era. RIP Olivia Sir Rod'

Sir Cliff Richard, met his 'Soulmate' Olivia in 1971

' I find myself at a loss as to what to say … We always had fantastic fun together, at parties or just chatting. Singing together was always special. She was pitch-perfect every time, and our voices blended well.

'Her heart of gold is the real legacy she leaves behind. She had so much love to give and everyone loved her back and I am happy that she considered me a friend.

'God bless you Livvy. Rest In Peace…Cliff xxx'

Frankie Valli

'She will be missed. She never changed, in that she didn't come on like she was a star or better than anybody else, and those are the things I like about her. She was a superstar, and she was one before *Grease*. She was selling records and having hits one right after the other. She will be missed, and I wish that we could have done more performances together.'

Richard Marx, a longtime friend

'My heart is broken. Rest now, sweet friend. You were as kind and loving a person as there's ever been. I'll miss you every day.'

Anni-Frid Lyngstad, ABBA

'What do you feel, what do you say when the nice, kindest and most loving woman leaves us to travel somewhere else. The heart aches to know Olivia's brave fight against an, in her case, invincible enemy. That she never gave up or complained about her situation, but instead told us her story so that we would understand and want to help others affected. I am grateful to have known a person like you Olivia and you will always be in my heart.'

Agnetha Fältskog, ABBA

'A fine person has left us – and there are many of us who mourn her now… My thoughts go out to the family, and her music and personality will always remain in memory.'

Nancy Sinatra

'I didn't know Olivia Newton-John personally, but I admired her for the way she faced her health battles. Beautiful & strong, she fought to the end. My heart goes out to her family & all who love her. It's just not fair. Godspeed, Olivia. We'll always be hopelessly devoted to you.'

Sheryl Crow, a breast cancer survivor herself

'Sad to hear of Olivia Newton-John's passing. She was a beautiful artist and a brave warrior as she battled breast cancer with grace.
Rest In Peace, Olivia.'

Peter Frampton, who recorded with Olivia

'One of the most genuinely beautiful souls has left us. Olivia Newton-John was an amazing artist in every way. She was a dear friend to me and to all. Olivia is the definition of the phrase 'Down to earth'. I love you Liv.'

Barbra Streisand, legendary singer and actress

'Too young to leave this world. May she RIP.'

Mariah Carey, performed '*Hopelessly Devoted To You*' onstage with Olivia in Melbourne.

'I first fell in love with Olivia's voice when I was a little girl and heard '*I Honestly Love You*'. Songs like '*Magic*', '*Suddenly*' and '*Have You Never Been Mellow*' showcased her beautiful airy tone and signature sound. And THEN there was *GREASE*. I was obsessed.

'I dressed up as Bad Sandy for Halloween in 5th grade and thought I was everything. Years later, THE Olivia Newton-John walked out onto my stage in Melbourne, Australia and we sang our hearts out together to '*Hopelessly Devoted To You*'. This is a moment I will never ever forget.

'I was also blessed to be in her presence on many other occasions and she was one of the kindest, most generous and lovely people I've ever met.'

Brian Wilson, Beach Boys legend.

'Sad news about Olivia Newton-John passing.'

Sophie B. Hawkins

'I got to work with Olivia Newton-John running after her up the stairs in the lighthouse, and with the kids. She was the kindest performer and such a generous person. I'm honored she graced my life.'

Melissa Etheridge

'Journey well, dear friend. She was one of the first to reach out to me after my cancer diagnosis. What a beautiful woman and special talent. Hard to know what to say. She will be missed.'

Dionne Warwick

'Another angelic voice has been added to the Heavenly Choir. Not only was Olivia a dear friend, but one of the nicest people I had the pleasure of recording and performing with. I will most definitely miss her. She now Rests in the Arms of the Heavenly Father.'

Darren Hayes, Savage Garden

'Oh dear, sweet, magical, eternal Olivia. You gave so much to this world and to this little boy who saw acceptance in your twinkling eyes and glittering world. You made us all feel held by the sweetness of your voice and the capacity of your heart. I hope you are in *Xanadu*.'

COUNTRY MUSIC

Dolly Parton

'My first memory of Olivia was when her song '*Let Me Be There*' was a hit. I have loved her ever since. We had many occasions that we got to share together, either backstage or performing on the same shows, and I loved every moment that I ever got to spend with her. My last memory of Olivia was when I sang with her on my song 'Jolene', which she recorded for an album not so very long ago. I cannot wait to hear that album and Olivia may you rest in peace. You left a spot that one else will ever fill.

'So sad to have lost my special friend Olivia Newton-John. So happy that our lives crossed paths. I know her voice is singing beautifully with the angels. With Love Dolly.'

Crystal Gayle and Loretta Lynn

'We will miss our dear friend. Sending love to Olivia's family.'

Wynonna Judd

'Her sweet spirit filled the room when she walked into the theater the day I met her. What a kind & beautiful woman.... #RIP.'

Kenny Rogers

'We honestly love you, Olivia! We know Kenny felt the same way. What a genuine and lasting impression you made on the world with your many talents, kindness and bravery. You are timeless. Your song will go on and on and on. –Team KR

Countrynow.com

'Our hearts are breaking at the loss of Olivia Newton-John. She was such a legend. #ripolivianewtonjohn #rip #olivianewtonjohn #hopelesslydevotedtoyou'

CMA Country Music

'We are deeply saddened by the passing of Olivia Newton-John, 1974 CMA Female Vocalist of the Year winner. Our thoughts are with her family and friends during this difficult time.'

AUSTRALIAN CELEBRITIES

Hugh Jackman

'I'm devastated to hear the news that @therealonj has passed away. One of the great privileges of my life was getting to know her. Not only was she one of the most talented people I've known … she was one of the most open hearted, generous and funny. She was a one of kind spirit. It's no secret Olivia was my first crush. I kissed her (poster) every night before bed. Her legacy will only grow stronger in the years to come. A fighter for healing from cancer that knows no bounds. I love you.'

Kylie Minogue

'Since I was ten years old, I have loved and looked up to Olivia Newton-John. And, I always will. She was, and always will be, an inspiration to me in so many, many ways. My deepest condolences to her family and loved ones. x ONJ 4EVER.'

John Farnham

Australian singer John Farnham, currently has his own battle to fight and who performed 'Dare to Dream' alongside Olivia at the opening ceremony of the 2000 Sydney Olympics, said in a statement:

'The Farnham family send love and sympathies to Olivia's family. Behind that iconic smile was a tenacious fighter. A beautiful voice and a loyal friend. She will be greatly missed.'

Rick Springfield

'She was a beautiful soul and I know of no one who didn't love her or know what a great humanitarian she was. God speed Livvy. We will all meet again.'

Rebel Wilson

'You were a true icon and I absolutely adored you.'

Keith Urban & Nicole Kidman

'Livvie brought the most divine light into the world… so much love, joy, inspiration and kindness... and we will always be hopelessly devoted to you.'

Delta Goodrem, who played Olivia in the 2018 biopic *Hopelessly Devoted to You*

'The whole world will feel this heartbreak today because the entire world felt Olivia's unmatched light. A force for good. A force of nature. Strong and kind. My mentor, my friend, my inspiration, someone who always guided me… she was always there for me. Family to me. I don't have all the words I would like to say today but I hope everyone will join in celebrating our beloved Olivia, her heart, soul, talent, courage, grace… I love you forever.'

Danni Minogue

'Dame Olivia Newton-John would illuminate a room, just with her presence. Her heart was full of love and light, and she made it her mission to share that beautiful energy with the world. I was lucky to meet Olivia many times over the years. I was honoured to be asked to assist in raising money to build the Olivia Newton-John Cancer & Wellness Centre in Heidelberg, Victoria. I know this hospital has helped — and will help — many people, and she was so very proud of making this dream come to life. Rest In Peace, lovely lady. You will never be forgotten.'

FAMILY

Tottie Goldsmith, Olivia's niece

'Liv is, and was, magic. She was a tornado of joy and action, a visionary, and a healer.'

Matt Lattanzi & wife Michelle

'Today we lost one of the world's greats Olivia Newton-John. Matt and I are so overwhelmed with the love and gratitude shared with us by friends, family and a deeply loving community of fans who will all miss Olivia's presence in this world.

'I have heard truly lovely stories and memories from people near and far, and honour in each of you where those feelings and memories come from.

'Nothing will replace the icon we lost, yet her legacy is alive and well in our hearts and memories, as well as her contributions to our global culture, her beloved daughter Chloe, and her cancer research and wellness centre in Melbourne.

'Please honour your sadness, and then celebrate the joy that Olivia's heart and lifetime achievements endowed in our world. Sending all kinds of love.'

John Easterling (Husband)

'Our love for each other transcends our understanding. Every day we expressed our gratitude for this love that could be so deep, so real, so natural. We never had to 'work' on it. We were in awe of this great mystery and accepted the experience of our love as past, present and forever.

'At Olivia's deepest essence she was a healer using her mediums of song, of words, of touch. She was the most courageous woman I've ever known. Her bandwidth for genuinely caring for people, for nature and all creatures almost eclipses what is humanely possible. It is only the grace of God that has allowed me to share the depth and passion of her being for so long. In her most difficult times she always had the spirit, the humor, and the will power to move things into the light.

'Even now as her soul soars, the pain and holes in my heart are healed with the joy of her love and the light that shines forward.'

James Driskill, Olivia's son-in-law

'I am so lucky and grateful that I had the opportunity to learn from such an amazing woman. You led an extraordinary life and touched so many. You taught me about grace and gratitude, love and light. You were always so generous and kind and I'm filled with joy thinking about spending the rest of my life with your beautiful daughter who also teaches me daily about how to be a more compassionate and forgiving man. Goodbye mama. I love you. I'll take care of our weasel.'

Chloe Lattanzi

'I love you forever my life giver, my teacher, my mama. It has been my honour and continues to be my honour to be your baby and best friend.

'You are an angel on earth and everyone touched by you has been blessed. I love you forever my life giver, my teacher, my mama.'

MEDIA/ GOVERNING BODIES

Spotify

'Olivia Newton-John, we'll always be hopelessly devoted to you.'

Debbie Shiell, divisional director, Olivia Newton-John Cancer Research Institute in Melbourne

'It is because of her that the centre is here. There's no two ways about it. This was her dream and this was her legacy, and it was something that she was really proud of.

'She was the light at the end of the tunnel for many, many people.'

Annabelle Herd, ARIA & PPCA CEO

'Olivia made a remarkable contribution to the global entertainment industry and will be greatly missed. From her first #1 hit in Australia, '*Banks Of The Ohio*', in 1971 to a string of hits across the 1970s and

1980s – including '*Physical*' and the extraordinarily successful *Grease* soundtrack – Olivia was a true superstar.'

Jordan Baker, chief reporter *SMH*

'Meeting one's idols is usually a bad idea, but Olivia was exactly as I had imagined her. She was funny, kind and generous, and wore her fame lightly. Beneath the Las Vegas sequins, there was an Aussie girl who loved nothing more than being surrounded by animals on her farm.'

Piers Morgan

'So sad to hear the fabulously gutsy, warm & talented Olivia Newton-John has died. At an auction of her *Grease* memorabilia in LA three years ago, she told me her favourite song from the movie was '*Hopelessly Devoted To You*'. Great song, great film, great lady. RIP.'

Zan Rowe, Double J broadcaster

'We lost these three giants this past fortnight, but we did not lose their legacies. Olivia, Judith, and Archie shared their Australia with the world and reflected it back to us. They made us proud, made us think, made us dance and made us sing. How extraordinarily lucky we are to live in the time of their talent.'

Rolling Stone

'FAREWELL, OLIVIA NEWTON-JOHN, the eternally beloved pop queen who died Monday at age 73. We loved Olivia Newton-John — we honestly loved her — and that's why pop connoisseurs are mourning for her today.'

CNN Entertainment

'She was the epitome of grace and style and such an unfortunate tragedy – a life gone too soon at just 73-years-old, leaving a hole in the hearts of her fans, her family, her daughter Chloe.'

POLITICAL

Julie Bishop, Australia's former Foreign Minister

'I admired her resilience, her determination, her energy. She was tenacious in all she fought for in terms of causes, yet she was an idolised singer and performer.'

Hillary Clinton

'As Ann Richards said, 'Ginger Rogers did everything that Fred Astaire did. She just did it backwards and in high heels."

Shingo Yamagami, Ambassador of Japan to Australia

Yamagami praised Olivia and mentioned her Order of the Rising Sun accolade for her contributions to developing Japan's musical culture as well as promoting friendly relations with Australia.

All tributes and @ sources are from Twitter/Instagram/Facebook/ Radio/ABC and World News networks.

Part Three

Achievements, Accolades, and Honours

'Nothing I have done professionally will top the feeling I got when singing with John Farnham at the 2000 Olympic games in Sydney.'

Olivia Newton-John [1]

When the Fire Fight Australia National appeal put through a call to Olivia Newton-John in 2020 to help them raise money for national bushfire victims, she said, 'I'm pretty much retired, but when I heard they were doing this, I had to be part of it. It's so important, and I feel privileged that I'm able to help in some way. Australians are tough. We have a wonderful sense of spirit and humour, and those things will get us through.' [2]

The Feb 16, 2020 concert saw Olivia join dear friend singer John Farnham on stage for a blistering and emotional set. It was an incredible feat to pull off: more than 75,000 people packed the stadium in Sydney, and more than 1 million watched 10 hours, 22 acts, with almost $10 million raised for bushfire relief. [3]

Olivia got one of the nights biggest cheers when she joined her old friend to perform the 1998 hit '*Two Strong Hearts*'. Later she joined John, Brian May, Mitch Tambo, fire fighters and volunteers for the '*You're The Voice*' finale. ONJ did not let her grave illness stop what would be her final performance in Australia.

Olivia connected to her fans, and their loyalty was a dear companion her whole life. When she received an award, everyone was totally rapt for her; when she toured, fans rushed to get tickets, and when she released a new song, her fans pushed that CD straight up the charts.

Olivia thrived on performing live, and singing for a cause gave her even more impetus to sing her heart out. 'When I look back on a life of live performances, it has been extraordinary. I step out on stage, and there's a rush of adrenalin. It just takes over and sweeps me away.' [4]

Part three of this book is about taking in the sheer volume of Olivia's work: all of her hit songs, duets, tours, awards, singles, albums, and compilations. For five decades, we have been travelling with Olivia, she let us into all aspects of her life, and her list of achievements is truly spectacular. Her Nobel prize-winning grandfather Max Born would have been as proud as punch.

'She took us along with her or at least showed us it was possible to fly. She embodied both glamour and goodness, the nice girl who got what she wanted, her angelic treble as sweet as her message.' [5]

Everyone remembers Olivia's time in the sun – fan or not! People who grew up in Melbourne emphatically embraced her success and jumped on board all her pop culture-inspired movements. These permanently embedded memories are her legacies to us all.

Those frenetic '80s years, when Olivia ruled the airwaves and the big screens, all the boys and girls loved it, and parents loved it as well – it reminded them of happier times. Leg warmers, headbands, roller skates … she changed our fashion as well.

'A woman for all seasons, Olivia will remain something specific and personal to each of us. In a career spanning six decades, Olivia Newton-John was a woman for all seasons: singer and songwriter, actor, activist, mother and health advocate.' [6]

Melissa

I was 7 when *Xanadu* came out – my neighbour saw it first and described the film as 'Olivia on roller skates, and then she revealed all the secrets of the universe.' I watched it, became obsessed, and recall wanting Olivia's hairstyle badly.

PB

He remembers as a boy dancing to 'let's get physical"' at the local Blue Light Disco and watching *Grease* the movie with his whole family, with his sisters loving it big time.

Elise

I was lucky enough to interview Olivia for a live-to-air TV show in 2002 about the launch of the Koala Blue label of Australian wines – Olivia had a hand in and was proud of the design of bottles – Ken Done-style, and she was so 'gracious and engaged during the interview'. P.S. Elise always wanted the 1980 Kira *Xanadu* tiger print outfit by Bobbie Mannix.

Denise

As a teenager knew every single *Xanadu* dance move and every word for every single song on the soundtrack and wanted to roller skate forever.

Jodie

Abba *Arrival* and *Grease* were the first two albums I owned, and I had both albums sitting on a heart-shaped pillow with a frilly border in my bedroom. Every single sleepover and birthday party revolved around Olivia – dressing in a pale blue sleeveless top with Physical written on it, necklace around my head for a headband and leg warmers.

Peter

1990 my first share house was Barry Street in Northcote and a few houses down was Olivia's sister Rona. Some dirtbag broke into my Holden HQ wagon, and when I was outside surveying the damage, these two ladies came out to chat and to offer some sympathy. I had no idea who they were initially, and then I realised I was talking to Olivia, who was very tiny and, I have to say, very lovely and kind!

Yans

I remembered seeing *Grease* and loved it, as it was a bit saucy.

JH

When Olivia came out with Physical, it just seemed a bit wrong as she was always seen as the good girl and the film clip was a bit sexy. A bit controversial. We all – pre-pubescent boys – liked the clip a lot!

Dave

We had the *Grease* soundtrack cassette, and my three younger teenage sisters would relentlessly play it in the car every week on a 3-hour drive from Melbourne to Euroa – I know every line. It was played so much it snapped, and I repaired it three times. We have it – it still works. My dad told me about a 21st he went to in the '70s – McHale Family, I think, horse owners in Sandringham. The backyard entertainment was Olivia and John Farnham. Best night ever.

Rachelle

All the bar mitzvah parties I went to at that age were *Grease*-themed. You could get *Grease* cat pants from Myer, and you wore these with a big Tee with a knot on the side. I bought the album and memorised the words (as back then you couldn't just look up the lyrics), so I remember one girl on the school bus singing, 'I've got the shoes they're multiplying.'

I went to see *Grease* on the Gold Coast and was rapt to find out she was from Australia. Then l heard she married Matt Lattanzi – he was hot. It was actually unbelievable to learn she was from Melbourne.

Let's Get Physical made everyone do aerobics and started a trend of '50s clothes – l had a swing skirt from Sussan in pastel colours.

Amanda

I remember seeing the '*Physical*' clip on *Countdown* – it was so full-on!

Olivia personified that indefinable essence that is Australian: a friend for life, a battler and, importantly, an egalitarian.

'Olivia represented Australia on the global stage at a time when no one knew much about us at all. She radiated optimism, authenticity and humility. What better image to the world could we have ever hoped for?' [7]

Olivia reached the peak of superstardom. She conquered male-dominated music and acting industries with strong but sweet determination, never compromising her core values. And because she was ambitious and proud of her ambitious drive, Olivia supported many other women on the same journey and was an intelligent and risk-taking businesswoman, a loving wife and a mother. She was always up for a laugh and clearly always up for a favour.

'I do have high standards, but I don't expect anything from anyone that I don't expect from myself.'
– Olivia Newton-John. [8]

She had high standards and she loved to move with the times, follow and create trends, and embrace 'the vibe' of everything current. In many ways, ONJ's remarkable, sustained victory can only be explained in the same terms John Lennon used at the height of Beatlemania:

'If we knew, we'd form another group and be managers.' [9]

Her touring history was a testament to her staying power – she had more than 50 years of gigs under her belt. Most were played in Vegas, then Sydney. She appeared on stage with John Farnham more than any other concert headliner and her most significant touring years were 2006 and 2014.

Olivia's music output was prolific. Her songwriters wrote for her, she wrote for herself, but she also loved to cover a song! 'It was hard to have a new record out every year of all originals, especially since she wasn't a prolific songwriter ... Newton-John has performed countless covers ... from classics to jazz to country to rock, Broadway show tunes, folk and traditional songs, Christmas songs and lullabies.' [10] Her first hit was a cover of Bob Dylan's '*If Not For You*' and the covers kept coming throughout the '70s. She did the Lennon/McCartney Beatles classic '*The Long and Winding Road*', Eddie Cochran's '*Summertime Blues*', and The Hollies original '*He Ain't Heavy, He's My Brother*'.

'Even her rendition of Peter Allen's ballad '*I Honestly Love You*' was technically a cover. He had recorded the song, but it was more like a demo. Newton-John made the song a hit.

'She was the first singer to cover the Andrew Lloyd Webber and Tim Rice song '*Don't Cry for Me Argentina*' from the original stage production of Evita. And often, while on tour, Newton-John would mix her shows up with a cover such as '*Love Is Alive*', the Gary Wright hit, '*Hollywood Nights*' by Bob Seger, and Louis Armstrong's '*What A Wonderful World*'.' [11]

Her acting resume is a wild read, with appearances on the majority of the world's iconic talk shows, throw in a few blockbuster movies and some hilarious comedy skits. Her honours list runs from being crowned a Dame by the Queen to being a National Treasure in Australia. And Queen Olivia was the goat of music videos – filming them before they were the thing to do.

One woman did all this – with her crew, of course – but Olivia Newton-John was a limitless force and she has left a clear trail of tiny footprints for others to follow.

'We lost part of our soundtrack, but the light lives on.' [12]

Chapter 20

Honours

1979 – Officer of the Order of the British Empire (OBE) in the Civil Division by Queen Elizabeth 11 in the 1979 New Year's Honours List.

1981 – Star on the Hollywood Walk of Fame at 6925 Hollywood Boulevard in the Recording Category on 5 August (outside Mann's Chinese Theatre).

1990 – Goodwill Ambassador to the United Nations Environment Program for two years.

1998 – Cadillac Concept to the world Humanitarian Award for breast cancer research.

1999 – Red Cross Humanitarian Award for breast cancer and environmental charity work.
Women's Guild of Cedar-Sinai Hospital – 'Woman of the 21st Century' Award for breast cancer and environmental charity work.

2000 – Environmental Media Association 'Ermenegildo Zegna International Environmental Award' for increasing public awareness of environmental problems.
Rainforest Alliance Green Globe Arts and Nature Award for her contribution to the preservation of rainforests.

2002 – Australian Recording Industry Association – Hall of Fame inductee.

2006 – Australia Day at Penfolds Black Tie Gala: Lifetime Achievement Award.
Decatur Memorial Hospital (Illinois) Humanitarian Award for her breast cancer awareness work.

Officer of the Order of Australia (AO) for 'service to the entertainment industry as a singer and actor, and to the community through organisations supporting breast cancer treatment, education, training and research, and the environment.'

2007 – American-Australian Association Black Tie Gala: Lifetime Achievement Award.
Kimmel Center (Philadelphia, PA) – Valour Award for raising funds for cancer research.

2008 – Project Angel Food – Marianne Williamson Founder's Award for her commitment to breast cancer awareness.

2012 – National Trust of Australia (NSW) – named a National Living Treasure of Australia ('an exceptional Australian').

2015 – Music Victoria Awards of 2015 – Hall of Fame.

2016 – Nevada Ballet Theatre Woman of the Year.

2018 – Honorary degree of Doctor of Letters (D. Litt) from La Trobe University in Melbourne on 14 May 2018.

2019 – Companion of the Order of Australia (AC) for services to community health, especially for people that are living with cancer, as well as her contributions as a musician and performer.
Dame Commander of the Order of the British Empire (DBE) in the 2020 New Year's Honours List.

2021 – Japan's Order of the Rising Sun, Gold Rays with Rosette, the country's highest civil honour (for her contribution to developing musical culture in Japan and promoting friendly relations with Australia).
Australian Women in Music Awards (Honour Roll inductee, joining inaugural AWMA inductee Helen Reddy, and Judith Durham AO).

MUSIC AWARDS

Grammy Awards (based on highest votes received by the US National Academy of Recording Arts and Sciences).

1973 – Best Country Vocal Performance, Female: *Let Me Be There.*

1975 – Record of the Year:
I Honestly Love You
Best female pop vocal performance: *I Honestly Love You.*

1983 – Video of the Year – '*Physical.*'
FOOTNOTE: John Farrar produced Newton-John's first American number-one hit single, *I Honestly Love You*, and was recognised in the Grammy Awards.

Grammy nominations

1975 – Best Female Pop Vocal Performance: *Have You Never Been Mellow.*

1978 – Album of the Year: *Grease.*
Best Female Pop Vocal Performance: *Hopelessly Devoted to You.*

1980 – Best Female Pop Vocal Performance: *Magic.*

1981 – Best Female Pop Vocal Performance: *Physical.*

1982 – Best Female Pop Vocal Performance: *Heart Attack.*

1983 – Best Long Form Music Video: *Olivia in Concert.*

1984 – Best Short Form Music Video: *Twist of Fate.*

American Music Awards (AMA)

1974 – Favourite Album – Country: *Let Me Be There.*
Favourite Female Artist – Country.
Favourite Female Artist – Pop/Rock.

Favourite Single – Pop/Rock: *I Honestly Love You.*

1975 – Favourite Album – Pop/Rock: *Have You Never Been Mellow.*

Favourite Female Artist – Country.

Favourite Female Artist – Pop/Rock.

1976 – Favourite Female Artist – Pop/Rock.

1978 – Favourite Album – Pop/Rock: *Grease.*

1982 – Favourite Female Artist – Pop/Rock.

AMA Nominations

1975 – Favourite Album – Country: *Have You Never Been Mellow*

1979 – Favourite Female Artist – Pop/Rock.

1980 – Favourite Female Artist – Pop/Rock.

***Billboard* Music Awards** (BMAs, based on performance on *Billboard* magazine charts compiled from sales, streaming, touring, airplay and social engagement)

1974 – Top Pop Singles Artist (Female).

1975 – Top Pop Albums Artist (Female).

1976 – Top Adult Contemporary Artist.

1979 – Top Soundtrack: *Grease.*

1982 – Top Pop Single: *Physical.*

Top Pop Singles Artist.

Top Pop Singles Artist (Female).

1997 – Top Pop Catalogue Album: *Grease.*

1998 – Top Pop Catalogue Album: *Grease.*

Cashbox Awards (trade publication for the music industry)

1974 – No.1 New Female Vocalist, Singles.

1975 – No.1 Female Vocalist, Singles.

No.1 Female Vocalist, Albums.

Australian Recording Industry Association (ARIA) Awards

1999 – ARIA Award for Highest Selling Album: *Highlights from The Main Event.*

ARIA Nominations

1999 – Best Adult Contemporary Album: *Highlights From The Main Event.*

2015 – Best Adult Contemporary Album: *Two Strong Hearts Live.*

King of Pop Awards (Australia)

1976 – Best Australian International Performer.

Record World

(US music industry trade magazines)

1974 – Top Most Promising Country Albums Artist (Female).

Top Most Promising Country Singles Artist (Female).

Top Pop Female Vocalist (Albums).

Top Pop Female Vocalist (Singles).

1975 – Top Country Female Vocalist (Albums).

Top Pop Female Vocalist (Albums).

Top Pop Female Vocalist (Singles).

1976 – Top Country Female Vocalist (Albums).

Top Pop Female Vocalist (Albums).

1978 – Top New Pop Duo (Singles) with John Travolta.

Record Mirror Awards

(British Music magazine)

1971 – Best British Female Vocalist.

Most Promising New Female Artist.

1972

Best British Female Vocalist.

American Guild of Variety Artists (AGVA) awards

1974 – Rising Star of the Year.

National Juke Box Awards (Favourite Juke Box artists, US Amusement Music Operators Association)

1980 – Top female artist.

American Society of Composers, Authors and Publishers (ASCAP)

1975 – Country Music Award, *Please Mr Please.*

Country Music Association (CMA) Awards

1974 – Female Vocalist of the Year.

CMA Nominations

1974 – Album of the Year: *If You Love Me Let Me Know.*

Entertainer of the Year.

Single of the Year: *If You Love Me (Let Me Know).*

Academy of Country Music (ACM) awards

1973 – Most Promising Female Vocalist.

ACM Nominations

1974 – Top Female Vocalist (won by Loretta Lynn).

British Country Music Association Award (BCMA)

1974 – Female Vocalist of the Year.

People's Choice Awards

(US awards show, recognising people in entertainment, voted online by the general public and fans)

1975 – Favourite Female Musical Performer (tied with Barbra Streisand).

1977 – Favourite Female Musical Performer.

1979 – Favourite Female Musical Performer.

Favourite Motion Picture Actress.

Golden Globe Awards

(Hollywood Foreign Press Association American and international film and television)

Nomination

1978 – Best Performance by an Actress in a Motion Picture Comedy or Musical: '*Grease.*'

Best Original Song in a Motion Picture – by John Farrar *You're The One That I Want.*

Mo Awards

(Australian entertainment industry)

1998 – Australian Performer of the Year.

Inside Film Awards

(IF annual awards for the Australian film industry)

2011 – Best Music Video: '*Magic 2011.*'

Daytime Emmy Awards

1999 – Best Original Song: *Love Is A Gift* feature on US TV soap opera '*As The World Turns.*'

Emmy Nomination

1977 – Outstanding achievement in technical direction and electronic camerawork: '*A Special Olivia Newton-John*' – ABC.

CableAce Awards Award for Cable Excellence by US National Cable Television Association (discontinued)

Nominations

1983 – Actress in a Variety Program ('*Olivia in Concert*').

1989 – Performance in a Music Special ('*Olivia Down Under*').

US Magazine Award

1983 – Favourite Female Pope Singer.

National Association of Retail Merchandisers (NARM, based on dollar volume)

1974 – Best Selling Album by a Female Country Artist: *If You Love Me, Let Me Know.*

Best Selling Album by a Female: *If You Love Me, Let Me Know.*

Other awards

Olivia's work and performances were recognised in many countries, including The Netherlands, Germany, Chile and Japan, in addition to the many accolades she received in the US, Australia and the UK. She received Golden Bravo awards in Germany as the Favourite Female Star; Top 40 Awards and Viewers' Favourite awards in The Netherlands; and a Lifetime Achievement award in Chile. In Japan, in 1976 she received a Toshiba/EMI award for 'excellent sales of music tapes.' In the US, she was also honoured for her work in cancer awareness by the Hubert H. Humphrey Institute of Public Affairs.

Chapter 21

The Hits

Olivia's Top 10 hit singles, ranked by *Billboard.*

10. *Heart Attack* (1982).

9. *Hopelessly Devoted to You* (with John Travolta) (1978).

8. *Let Me Be There* (1974).

7. *I Honestly Love You* (1974)

6. *Have You Ever Been Mellow* (1975)

5. *Please Mr. Please* (1975)

4. *A Little More Love* (1979)

3. *You're the One That I Want* (with John Travolta) (1978)

2. *Magic* (1980)

1. *Physical* (1981)

NOTE: *Billboard* ranks songs on an inverse point system, with weeks at No. 1 earning the greatest value and weeks at No. 100 earning the least. Due to changes in chart methodology over the years, certain eras are weighted to account for different chart turnover rates over various periods.

HITS IN AUSTRALIA

Olivia had many hits in Australia, starting with *If Not for You* in 1971 which peaked at No. 17 on the Top 40 charts and stayed in the charts for 19 weeks. Some of her singles that made it into overseas charts didn't make it in Australia. One of those was *What is Life*, written by George Harrison, which was only a hit in the UK and Ireland.

After *If Not for You*, Olivia's Australian Top 40 hits included:

Banks of the Ohio. 1971. Was No.1 for 5 weeks and styed in the charts for 25 weeks.

Let Me Be There. 1973. Reached No. 11 and stayed in the charts for 30 weeks.

Long Live Love. 1974. Reached No. 11 and stayed in the charts for 22 weeks.

If You Love Me (Let Me Know). 1974. Reached No. 2 and stayed in the charts for 22 weeks.

I Honestly Love You. 1974. Was No. 1 for 4 weeks and stayed I the charts for 23 weeks.

*Have You Never Been Mellow.*1975. Reached No. 10 and stayed in the charts for 10 weeks.

Please Mr. Please. 1975. Reached No. 35 and stayed in the charts for 16 weeks.

You're the One That I Want. 1978. Stayed No. 1 for 9 weeks and was in the charts for 32 weeks.

Hopelessly Devoted to You. 1978. Reached No. 2 and was in the charts for 21 weeks.

Summer Nights. 1978. Reached No. 6 and was in the charts for 16 weeks.

A Little More Love. 1978. Reached No. 9 and was in the char5ts for 20 weeks.

Magic. 1980. Reached No. 4 and was in the charts for 18 weeks.

Don't Cry for me Argentina. 1980. Reached No. 32 and stayed in the charts for 14 weeks.

Xanadu. 1980. Reached No. 2 and was in the charts for 17 weeks.

Suddenly. 1980. Reached No. 32 and was in the charts for 12 weeks.

Physical. 1981. Was No. 1 for 5 weeks and stayed in the charts for 28 weeks.

Make a Move on Me. 1981. Reached No. 8 and was in the charts for 15 weeks.

Heart Attack. 1982. Reached No. 22 and was in the charts for 16 weeks.

Twist of Fate. 1983. Reached No. 4 and was in the charts for 20 weeks.

Soul Kiss. 1985. Reached No. 20 and was in the charts for 14 weeks.

Rumour. Reached No. 35 and was in the charts for 7 weeks.

The Grease Megamix. 1990. Was No. 1 for 5 weeks and was in the charts for 24 weeks.

No Matter What You Do. 1995. Reached No. 35 and was in the charts for 4 weeks.

Grease - the Remix EP. 1998. Reached No. 27 and was in the charts for 13 weeks.

THE SONG WRITER

Olivia Newton-John put her name to at least a dozen songs as songwriter or co-writer.

Changes (1972).

Rosewater (1973).

Love You Hold the Key (1976) with John Farrar.

Don't Ask a Friend (1977).

Borrowed Time (1978).

The Promise (*The Dolphin Song*). (1981).

Let's Talk About Tomorrow (1988) with Amy Sky and John Capek.

Warm and Tender (1989) with John Farrar.

No Matter What You Do (1994).

Precious Love (1998) with Anne Roboff.

Sunburned Country (2002) with Keith Urban.

Stronger Than Before (2005) with Annie Roboff and Beth Nielsen Chapman.

Grace and Gratitude (2006) with Amy Sky.

Chapter 21

Filmography

Olivia Newton-John had more than 80 credits as an actress for appearances in cinema and television programs around the world.

FILM

1965: '*Funny Things Happen Down Under*' Role: Olivia.

1970: '*Toomorrow*' Role: Liv.

1972: '*The Case*' (TV movie). Role: Olivia.

1978: '*Grease*' Role: Sandy Olsson.

1980: '*Xanad.*' Role: Kira.

1983: 'Two *of a Kind*' Role: Debbie Wylder.

1988: '*She's Having a Baby*' Role: Herself.

1990: '*A Mom For Christmas*' (TV movie). Role: Amy Miller.

1991: '*Madonna: Truth or Dare*' (documentary). Role: Herself.

1994: '*A Christmas Romance*' (TV movie). Role: Julia Stonecypher.

1996: '*It's My Party*' Role: Lina Bingham.

2000: '*Sordid Lives*' Role: Bitsy Mae Harling.

2001: '*Wilde Girls*' (TV movie). Role: Jasmine Wilde.

2010: '*1 a minute*' Role: Herself.

2010: '*Score: A Hockey Musical*' Role: Hope Gordon.

2011: '*A Few Best Men*' Role: Barbara Ramme.

2017: '*Sharknado: Global Warming*' (TV movie). Role: Orion.

2020: '*The Very Excellent Mr Dundee*' Role: Olivia.

TELEVISION

1963: Contestant on 'New Faces' Australian talent quest.

1963: 'Kevin Dennis Auditions' Australian talent show.

1964: '*Sunnyside Up*' Australian TV series.

1964: '*Teen Scene*' Australian music program.

1964-65: '*Sing Sing Sing*' Australian music program.

1964: '*The Kevin Dennis New Faces Show*' Australian variety program. Later became 'New Faces.'

1964: '*Teen Time Ten*' Australian music program.

1964-65: '*The Happy Show*' Co-host as Lovely Livvy. Australian program

1965: '*Boomeride*' Sings *When I Grow Up and Crawl Baby, Crawl*. Pioneer lip-synced pop music show, Australia.

1965-1966: '*The Go!! Show*' Australian pop music series (16 episodes).

1965: '*Kommotion*' Australia music series.

1965-66: '*Time for Terry*' Australian variety show.

1966: '*Dick Emery Show*' BBC UK series.

1967: '*Pat and Olivia*' with Pat Carrol. Australian special.

1967: '*News Conference*' Australian series.

1967: '*The Young Entertainers*' Australian series.

1969: '*Bandstand*' Australian music program. Performs *Here, There And Everywhere / I Can't Do Without You Today* with Pat Carroll.

1969: '*ABC News*' with Pat Carroll. Australian program.

1970: 'T*he Cliff Richard Show*' BBC, UK (one episode).

1971-72: '*disco*' – guest for two episodes, German TV. Sings *If Not For You / Banks Of The Ohio.*

1971: '*Grand Amphi*' French series. Sings *Love Song.*

1971: '*The Golden Shot*' UK series (one episode).

1971: '*Getaway with Cliff*' UK series.

1971: '*Lift Off with Ayshea*' UK series.

1971: '*GTK*' Australian pop music show.

1971: '*15 Years of Channel Nine*' Australian special. Sings *If Not For You / Banks Of The Ohio.*

1972: '*Top of the Pops*' UK music series (2 episodes). Sings *What is Life.*

1972: '*The Case*' BBC movie. Plays herself alongside Cliff Richard and Tim Brooke-Taylor.

1972: '*Sacha's In Town*' UK series (2 episodes). Plays herself.

1972: '*The Dean Martin Show*' US series. Sings *If / Just A Little Lovin'/ True Love* with Dean Martin.

1972: '*The Harry Secombe Show*' UK series. Guest, sings *Take Me Home, Country Roads.*

1972: '*Top of the Pops*' UK series. Sings *Take Me Home, Country Roads.*

1972: '*The Reg Varney Revue*' – Guest for one episode, '*The Christmas Revue.*'

1974: '*Eurovision Song Contest*' UK entry. Sings *Long Live Love.* Fourth Place.

1976: '*A Special Olivia Newton-John*' ABC America special.

1977: '*Only Olivia*' BBC Special.

1978: '*Olivia*' ABC US. Special . Guests ABBA, Andy Gibb. During 'ABBA Month' in the US.

1980: '*Hollywood Nights*' ABC US Special.

1982: '*Let's Get Physical*' ABC US special.

1982: '*Saturday Night Live*' – Host and musical guest. US variety show.

1982 '*Olivia in Concert*' HBO in US special.

1982. '*Olivia*' Australian TV special.

1988: '*Olivia Down Under*' HBO in US special.

1990: '*Timeless Tales From Hallmark*' host. Six Episodes.

1995: '*Banjo Paterson's The Man From Snowy River*' Role: Joanna Walker for 3 episodes. Australian adventure drama television series based on Banjo Paterson's poem '*The Man from Snowy River.*' Released in US and the UK as '*Snowy River: The McGregor Saga.*'

1995: '*Ned and Stacey*' US series. Herself in episode 'Reality Check.'

1995: '*Is This Your Life?*' Extended interview with Andrew Neil on Channel 4 in the UK.

1997: '*Tracey Takes On ...*' Herself in 'Childhood' episode.

1997: '*Murphy Brown*' – herself in 'I Hear a Symphony' episode.

2001: '*Bette*' – herself in 'The Invisible Man' episode.

2002: '*A Night With Olivia*' Channel 9 Australia special.

2003: '*Live in Japan 2003*' BS-Hi Japan special.

2003- 2007: '*American Idol*' Fox network series. Guest judge for three episodes.

2004: '*This is Your Life*' Australian series.

2005: '*Olivia Newton-John Gold*' Australian special Nine Network. Filmed at Melbourne's Austin Hospital where she was working on a fundraiser for Austin Health.

2008: '*Sordid Lives: The Series*' – US prequel spin-off from movie. Role: Bitsy Mae Harling. Supporting role in 12 episodes.

2009: '*Kathy Griffin: My Life on the D-List*' US reality series. Herself in episode 'Fly the Super Gay Skies.'

2010: '*Glee*' – US musical comedy drama series. Herself in episodes 'Bad Reputation' and 'Journey to Regionals.'

2015: '*Rue Paul's Drag Race*' – US reality competition series. Guest judge in episode 'Glamazonian Airways.'

2015: '*Dancing with the Stars*' US reality series. Guest Judge "'Famous Dances Night."'

MUSIC VIDEOS

1975: *Follow Me.*

1976: *Don't Stop Believin', Every Face Tells a Story, Sam.*

1977: *Making a Good Thing Better.*

1978: *You're the one That I Want* (with John Travolta), *Summer Nights* (with John Travolta), *Hopelessly Devoted to You* (all with clips from '*Grease*'), *Deeper Than the Night, A Little More Love* (live version).

1979: *Totally Hot*.

1980: *Xanadu* (including excerpts from the movie).

1981-1982: *Physical, Landslide, Magic, Carried Away, A Little More Love, Recovery, The Promise (The Dolphin Song), Love Make Me Strong, Stranger's Tough, Make a Move on Me, Falling, Silvery Rain, Hopelessly Devoted to You* (1982 version). Filmed for the '*Olivia Physical*' video collection.

1982: *Heart Attack, Tied Up*.

1983: *Twist of Fate, Take A Chance* (with John Travolta), *Livin' in Desperate Times, Shaking You*. Filmed for the '*Twist of Fate*' collection.

1985: *Soul Kiss, Toughen Up, Emotional Tangle, Culture Shock, The Right Moment*. Filmed for the '*Soul Kiss*' video collection.

1986: *The Best of Me* (David Foster with Olivia). Filmed at David Foster's house.

1988: *The Rumour, Can't We Talk it Over in Bed. Tutta la vita, Click Go the Shears, Walk Through Fire, Old Fashioned Man, Let's Talk About Tomorrow, Winter Angel, Get Out, Big and Strong, Love and Let Live, It's Always Australia for Me*. Filmed for the '*Olivia Down Under*' video collection.

1989: *Reach Out for Me*.

1992: *I Need Love*. Includes snippets from the music videos for '*Can't We Talk It Over in Bed*' and '*Love and Let Live*.'

1994: *No Matter What You Do*. Filmed at Olivia Newton-John's house, Byron Bay, Australia.

1995: *Had to be* (Cliff Richard and Olivia Newton-John).

1997: *Falling* (Raybon Brothers and Olivia Newton-John).

1998: *One Heart at a Time* (with various artists), *I Honestly Love You* (filmed at Los Angeles including Malibu house), *Precious Love* (made for Country Music Television).

2011-2012: *Magic* (Peach and Murphy remix), *Mickey* (Chu Fu Fix). Do not feature an Olivia Newton-John appearance.

2012: *Weightless* (fan-made with clips from the movie '*A Few Best Men*'). *I think You Might Like It* (With John Travolta).

2015: *You Have to Believe* (with daughter Chloe Lattanzi; Chloe released a re-working of *Magic* with Olivia in the video and singing in the chorus).

2016: *Live On* (with Amy Sky and Beth Nielsen Chapman).

MUSIC VIDEO COLLECTIONS

1982: '*Olivia Physical.*' Includes *Landslide, Magic, Physical, Carried Away, A Little More Love* (1982 version), *Recovery, The Promise (The Dolphin Song), Love Makes Me Strong, Stranger's Touch, Make a Move on Me, Falling, Silvery Rain* and *Hopelessly Devoted to You* (1982 version).

1983: '*Twist of Fate.*' Includes *Twist of Fate, Take a Chance, Livin' in Desperate Times* and *Shaking You.*

1985: '*Soul Kiss.*' Includes the music videos of *Toughen Up, Emotional Tangle, Culture Shock, Soul Kiss* and *The Right Moment.*

1989: '*Olivia Down Under.*' Includes the music videos of *Tuta la vita, Click Go the Shears, Walk Through Fire, Old Fashioned Man, Let's Talk About Tomorrow, Winter Angel, Get Out, Big and Strong, Love and Let Live, It's Always Australia for Me* and *The Rumour.*

MUSIC VIDEO COMPILATIONS

2005: '*Video Gold I*'" (Geffen Home Video). Promotional music videos from 1978 to 1983. Includes *Deeper Than the Night, A Little More Love, Totally Hot, Landslide, Magic, Physical, Carried Away, A*

Little More Love (1982 version), *Recovery, The Promise (The Dolphin Song), Love Makes Me Strong, Stranger's Touch, Make a Move on Me, Falling, Silvery Rain, Hopelessly Devoted to You* (1982 version), *Let Me Be There* ('*Olivia in Concert*'), *Please Mr. Please* ('*Olivia in Concert*') and *If You Love Me (Let Me Know)* ('*Olivia in Concert*').

2005: '*Video Gold II*' (Geffen Home Video). Promotional music videos from 1983 to 1998. Includes *Twist of Fate*, Take a Chance, Livin' in Desperate Times, Shaking You, *Heart Attack*, Tied Up, *Soul Kiss*, Culture Shock, Emotional Tangle, Toughen Up, The Right Moment, The Rumour, Can't We Talk It Over in Bed, Reach Out for Me, I Need Love, *I Honestly Love You* (1998 version), Sam ("'Olivia in Concert'"), Suddenly ("'Olivia in Concert'"), *You're the One That I Want* ("'Olivia in Concert'") and *Xanadu* ("'Olivia in Concert'").

2004: '*Video Gold 1 and II.*' Universal Home Entertainment. DVD release, containing the music videos from both I and II editions. (mostly Europe).

TV SPECIAL VIDEOS

1978: '*Olivia.*' MCA. Contains the '*Olivia*' TV special, originally broadcast on ABC (US) in May 1978. Laserdisc-only release.

Chapter 23
Tours

Olivia Newton-John undertook 17 headlining concert tours over 45 years in her career, with a total set list of 952 songs. She co-headlined another three tours.

HEADLINING TOURS

If Not for You Tour (1972). London venues.

Clearly Love Tour (1975) . United States.

Love Performance Tour/ *Don't Stop Believin'* (1976). Japan.

Totally Hot World Tour (1978). North America, Japan, Australia and Europe.

Physical Tour (1982–1983). North America.

Greatest Hits Tour (1999). United States.

One Woman's Live Journey Tour (1999). United States.

Millennium Tour (2000). Hong Kong, Korea.

30 Musical Years Tour (2001). United States, Canada.

Heartstrings World Tour (2002–2005). North America, Australia, Japan.

2006 World Tour (2006). Japan, Australia, United States.

Grace and Gratitude Tour (2006). United States, Canada.

Body Heart & Spirit Tour (2007). Asia, North Amercia.

An Evening with Olivia Newton-John (2007–2009). North America.

2010 World Tour (2010). Chile and Japan.

2011 United States Tour (2011).

A Summer Night with Olivia Newton-John (2012–2013). United Kingdom.

CO-HEADLINING

The Main Event Tour (with John Farnham and Anthony Warlow) (1998). Australia.

Two Strong Hearts Tour (with John Farnham) (2015). Australia.

Liv On In Concert (with Beth Nielsen Chapman and Amy Sky) (2017). United States, United Kingdom.

RESIDENCY SHOW

Summer Nights (2014–2016). Las Vegas.

Chapter 24
The Duets

One special album was Elvis Presley's *Christmas Duets* released in 2008, 31 years after his death. Digital technology enable his recordings to be 'mashed' with others - Olivia Newton-John joined him for *O Come all Ye Faithful.*

Olivia's other duet albums included *Olivia Newton-John – Your Duets.* MCA. CD.

These are some of the duets from her own releases and guests on those of other performers:

Will you Still Love me Tomorrow (with Georgie Fame) 1973.

Silver Bells (with Bob Hope) 1974.

Summer Nights (with John Travolta) 1978.

You're The One That I Want (with John Travolta) 1978.

Whenever You're Away From Me (with Gene Kelly) 1980.

I Can't Help It (with Andy Gibb) 1980.

Suddenly (with Cliff Richard) 1980.

*Rest Your Love On M*e (with Andy Gibb) 1980.

Take a Chance (with John Travolta) 1983.

Face to Face (with Barry Gibb) 1984.

You Were Great, How Was I (with Carl Wilson) 1985.

I Do Not Love You Isabella (with Cliff Richard and Kristina Nichols) 1995.

Marked With Death (with Cliff Richard) 1995.

Choosing When It's Too Late (with Cliff Richard) 1995.

You're The One That I Want (with Francis Lalanne) 1996.

Age of Reason (with John Farnham & Anthony Warlow) 1998.

Heart's On Fire (with John Farnham & Anthony Warlow) 1998.

Don't Move Away (with Cliff Richard) 1998.

I Honestly Love You (with Anthony Warlow) 1998.

If Not For You (with John Farnham & Anthony Warlow) 1998.

Let Me Be There (with John Farnham & Anthony Warlow) 1998.

You're The One That I Want (with John Farnham) 1998.

You're The Voice (with John Farnham & Anthony Warlow) 1998.

You've Lost That Lovin' Feeling (with John Farnham & Anthony Warlow) 1998.

Long And Winding Road (with Anthony Warlow) 1998.

Love is a Gift (with Anthony Warlow) 1998.

Not Gonna Give in to It (with Anthony Warlow) 1998.

Take Me Home Country Roads (with Anthony Warlow) 1998.

Please Don't Ask Me (with John Farnham) 1998.

Raindrops Keep Falling On My Head (with John Farnham & Anthony Warlow) 1998.

Summer Nights (with John Farnham & Anthony Warlow) 1998.

Dare To Dream (with John Farnham) 2000.

Away In A Manger (with Vince Gill) 2000.

Flying Dreams (with Kenny Loggins) 2000.

Home For The Holidays (with Vince Gill) 2000.

Let it Snow (with Kenny Loggins and Clint Black) 2001.

Have Yourself a Merry Little Christmas (with Kenny Loggins) 2001.

White Christmas (with Kenny Loggins and Clint Black) 2001.

I Love You Crazy (with Human Nature) 2002.

I Will Be Right Here (with David Campbell) 2002.

Act of Faith (with Michael McDonald) 2002.

Bad About You (with Billy Thorpe) 2002.

I'll Come Runnin' (with Tina Arena) 2002.

I'm Counting On You (with Johnny O'Keefe) 2002.

Sunburned Country (with Keith Urban) 2002.

Tenterfield Saddler (with Peter Allen) 2002.

Lift Me Up (with Darren Hayes) 2002.

Never Far Away (with Richard Marx) 2002.

This Can't Be Real (with Barry Manilow) 2004.

Let It Be Me (with Cliff Richard) 2004.

Wishin' and Hopin' (with Dionne Warwick) 2006.

Silent Night (with Jann Arden) 2007.

All Through The Night (with Michael McDonald) 2007.

Somewhere over the Rainbow (with Les Paul) 2007.

Cotton Jenny (with Anne Murray) 2007.

Every Time it Snows (with Jon Secada) 2007.

Angel In the Wings (with Jann Arden) 2008.

A Mother's Christmas Wish (with Amy Sky) 2008.

Beautiful Thing (with Belinda Emmett) 2008.

Courageous (with Melinda Schneider) 2008.

Everything Love Is (with Jimmy Barnes) 2008.

Every Time it Snows (with Mark Masri) 2008.

Find a Little Faith (with Cliff Richard) 2008.

Never Far Away (with Richard Marx) 2008.

Isn't It Amazing (with Sun Ho) 2008.

Reckless (with John Farrar) 2008.

Right Here With You (with Delta Goodrem) 2008.

Sunburned Country (with Keith Urban) 2008.

The Heart Knows (with Barry Gibb) 2008.

The Water is Wide (with Amy Sky and RyanDan duo) 2008.

Amoureuse (with Elaine Paige) 2010.

Auld Lang Syne (with John Travolta) 2012.

Baby It's Cold Outside (with John Travolta) 2012.

Deck The Halls (with John Travolta) 2012.

Have Yourself a Merry Little Christmas (with Cliff Richard) 2012.

Rockin' Around The Christmas Tree (with John Travolta) 2012.

This Christmas (with Chick Corea) 2012.

I'll Be Home For Christmas (with Barbra Streisand and John Travolta) 2012.

Canadian Summer Dream (with Liona Boyd) 2013.

Have to Believe (with Chloe Lattanzi) 2016.

How Can You Mend a Broken Heart (with Kelly Lang) 2016.

Let Me Be There (with Delta Goodrem) 2018.

Love Is a Gift (with Delta Goodrem) 2018.

Put Your Head on My Shoulder (with Paul Anka) 2021.

Rest Your Love on Me (with Barry Gibb) 2021.

Window in the Wall (with Chloe Lattanzi) 2021.

DUETS ON STAGE

Olivia sang several memorable duets on stage that weren't recorded for albums.

You're the one That I Want (with Donny Osmond). *Donny and Marie Variety Show* 1978.

Rest your Love on Me (with Andy Gibb). Music for UNICEF Concert in New York 1979.

Candle in the Wind (with Elton John). Hollywood Nights 1980.

Hopelessly Devoted to You (with Mariah Carey). Melbourne Australia (Mariah Carey Tour) 1998.

Summer Nights (with rescued Chilean Miner Edison Pena). Santiago, Chile, 2010.

Chapter 25
The Singles

13 May 1966: First single release *Till You Say You'll Be Mine/For Ever.* Decca records. Writer Jacki DE Shannon (non-album single).

March 1971: *If Not For you* - B side *The Biggest Clown.* Festival. Writer Bob Dylan.

October 1971: *Banks of the Ohio* - B side *Love Song.* Festival. Unknown writer/s. Album: *If Not For You* (first album).

March 1972: *What is Life* - B side *I'm Small and Lonely Tonight.* Festival. Writer George Harrison. Album *Olivia.*

August 1972: *Just a Little Too Much* - B side *Changes.* Festival. Writer Johnny Burnett. Album *Olivia.*

January 1973: *Take Me Home Country Roads* - B side *Sail into tomorrow.* Decca. Writers Danoff, Nivert, Denver. Album *Let Me Be There.*

September 1973: *Let Me Be There* - B side *Maybe Then I'll Think of You.* Festival. Writer John Rostill. Album *Let Me Be There.*

March 1974: *Long Live Love* - B side *Angel Eyes.* EMI. Writers Avon, Spiro. Album *Long Live Love.*

May 1974: *If You Love me (Let Me Know)* - B side *Rosewater* (Australia), *Brotherly Love* (US, Canada and rest of world). Writer John Rostill. Album *If You Love Me Let Me Know.*

August 1974: *I Honestly Love You* - B side *Home Ain't Home Anymore.* Writers Barry, Allen. Festival. Album *Long Live Love* (UK) and *If You Love Me, Let Me Know* (US).

February 1975: *Have you Never Been Mellow* - B side *Water Under the Bridge.* EMI. Writer John Farrar. Album *Have You Never Been Mellow.*

June 1975: *Please Mr. Please* - B side *Don't Cry for Me Argentina*. EMI. Writers Welch, Rostill. Album Have You Never been Mellow.

July 1975: *Follow Me* - B side *Summertime Blues*. EMI. Writer John Denver. Album *Have You Never Been Mellow.*

September 1975: *Something Better to Do* - B side *He's My Rock*. EMI. Writer John Farrar. Album *Clearly Love.*

December 1975: *Let it Shine* - B side *He Ain't Heavy He's My Brothe*r. EMI. Writer Linda Hargrove. Album *Clearly Love.*

February 1976: *Come on Over* - B side *Small Talk and Pride*. EMI. Writers Barry and Robin Gibb. Album *Come on Over.*

March 1976: *Jolene* - B side *Wrap Me in Your Arm*s. EMI. Writer Dolly Parton. Album *Come on Over.*

August 1976: *Don't Stop Believin'* - B side *Greensleeves*. EMI Capitol. Writer John Farrar. Album *Don't Stop Believin'*

November 1976: *Every Face Tells a Story* - B side *Love You Hold the Key.* EMI. Writers Allison, Black, Sills. Album *Don't Stop Believin'.*

January 1977: *Sam* - B side *I'll bet You a Kangaroo*. EMI. Writers Black, Marvin Farrar. Album *Don't Stop Believin'.*

June 1977: *Making a Good Thing Better* - B side *Compassionate Man.* EMI. Writer Pete Wingfield. Album *Making a Good Thing Better.*

December 1977: *Don't Cry for Me Argentina* - B side *Rainbow High*. EMI. Writers Webber, Rice. Album *Making a Good Thing Better.*

May 1978: *You're the One That I Want* (with John Travolta) - B side *Alone at a Drive-In Movie* (instrumental). RSO. Writer John Farrar. Album. *Grease.*

August 1978: *Hopelessly Devoted to You* - B side *The Anthem Melody.* RSO. Writer John Farrar. Album *Grease.*

August 1978: *Summer Nights* (with John Travolta) - B side *Rock and Roll Party Queen* (performed by Louis St. Louis). RSO. Writers Jacobs, Casey. Album *Grease.*

October 1978: *A Little More Love* - B side *Borrowed Time.* EMI, MCA. Writer John Farrar. Album *Totally Hot.*

April 1979: *Deeper Than The Night* - B side *Please Don't Keep Me Waiting.* EMI, MCA. Writers Snow, Vastano. Album *Totally Hot.*

November 1979: *Totally Hot* (released as double A sided single) - B side *Dancin' Round and Round.* EMI, MCA. Writer John Farrar. Album *Totally Hot.*

November 1979: *Dancin' Round and Round* - B side *Totally Hot.* MCA. Writer Adam Mitchell. Album *Totally Hot.*

March 1980: *I Can't Help It* (with Andy Gibb) - B side *Someone I Ain*'t. RSO. Writer Barry Gibb. Album *After Dark.*

May 1980: *Magic* - B side *Fool Country* (US), *Whenever You're Away from Me* (with Gene Kelly, UK). MCA, Jet. Writer John Farrar. Album *Xanadu.*

June 1980: *Xanadu* (with ELO) - B side *Whenever You're Away from Me* (with Gene Kelly, US), *Fool Country* (UK). MCA, Jet. Writer Jeff Lynne. Album *Xanadu.*

October 1980: *Suddenly* (with Cliff Richard) - B side *You Made Me Love You.* MCA, Jet. Writer John Farrar. Album *Xanadu.*

September 1981: *Physical* - B side *The Promise* (The Dolphin Song - written by Olivia Newton-John). EMI, MCA. Writers Kipner, Shaddick. Album *Physical.*

January1982: *Make a Move on Me* - B side *Falling.* MCA. Writers Farrar, Snow. Album *Physical.*

April 1982: *Landslide* - B side *Recovery.* EMI, MCA. Writer John Farrar. Album *Physical.*

August 1982: *Heart Attack* - B side *Stranger's Touch.* EMI, MCA. Writers Bliss, Kipner. Album *Olivia's Greatest Hits Vol. 2.*

January1983: *Tied Up* - B side *Silvery Rain.* MCA. Writers Farrar, Ritenou. Album *Olivia's Greatest Hits Vol. 2.*

October 1983: *Twist of Fate* - B side *Jolene* (UK), *Take A Chance* (with John Travolta, US). EMI, MCA. Writers Beckett, Kipner. Album *Two of a Kind.*

October 1983: *Take a Chance* (with John Travolta) - B side of *Twist of Fate*. MCA. Writers Foster, Lukather, Olivia Newton-John (reached charts as B side). Album *Two of a Kind.*

February1984: *Livin' in Desperate Times* - B side *Landslide.* MCA. Writers Alfonso, Snow, Williams. Album *Two of a Kind.*

September 1985: *Soul Kiss* - B side *Electric.* MCA. Writer Mark Goldenberg. Album *Soul Kiss.*

January 1986: *Toughen Up* - B side *Driving Music.* MCA. Writers Britten, Lyle. Album *Soul Kiss.*

June 1986: *The Best of Me* (with David Foster) - B side *Saje.* Atlantic. Writers Foster, Lubbock, Marx. Album *David Foster.*

April 1988: *The Rumour* - B side *Winter Angel.* Mercury. Writers Elton John, Bernie Taupin. Album *The Rumour.*

August 1988: *Can't We Talk it Over in Bed* - A and B side. MCA. Writers Linzer, Levine. Album *The Rumour.*

September 1989: *Reach Out for Me* (With Brahms Lullaby Intro and Reprise) - B side *The Flower That Shattered the Stone* (LP Version). Geffen. Writers Bacharach, David. Album *Warm and Tender.*

September 1989: *When You Wish Upon a Star* - B side *Rocking.* Mercury. Writers Harline, Washington (1940). Cover credit Chloe Lattanzi. *Album Warm and Tender.*

December 1990: *The Grease Megamix* (with John Travolta). Tracks in mix: *You're the One That I Want, Greased Lightning* and *Summer Nights* - B side *Alone at the Drive-in-Movie, Love Is a Many Splendored Thing.* Polydor. DJ mix, Harding Curnow. Non-album single.

March 1991: *Grease the Dream Mix* (with Frankie Valli and John Travolta) - B side *We Go Together.* From 1978 recordings. Polydor. Non-album single.

July 1992: *I Need Love* - B side *Warm and Tender.* Mercury. Writers Parker, Kipner. Album *Back to Basics: The Essential Collection 1971-1992.*
June 1992: *Deeper Than a River* - B side *The Promise.* Geffen. Writer Diane Warren. Album. *Back to Basics: The Essential Collection 1971-1992.*
July 1994: *No Matter What You Do* - B side *Silent Ruin.* Festival. Writer Olivia Newton John. Album. *Gaia: One Woman's Journey*
September 1994: *Don't Cut Me Down* - B side *Do You Feel Like I Do.* Festival. Writer Olivia Newton-John. Album. *Gaia: One Woman's Journey.*
November 1995: *Had to Be* (with Cliff Richard) - B side *Don't Move Away.* EMI. Writers Farrar, Rice. Album *Songs from Heathcliff* (Cliff Richard).
July 1998: *You're the One That I Want* (Martian remix with John Travolta). Contains *You're the One That I Want, Greased Lightnin', You're the One That I Want* (original version), *Hopelessly Devoted to You.* Polydor. *Grease: The Remix EP.*
May 1998: *I Honestly Love You* (1998 version). MCA. Version featured Babyface (Kenneth Brian Edmonds) on background vocals. Album *Back with a Heart.*
October 1998: *Back with a Heart; Precious Love.* Universal/MCA. Writers Olivia Newton-John, Burr. Album *Back with a Heart.*
August 2000: *Change of Heart* (with Jim Brickman, live version) Windham Hill. Writers James Brickman, Olivia Newton-John. Album *My Romance: An Evening with Jim Brickman.*
February 2001: *Valentine* (with Jim Brickman). Windham Hill. Writers Brickman, Kugel. Album *My Romance: An Evening with Jim Brickman.*
October 2006: *Instrument of Peace.* EMI. Writers Sky, Jordan, Moccio. Album *Grace and Gratitude.*
June 2008: *Angel in the Wings* (featuring Jann Arden) . UMG. Writer Amy Sky. Album *A Celebration in Song* EP.

November 2009: *Hope is Always Here* (featuring David Foster). Edge Health. Writers Foster, Olivia Newton-John. Non-album single.
October 2010: *Help Me to Heal.* (Proceeds to Olivia Newton-John Cancer & Wellness Centre and City of Hope). Olivia Productions. Writers Sky, Olivia Newton-John. Album *Grace and Gratitude: Renewed*
June 2011: *Magic* (Peach & Murphy mix featuring Wacci). Proceeds to Olivia Newton-John Cancer & Wellness Centre. Olivia Productions. Non-album single.
May 2011: *When You Wish Upon a Star* (2011 version). Phyz. Non-album single.
January 2021: *Window in the Wall* (with Chloe Lattanzi). Green Hill. Writers Paden, Kilgallon, Cameron. Non-album single.
May 2021: *Put Your Head on My Shoulder* (with Paul Anka). iTunes Plus AAC M4A. Writer Paul Anka (first recorded 1958). Non-album single.
February 2022: *Valentine* (25th anniversary mix with Jim Brickman). Non-album single.

AS FEATURED ARTIST

May 2010: *Physical* (with Glee cast). Album *Glee: The Music, Volume 3 Showstoppers.*
April 2014: *I Touch Myself* (part of I Touch Myself project). Album *I Touch Myself Project.*
August 2015: *You Have to Believe* (Dave Aude and Chloe Lattanzi). Cover of Olivia's hit single *Magic* from *Xanadu.* Non album single.

Chapter 26

The Albums

Genres

Pop, Pop Rock, Country Pop, Adult Contemporary, Film Soundtrack, Soft Rock.

First airing

Toomorrow movie soundtrack. RCA. August 1970. First album on which Olivia featured – as a member of the group formed to star in the sci-fi musical movie of the same name with three male members, Ben Thomas, Karl Chambers and Vic Cooper. Re-issued in July 2021.

STUDIO ALBUMS

Olivia Newton-John first solo album. Pye. November 1971; released in Australia and the US as ***If Not for You***. Producers John Farrar and Bruce Welch.

Olivia: August 1972. Pye. Featured her own song, Changes. Producers Farrar, Welch. Digitally remastered version released in 1995.

Let Me Be There: March 1973. (LP, CD, cassette, 8-track). MCA. Also released with an alternative tracklist, including songs from previous albums. Released as *Music Makes My Day* (UK) with some different tracks. Producers Farrar, Welch. Sales: 689,130.

Long Live Love: June 1974. EMI. Producers Farrar, Welch.

Have You Never Been Mellow: February 1975 EMI. Sales 869,380. Producer John Farrar.

Clearly Love: September 1975. EMI. Sales 710,450. Producer Joh Farrar.

Come on Over: February 1976. Emi. Sales: 1,015,450. Producer John Farrar. Title song written by Barry and Robin Gibb of the Bee Gees.

Don't Stop Believin': October 1976. Emi. Sales: 684,190. Producer John Farrar.

Making a Good Thing Better: June 1977. EMI. Sales: 159,820. Producer John Farrar.

Totally Hot: November 1978. EMI. Sales 1,297,280. Producer John Farrar.

Physical: October 1981. Emi. Sales: 2,913,310. Producer John Farrar.

Soul Kiss: October 1985. Sales: 617,090. Producer John Farrar.

The Rumour: August 1988. Festival. Sales: 19,340. Producers Elton John, James Newton Howard, Davitt Sigerson, Hank Medress, Sandy Linzer, Randy Goodrum.

Warm and Tender: September 1989. Mercury. Sales: 12,570. Producer John Farrar.

Gaia. One Women's Journey: July 1994. Festival. Sales: 35,000. Producers Olivia Newton-John, Murray Burns, Colin Bayley.

Back With a Heart: May 1998. MCA Nashville. Producers Tony Brown, Gary Burr, Don Cook, John Farrar, Chris Farren, David Foster.

'Tis The Season (with Vince Gill): September 2000. Olivia's first Christmas album, Vince's third. Featuring London Symphony Orchestra. Hallmark. Producer Carter Co's Inc.

(2): November 2002. First duets album. Sales BMG-US 70,000. Producers Charles Fisher, Richard Marx, Rick Nowels.

Indigo. Women of Song: October 2004. Festival (Mushroom). Sales: 35,000. Producer Phil Ramone. Released in US as Portraits.

Stronger Than Before: August 2005. Hallmark. Producers Kim Bullard, Chong Lim, Amy Sky.

Grace and Gratitude: August 2006. EMI. Producers Amy Sky, Tracy Young (Pink edition bonus). Re-released 2010 with extra tracks.

Christmas Wish: November 2007. Compass.Producer Amy Sky.

A Celebration in Song: June 2008. Warner. Producers Amy Sky, Mike Clute, Melinda Schneider, Barry Gibb, Eddie Schwartz, Charles Fisher,

Richard Marx, John Farrar, Greg Johnson, Daniel Denholm, Phil Buckie.
This Christmas (with John Travolta): November 2012. Universal. Producers Randy Waldman, John Farrar, Dave Grusin, Phil Ramone, James Taylor. Christmas CD raised money for Olivia's Wellness Centre and John Travolta's Jett Travolta Foundation.
Liv On (with Amy Sky and Beth Nielsen Chapman). October 2016. OBA Productions. Producers Amy Sky, Beth Nielsen Chapman, Olivia Newton-John.
Friends for Christmas (with John Farnham). November 2016. Sony Music. Sales: 140,000. Producer Chong Lim.

SOUNDTRACK ALBUMS

Grease (with John Travolta): April 1978, two months before the movie was released. RSO. Double album. Re-released as an anniversary edition after 25 years. One of the biggest selling albums of all time and still selling. Estimated sales of 30 million. Producer
Xanadu (with Electric Light Orchestra): June 1980. Jet. Sales: 2,896,790 (double platinum certification in US). Producers John Farrar and Jeff Lynne.
Two of a Kind (With John Travolta): December 1983. MCA Sales: 1,085,120 Producer David Foster.
Sordid Lives: May 2001. Olivia performed six songs (plus two revises) on the soundtrack.
Sordid Lives, The Series: July 2008. The TV series only ran for one season. Olivia performed six songs on the soundtrack.
A Few Best Men (Original Motion Picture Soundtrack): January 2012. Universal. Most of the songs performed for the Movie (Australian) were by Olivia Newton-John. Producers Warren Fahey and Stephan Elliott.

LIVE ALBUMS

Love Performance: 1981. EMI. First live album performance recorded December 1976 on tour of Japan to promote album *Don't Stop Believin'*; not released for 5 years. Sales: 123,590. Producer John Farrar.

Highlights from the Main Event (with John Farnham and Anthony Warlow): December 1998. Re-released 2001. BMG. Sales: 350,000 (Australia).

One Women's Live Journey: September 2000 (Australia) and 2001 in US. Recorded recorded live at the Taj Mahal, Atlantic City, 26 August 1999. Festival Mushroom. First live CD. Producers Oliva Newton-John, Eliot Scheiner.

Olivia's Live Hits: Recorded March 2006, Sydney Opera House, with the Sydney Symphony Orchestra over four performances. Not all songs were included on the album. Released January 2008. A DVD called Live at the Sydney Opera House was also recorded. Capitol/EMI.

Summer Nights – Live in Las Vegas: Double album. Recorded live at the Donny & Marie Showroom Hotel Flamingo April 2014. Released April 2015. Olivia/Universal. Producers Olivia Newton-John, Mark Hartley.

Two Strong Hearts Live (with John Farnham) Recorded with Philharmonia Australia in Melbourne April 2015, released June 2015. Sony Music Australia. Sales: 50,000.

BOX SETS

Olivia Newton-John Box. December 1983. EMI Ten vinyl LPs.

40th Anniversary Collection. Universal Music. October 2010. Universal Japan released a 40th anniversary Olivia Newton-John box set of 10 CDs. Includes Booklet 'The Single Collection.' Two bonus tracks from each album plus bonus DVD with six tracks.

COMPILATION ALBUMS

1974: '*If You Love Me Let Know.*' North America only. MCA.

1974: '*First Impressions.*' Australia and New Zealand subtitle 'Great Hits'. Festival. 1971 to 1974 – songs from the first three studio albums and the compilation '*If You Love Me, Let Me Know.*' Released in Japan as '*Let Me Be There.*'

1976: '*Crystal Lady.*' Japan. EMI.

1977: '*Olivia Newton-John's Greatest Hits.*' MCA. First hits album comprising American Top 40 singles released between 1971 and 1977. Received her first Platinum award and reached double Platinum in US.

1982: '*Olivia's Greatest hits Vol. 2.*' MCA. Contains most singles released since 1977 album. Multi-platinum in US and Canada.

1982: '*Greatest Hits Vol. 3*'. Hits from 1978-82. Festival.

1992: '*Back to Basics: The Essential Collection 1971-1992.*' Geffen. First compilation to include country and pop hits.

2001: '*Magic: The Very Best of Olivia Newton-John.*' Universal. First compilation to include all 15 of her Top 10 hits on the *Billboard* Hot 100 and the first to include *The Grease Megamix.*

2001: '*The Definitive Collection.*' (Europe 2002). Sony BMG.

2002: '*The Best of Olivia Newton-John - The Millennium Collection.*' Hip-O. Ten of her best hits from 1973 to m1983 from studio recordings.

2005: '*Gold.*' Hip-O. Comprehensive double album of songs recorded 1970-1988.

2010: '*40/40: The Best Selection.*"' Universal. Double album. Japan. Tracks chosen based on votes from Japanese fans.

2018: '*Hopelessly Devoted Hits.*' Sony Music Australia. Includes songs from '*Grease*' and '*Xanadu*' as well as her record-breaking solo releases.

FOOTNOTE: Compilation albums comprise singles and tracks from other albums. Some compilation albums may be listed under Studio Albums if they were recorded specifically for the album. Some were released under different titles and labels in some countries. Her songs also appeared on compilation albums by other artists and special releases.

EPs

A Window to the Sky. 1976. Tracks: *A Window in the Sky* and *A Window in the Sky* narrative. Released as an LP in Japan only, with extra tracks.

4 Successos. 1977 (Brazil). EMI. Tracks: *Sam, Every Face Tells a Story; Sad Songs, Slow Dancing.*

Hotel Sessions. 2014. ONJOlivia Productions. Produced by Brett Goldsmith. Tracks: *Ordinary Life, Best of my Love, End in Peace, Bow River, Broken Wings*. Bonus tracks: Dance remixes *Bow River* and *Broken Wings.*

UPDATED POSTHUMOUS DISCOGRAPHY ADDITIONS

ALBUMS

Aug 12 2022: *If Not For You 50th Anniversary Deluxe Edition* Primary Wave*

21st Oct 2022: *Olivia Newton-John's Greatest Hits 45th Anniversary (Deluxe Edition)* Primary Wave*

5 May 2023: *Just the Two of Us: The Duets Collection (Vol. 1)* Primary Wave*

6 October 2023: *Just the Two of Us: The Duets Collection (Vol. 2)* Primary Wave*

6 Jan 2023: *Olivia's Greatest Hits Vol 2 (Deluxe Edition)* Primary Wave*

29 November 2024: *Angels in the Snow Release* Universal

21 Jun 2024: *Grace And Gratitude (Deluxe Edition)* Green Hill Music

SINGLES

May 5, 2023: *Jolene* with ONJ and Dolly Parton

Album *Just the Two of Us: The Duets Collection*

first single out Feb 2023 Primary Wave

20 September, 2024: *My Dream* - Single

NEW LOST WORK Discovered with Jim Brickman and Il Volo) and ONJ

Sept 26 2024: *Phoenix* Chloe Lattanzi In honour of Olivia

22 Nov 2024: *Oh Come All Ye Faithful* (ONJ and Jane Lynch)

Single release from re release album Angles in the snow

Posthumous Releases

Primary Wave* remastered back catalogue

ADDITIONAL EPS/CD/PICTURE DISC REMASTERS AND EXCLUSIVES

21 oct 2022: *Greatest Hits* Japan Deluxe Edition

Comes with a poster and a message from Olivia to Japanese fans/with translation.

18 Nov 2022: *Olivia Newton John's Greatest Hits 1971-1982* (2LP) (Target Exclusive, Pink/Blue Vinyl) exclusive Target collection produced by Vinny Vero for So Hip It Hurts Productions and Oblivion Entertainment /Primary Wave*

September 8, 2023: *I Need Love: The Back To Basics Bonus EP* Digital/ Primary Wave*

September 25, 2023: *Happy 75th Birthday* Digital /Streaming services only /Universal

10 Nov 2023: *Soul Kiss Picture Disc* Primary Wave*

17 Nov 2023: *Totally Hot* Coral red vinyl / UK CD includes a mini poster. Primary Wave*

Mar 15th, 2024: *2* (Olivia Newton-John Album)

Digital release includes bonus track "Let It Be Me" with Cliff Richard and Olivia's Bossa Nova version of "Physical."

August 23 2024: *Long Live Love album* Digital Primary Wave *

Chapter 27

Timeline of the Life of Olivia Newton-John

Dame Olivia Newton-John AC DBE OBE

(26 September 1948 – 8 August 2022)

From England to Australia and the World

1948: Born to Irene and Brin Newton-John 26 September, Cambridge, UK; the youngest of three children, sister of Rona and brother of Hugh. The family lived in Cambridge until leaving for Australia. Her father was a headteacher at the Cambridgeshire High School for Boys and later became Professor of German at Kings College.

1953: Brin Newton-John accepts position as master of Ormond College, University of Melbourne, Australia. Family (Brin, Irene and children Hugh, Olivia and Rona) leaves Cambridge and sails from London to Australia aboard the '*SS Strathaird*'.

1954-60: 1954 Newton John family of 5 arrives arriving in Fremantle on 25 January 1954 before going on to Melbourne.

Olivia attends Christ Church Grammar School (primary school) in Melbourne.

1958: Brin and Irene Newton-John divorce. Brin accept position as associate professor of German at the University of Newcastle, NSW.

1961-64: Attends University High School, in Parkville, Melbourne.

1963: Forms 'The Sol Four' group with three other schoolgirl friends. Group disbanded because it interfered with schoolwork. Olivia continued to sing in her brother-in-law's coffee lounge.

1964: Portrays Lady Mary Lasenby in University High School's production of *The Admirable Crichton*. Became the '*Young Sun*' (newspaper) Drama Award best schoolgirl actress runner-up.

1964: April, wins a Sitmar Talent Quest on Australian Channel Seven's popular '*Sing Sing Sing*"' show, hosted by Australian rock icon Johnny O'Keefe. Delayed acceptance of prize – trip to London – to continue at school.

1964-65: Stands in as host 'Lovely Livvy' on Channel Seven's '*Happy Show*' during summer. Also a regular on '*Time for Terry*' variety show (HSV-7), hosted by English comedian, entertainer and jazz musician Terry O'Neill 1964-66.

1965: First movie role in the Australian film '*Funny Things Happen Down Under*'. Reportedly dated Turpie during filming. Sang *Christmas Time Down Under.*

1965: Took her Sitmar talent Quest prize trip to London with her mother, Irene.

1966: Released debut 45 rpm single (recorded 1965) *Till You Say You'll be Mine*, in Britain for Decca Records. Offered role to play Cinderella in a Christmas show but opted to return to Australia for Christmas.

CAREER BEGINS

1967: Returned to England to pursue singing career.

1967-68: Dated and got engaged to The Shadows guitarist Bruce Welch. Named as 'other woman' when Welsh's wife sues him for divorce.

1969-1970: Approached by Don Kirshner (inventor of Monkees and Archies groups) to take part in '*Toomorrow*,' also a manufactured film/band combination for the movies. Joined Karl Chambers, a drummer from Philadelphia, Vic Cooper, a multi-instrumentalist from London and Ben Thomas, a Georgia-born singer and guitarist. The movie runs for a week at one London theatre in 1970. The soundtrack fails to sell.

1971: Performs duet with Cliff Richard, *Don't Move Away.* Tours The Netherlands, Belgium, Switzerland and Germany with Richard. Records and releases first Top 40 single, *If not for you* (Pye). Guest on Cliff Richard's holiday TV special '*Get Away with Cliff*.' First album Olivia Newton-John released by Pye. Performs at 1971 Tokyo Music Fair.

1972: Second album, *Olivia*, released in UK. Becomes resident guest for 13 weeks on Cliff Richard's BBC TV musical variety show. Performs live around London. Single *What is Life* (Pye, written by George Harrison of the Beatles) reaches No. 16 in UK but isn't a hit in Australia. Single *Just a Little Too Much* released but fails to reach charts. Breaks engagement to Bruce Welch but he continues to produce her records and she accompanies him in ambulance to hospital after he took a drug overdose. Appears in West End stage show with Sacha Distel. Lives in London in a flat nor far from her sister Rona. Writes her first tune, for a new album that's planned.

1973: Take Me Home Country Roads (written by John Denver and recorded for her album Let Me be There) reaches No. 15 in UK. Single *Let Me Be There* fails to reach charts there but becomes her first Top 10 single in the US and No. 11 in Australia. Has a session musician credit playing recorder on Marvin, Welch (ex Shadows) and Farrar's (ex Strangers) album Music Makes My Day. Her main instruments are piano and guitar.

1974: Wins her first Grammy, for 'Best Country Vocal Performance, Female,' for *Let Me Be There*. Moves to EMI records from Pye. *Long Live Love* album charts at No. 40 in UK. She sings *Long Live Love* (a song she says she didn't really like) as UK's entry in the Eurovision song contest and the single charts at No. 11 in UK, but is beaten in Eurovision by Sweden's ABBA with *Waterloo*. Gets own poetry and music show on BBC TV – guests include Cliff Richard, Labi Siffree and Neil Sedaka. *I Honestly Love You* (also recorded by Australian Peter Allen) becomes first No. 1 hit in the US and No. 2 in Australia and wins a Grammy for 'Record of the Year.' Album *If You Love Me, Let Me Know* tops the album charts and reaches No. 2 in Australia.

1975: Moves to the United States with then boyfriend/manager Lee Kramer and singer/songwriter John Farrar hoping to capitalise on the recoding success she's had there. *Have You Never Been Mellow* is No. 1 and the album of the same name tops the charts, earning a gold disc. Controversy is sparked when she is named Country Music Association Vocalist of the Year – some CMA stalwarts were upset that she was classified a country music singer. *Please Mr Please* (written by Welch) becomes her fifth million-selling album in the US, charting at No. 3. Earns another gold disc for *Clearly Love* album that charts at No. 13 in the US. Named top vocalist of 1975 by the recording industry trade magazine *Cashbox* in both singles and albums category.

1976: In January suffers minor back injury after falling from her horse near Malibu Beach in Los Angeles when the horse bolted. She recovers quickly after treatment at home and rest. First TV special '*A Special Olivia Newton-John*' airs on American TV, with Rona Barrett and Tom Bosley. Tours with '*Don't Stop Believin*' show. Performs at Tokyo Festival Hall. Official recording (her only live recording) released in 1981 as '*Love Performance*.'

YEAR OF THE SMASH HIT

1977: Makes live debut at New York Metropolitan Opera House (gave each guest a red de-thorned rose). Stars in the 'Big Top Show' at Windsor Castle, UK, with Elton John in Silver Jubilee celebrations. '*Only Olivia*' TV special screens on BBC in UK. Flies to Namibia in southwest Africa with conservationist Dr Laurie Marker to film a segment about the plight of the cheetah. Co-hosts the third annual *Rock Music Awards* show with Peter Frampton in October at the Hollywood Palladium in California.

1978: *Olivia Newton-John's Greatest Hits* released, selling more than a million. Second '*Olivia*' TV special airs in US. '*Grease*' opens in the US followed by UK, Australia and other countries. Soundtrack tops album charts. *Summer Nights* tops UK charts for seven weeks and reaches No. 5 in the US. Solo *Hopelessly Devoted to You* makes No. 3 in US and No. 2 in UK. Makes No. 89 in '*Premiere*' magazine's 100 Greatest Movie Characters of All Time (Sandi in '*Grease*'). Re-records *I Honestly Love You* for the album *Back With A Heart.* Suffers rib injuries after being mobbed at the release of the movie '*Grease*' in Chicago in June (her dress was torn also). A judge prevents her from leaving MCA records until the expiry of her contract in 1982. Cancels Japan tour in June in protest at the killing of dolphins by Japanese fishermen but goes ahead in October/November, donating part of her fee to the Japanese Marine Science and Technology Centre.

1979: Performs a duet in January with Andy Gibb (another Australian singer of English descent) at the concert 'Music for Unicef' in the General Assembly Hall of the United Nations in New York, marking 'The International Year of the Child.' The concert is aired on TV and an album released with royalties going to Unicef. Awarded Order of the British Empire (OBE) in the Queen's New Year's Honours List. Performs *Hopelessly Devoted to You* at the Oscars before going home to bed, then to hospital; spends four days in hospital (14-18 April) in Los Angeles after a virus affected her liver (no lasting effects).

SUCCESS AND A FLOP

1980: The movie '*Xanadu*' was a flop among critics and at the theatre, but its soundtrack in collaboration with supergroup Electric Light Orchestra was a major hit. Third TV special, *Hollywood Nights*, airs on TV (first met future husband Matt Lattanzi who appeared briefly in the finale). Lattanzi, then 20, was hired as a dancer and Newton-John, then 31, was starring as Greek muse Kira.

As a member of the Screen Actors' Guild in the US she finds herself caught up in an industrial dispute and in Australia to promote the film '*Xanadu*' is unable to speak about it while Guild members are on strike. She is able to promote the music soundtrack.

Performs *Hopelessly Devoted to You* from the movie *Grease* at the Royal Command Performance in May at the Sydney Opera House in the presence of Her Majesty Queen Elizabeth II and Prince Phillip. Receives a special mention in the series episode '*The Goodies: Saturday Night Grease*.'

GETTING PHYSICAL

1981: Hollywood's 'Walk of Fame' honours her with a star outside Mann's Chinese Theatre on Hollywood Boulevard. Gets Physical – the single *Physical* is an instant hit, reaching No. 1 in Australia and staying in the US charts for more than two months. The album *Physical* peaks at No. 6 in the US and No. 11 in the UK. TV special featuring songs from the album is shown on American TV. The song was temporarily banned by some radio stations for its 'suggestive' content – those in Utah and Idaho, were disturbed by the lines: 'I took you to an intimate restaurant, then to a suggestive movie, There's nothing left to talk about. Let's get physical.' Application for Australian citizenship expedited by then Prime Minister Malcolm Fraser.

1982: More physicality. Singles from the album continue to flow on to the music charts. Starts '*Physical*' tour of the US and film of it becomes a home video hit, *Olivia Live!*
Heart Attack, a single from her *Greatest Hits Vol. 2* album reaches No.3 in the US and No. 46 in the UK. The album reaches No. 16.

1983: Wins the very first Grammy Award in the 'Video of the Year' category for *Physical.* Joins John Travolta for another movie, '*Two of a Kind*', which turns out to be a box office flop with the soundtrack saving the day again as the single *Twist of Fate* charts at No. 52 in the UK. With friend Pat Farrar opens first

Koala Blue store (described as an upmarket boutique/milk bar stocking Australian items, from hand-knit one-of-a-kind sweaters to products such as Vegemite and Violet Crumble) on Melrose Avenue in Los Angeles. Sixty more stores open within four years, including outlets in Europe and Asia.

1984: Hosts reception for the Australian team in the US for the 1984 Los Angeles Olympic Games and performs *I Still Call Australia Home* (written and originally performed by Australian Peter Allen in 1980 and popular among homesick Australians) for an Olympic TV Gala. Married her long-time, live-in boyfriend, actor Matt Lattanzi, in December.

STARTING A FAMILY

1985: Single *Soul Kiss* reaches No. 20 in the US. Album of same name reaches No. 29 in US. Pregnant to Matt Lattanzi, after suffering three miscarriages.

1986: Gives birth to daughter Chloe Rose Lattanzi on 17 January at Cedars-Sinai Medical Center in Los Angeles, California. Performs the Australian National Anthem at the VFL (now AFL) Grand final in September between Hawthorn and Carlton at the Melbourne Cricket Ground (won by Hawthorn). Visits Australia with baby Chloe for the first time.

1987: With husband Matt and daughter Chloe films 1987-88 New Years special *It's Always Australia for Me* in the living room of her home. Attends 75th Paramount anniversary celebrations. Invites Americans to 'Say G'day to Melbourne' in a $3 million Victorian Tourism Commission

1988: Performs with Cliff Richard at the Bicentennial Concert in January at the Sydney Entertainment Centre, attended by

HRH Prince of Wales and Princess Diana. Performs several of her songs from album *Rumour* for TV movie '*Olivia Down Under.*'

1989: Records album of children's songs, *Warm and Tender*, with Geffen Records. Voted Celebrity Businesswomen of the Year in US for Koala Blue stores.

1990: Appointed United Nations Goodwill Ambassador for the Environment. Stars in Disney movie, '*A Mom for Christmas.*' *The Grease Megamix* released. Returns to Australia to perform her first live concert there since Australia Day 1988 – a fundraiser at the Sydney Entertainment Centre on 4 February for victims of the Newcastle earthquake in December 1989.

1991: Appears in Madonna's '*Truth or Dare*' documentary. *The Dream Mix* produced to launch the video release of '*Grease*,' single (mix of *Grease* and Sandy tracks) also credited to Frankie Valli and John Travolta. Koala Blue chain, after reaching $US 25 million sales annually, reports trading difficulties and is put into receivership. She describes 1991 as 'the worst year of my life.' A positive was that a remix of her and John Travolta's 1970 '*Grease*' soundtrack topped the ARIA album music charts in July.

BAD NEWS, GOOD NEWS

1992: Comeback album *Back to Basics* released. Major tour planned for the US cancelled on 2 July when diagnosed with breast cancer (aged 44). The bad news comes less than two weeks after her father Brin dies of cancer. Undergoes emergency surgery at Cedars-Sinai Medical Centre in Los Angeles and eventually goes into remission. Helps launch CHEC (later known as Healthy Child Healthy World) charity with friend Nancy Chuda after Nancy's daughter (Olivia's Goddaughter) Collette dies with a rare form of childhood cancer. Establishes the Olivia Newton-John Cancer Wellness and Research Centre in Melbourne that opens as part of the Austin Hospital in Heidelberg, with $A 189 million in government and philanthropic funding. Koala Blue with 60 stores world-wide at one stage files for bankruptcy in the US, goes into liquidation and she takes a big financial hit.

1993: Recuperates from cancer treatment in Australia. Begins writing material for a new album. Co-writes a children's book, '*A Pig Tale*,' with Brian S. Hurst (saving-the-environment theme). First met future husband John Easterling through a mutual friend. Daughter Chloe Lattanzi follows her mother into acting.

1994: Writes and produces 'new-age' album *Gaia: One Woman's Journey* (her 15th studio album) in Australia, released via small record companies as she doesn't have a record label at this time. First album since cancer diagnosis. Performs songs from the album at 'Best for the Bush' charity concert to aid drought-stricken Australian farmers. Album reaches No. 7 in Australia and No. 33 in UK (not released in US). Appears in three episodes of Australian soap '*The Man From Snowy River*' (released in the US and UK as '*The McGregor Saga: the Man from Snowy River*') as Joanna Walker. Appears in TV movie '*A Christmas Romance*.' Performs *Away in a Manger* on a limited-edition Christmas album, *Spirit of Christmas '94*, released by Myer Grace Bros (an Australian department store) with the profits in aid of the Salvation Army. Rumours of trouble in her marriage.

1995: Guest appearance on five tracks of the soundtrack for Cliff

Richard's stage show '*Heathcliff*.' Performs *Had to Be* with Cliff Richard on the Royal Variety Show in London. *Gaia* album released in Europe and Japan. Hosts Australian wildlife series '*Human/Nature*.' Has small part in Randal Kaiser low-budget movie '*It's My Party*.' She and Matt Lattanzi separate, then divorce.

1996: Hosts Lifetime TV's '*Lifetime Applauds – the Fight Against Breast Cancer*' and performs songs from Gaia to an American audience for the first time. Appears on Home Shopping channel promoting Marae range of beauty products. Performs *You're The One That I Want* with French singer Francis Lalanne for a French small-edition dance club CD , recorded in France in late 1995 to promote *Gaia*. With friend Jon Dee through Planet Ark co-founds National Tree Day in Australia and backs the One Tree Per Child campaign. Appears in the film '*It's My Party*' (renamed '*A Party for Nick*') one of the first feature films dealing with AIDS patients dying without dignity. Moves in with boyfriend Patrick (Kim) McDermott.

1997: Signs on to the country division of her old record label MCA/ Universal. Performs duet with Raybon Brothers on their self-titled album, (including music video). Guest appearance on episode of *Murphy Brown* TV show and recording of *New Hometown* included in soundtrack for Christmas movie '*Snowden on Ice*'.

1998: Through MCA Nashville, releases first studio album in four years and her 16th, *Back with a Heart*, in return to country music after two decades. Single released is remix of *I Honestly Love You*. Receives Daytime Emmy Award for song *Love is a Gift*. Tours Australia with Cliff Richard. Tours Australia with Anthony Warlow and John Farnham in '*Main Event: A Night of Aussie Magic!*' Performs new single *Precious Love*. '*Grease*' re-released world-wide on 20th anniversary. Listed as president of the conservation group Isle of Man Basking Shark Society from 1998 to 2005. Chosen by '*People*' magazine as one of the '50 Most Beautiful People in the World.'

1999: Receives awards from American Red Cross (Humanitarian) and the Women's Guild of Cedars-Sinai Hospital for her charity support. Is cast in the film version of the stage play '*Secret Lives*' as ex-con and barfly singer Bitsy Mae. Performs at live concert in Las Vegas. Performs in small American venues on '*Greatest Hits*' tour, then makes 30-date '*One Woman's Journey Tour*,' her eighth concert tour, to promote *Back With a Heart* album.

NEW MILENNIUM

2000: Teams with fellow Australian John Farnham (who had just had a major hit with *You're the Voice*) to perform *Dare to Dream* at the opening ceremony of the Olympic Games before the biggest audience of her career, in Sydney. Undertakes 14-date *Millennium Tour* based on her *Greatest Hits* album. Tours Hong Kong and Korea. Joins Vince Gill on a Christmas CD for Hallmark stores in the US. Continues to promote CHEC charity. Performs *Somewhere over the Rainbow* at a charity concert before the Pope in Vatican City. Supported former fiancée Bruce Welch who became a prostate cancer patient, encouraging him to fight the disease as he faced surgery.

2001: Teams again with Anthony Warlow and John Farnham on a '*Main Event*' tour for the centenary of Australian Federation celebrations. Attends 10th Annual Human Rights Campaign Gala in February in Los Angeles with cameraman boyfriend Patrick McDermott. Films TV movie '*Wilde Girls*' with daughter Chloe (shown on Showtime in US). Films wildlife TGV *One World* documentary about the Galapagos Islands. Undertakes 27-date tour of the US and Canada. Releases greatest hits album *Magic* and her first Christmas album, *The Christmas Collection*. Appears on her charity's educational video and continues promotion of CHEC's Childproofing campaign. Spends Christmas in Australia with Chloe who works on her own acting and music career. Daughter Chloe makes first recording deal.

2002: Begins '*Heartstrings World Tour*,' her 12th concert tour (and third world-tour) with shows in North America, Australia and Japan. Receives award in Australia for services to Australian music. Performs charity work for Planet Ark. With friend Pat Farrar launches Koala Blue wine in the US in a three-way deal between Snowdon Wines Pty Ltd and US wine importer Distillerie Stock. Launches cancer support centre project with appeal for donations. Chloe portrays Chrissy in a Melbourne stage production of the 1960s musical '*Hair*.'

2003: '*Heartstrings World Tour*' continues on the East Coast of the US. Tours Australia and Japan and back to US. '*Grease*' album re-released for 25th anniversary. Mother Irene dies in Melbourne on 29 August, aged 89.

2004: Releases first music video DVD containing five videos. Indigo CD released in Australia (covering female artists that have influenced her career). Performs with Cliff Richard at Royal Variety performance in UK. '*Heartstrings World Tour*' continues. Promotes Liv-Kit, a breast self-examination product, in Australia. Chloe starts treatment for eating disorder (anorexia).

2005: Sings *Magic* at Australian Open men's tennis final in Melbourne. *Indigo* CD released in UK and undertakes promotional tour there. *Stronger than Before* album released in Hallmark stores in North America, includes *Can I trust Your Arms* written by daughter Chloe. Tours US. Opens Gaia retreat in Byron Bay, a 22-room boutique on 8 ha of hinterland offering a day spa, saltwater pool and walking tracks. Her Korean-born American cameraman boyfriend Patrick McDermott, 48, goes missing on an overnight boat trip off California, sparking a decades-long mystery over his whereabouts. The US Coast Guard rules that McDermott most likely was lost at sea but rumours persist that he faked his own death and went to live in Mexico.

2006: Appeal for cancer support centre in Melbourne reaches $A50 million, half its goal. *Stronger Than Before* released in Australia and Japan. Tours Japan and Australia, then the US. '*Grease*' re-released on DVD. *Grace and Gratitude* CD released in Walgreen Stores in the US. Takes share in an Australian racehorse named *I Got Chills*. Receives Lifetime Achievement Award during Australia Day gala. Awarded the AO (Officer of the Order of Australia) in the Queen's Birthday Honours List for her services to the entertainment industry as a singer and actor, and to the community through organisations supporting breast cancer treatment, education, training and research, and the environment.

2007: *Christmas Wish* CD released. '*Live in Sydney*' DVD from 2006 Australian Tour airs on PBS television. Attends '*Xanadu*' stage play premiere in New York with John Easterling. Helps daughter Chloe recover from anorexia. Friend and Australian musician Billy Thorpe dies suddenly.

MUCH TO DO

2008: Takes part in the in the Great Walk to Beijing to raise money and awareness for the Olivia Newton-John Cancer Centre. Marries John Easterling, a natural-health businessman and conservationist, with shared interest in spirituality and holistic cures. Supports friend Australian actor Hugh Jackman for the premiere of the film *'Australia.'* Releases 23rd and final studio album in Australia (including duets with Richard Marks and Keith Urban), then world-wide to coincide with cancer wellness centre fundraising. Has role in *'Sordid Lives: The Series'* launched on American TV (as a prequel to the 2000 film *'Sordid Lives.'* Album *Olivia's Live Hits* released. Takes part in the BBC Wales program *'Coming Home'* about her Welsh family history. Joins Anne Murray on Murray's last album, *Duets: Friends & Legends*. Releases *'Olivia Newton-John and the Sydney Symphony Orchestra: Live at the Sydney Opera House'*.

2009: Hosts Olivia Newton-John & Friends in Concert, a fundraising gala event in Sydney, for the Olivia Newton-John Cancer and Wellness Centre. With husband John Easterling purchases a new $US 4.1 million home in Jupiter Inlet, Florida.

2010: Stars in the film *'Score: A Hockey Musical'*, released in Canada, portraying Hope Gordon, mother of a home-schooled hockey prodigy. Film opens the 2010 Toronto International Film Festival. Attends (with husband) 'G'Day USA Gala' with John Travolta. Makes first appearance on '*Glee*' a musical comedy-drama TV series on US Fox network, recreating her '*Physical*' video with Jane Lynch. Performance released as a digital single which peaks at No. 89 on the *Billboard* Hot 100. Hosts the animal and nature series '*Wild Life*' in Australia. Daughter Chloe releases debut single *Wings and a Gun*.

2011: Begins filming the comedy '*A Few Best Men*' in Australia with director Stephan Elliott, in the role of mother of the bride. Releases '*Tre uomini e una pecora*', shown out of competition at the Rome Film Festival, performing much of the soundtrack and the closing song, *Weightless*.

2012: Australia issues a 60 cents postage stamp to help raise funds for the Olivia Newton-John Cancer & Wellness Centre Appeal. Begins '*A Summer Night with Olivia Newton-John*' tour, her 18th concert tour, in support of for her sixth soundtrack '*A Few Best Men*.' Teams with John Travolta to make the charity album *This Christmas*, in support of The Olivia Newton-John Cancer & Wellness Centre and the Jett Travolta Foundation.

THE VEGAS YEARS

2013: Pictured on an Australian commemorative postage stamp in the 'Living Legends' series. Her continuing UK tour takes in Bournemouth, Brighton, Birmingham, Manchester and Cardiff. Tours Asia as well as UK. A residency at the Flamingo Las Vegas is postponed due to the death in May of her elder sister, Rona (aged 72), from a brain tumour. It is later revealed that despite a successful operation earlier her cancer had returned but keeps details private at the time.

2014: Resumes performing with 45 shows in her '*Summer Nights*' concert residency in the Donny & Marie Showroom at the Flamingo Las Vegas, accompanied by an eight-piece band. Compiles a new EP, *Hotel Sessions*, including seven tracks of unreleased demos recorded between 2002 and 2011 with her nephew Brett Goldsmith and released independently by Olivia Productions, her own production company. It was also her last album from her company before she signs with Sony Music Australia. Album is dedicated to Rona, her sister and Brett Goldsmith's mother.

2015: Inducted into the Music Victoria Hall of Fame. With husband John Easterling purchases a 4.8 hectares (12 acres) ranch, in Santa Ynez, California, for $US 4.69 million. Appears as a guest judge on an episode of '*RuPaul's Drag Race*.' Vegas residency show extends through 2015 to 2016, resulting in a live album, *Summer Nights: Live in Las Vegas*. Performs 117 concerts. Has her first number-one single on *Billboard*'s Dance Club Songs chart with *You Have to Believe* with daughter Chloe and producer Dave Audé. The song is a re-imagining of her 1980 single *Magic*, to celebrate both the 35th anniversary of '*Xanadu*' and as a dedication to her daughter. It is the first mother-daughter single to reach No. 1 on the *Billboard* Dance Club Play chart.

2016: Las Vegas concert residency ends. Performs 78 concerts in Vegas and other venues in the USA and Canada. Tours Brazil, Argentina, Peru, Chile and Ecuador. Releases a new album with Beth Nielsen Chapman and Amy Sky called *Liv On*, inspired by their experiences of grief, loss and illness. Performs at Montclair, New Jersey's Wellmont Theatre, including a '*Grease*' medley with Didi Conn ('Frenchy') called up from the audience to recreate some 'Pink Ladies' memories.

MORE BAD NEWS

2017: Performs at the Viña del Mar International Song Festival (also known as Viña 2017) at Quinta Vergara Amphitheatre, in Viña del Mar, Chile, in March. Commits to a joint concert tour with American singer-songwriters Beth Nielsen Chapman and Amy Sky to promote *Liv On* and produces a CD of the same name. After beating off breast cancer twice, there's bad news in May: the cancer has returned and metastasised (spread to a new site via blood or lymph vessels) to her lower back. Starts treatment with medical cannabis. Tours to promote *Liv On* album but is forced to cancel concerts in the US and Canada because of sciatica complications and treatment. It is revealed that back pain is caused by the return of breast cancer that's reached stage IV. Appears alongside daughter Chloe in in '*Sharknado 5: Global Swarming.*'

2018: Receives an Honorary Doctorate of Letters from La Trobe University, Melbourne, in June, recognition for her 'significant and ongoing support of cancer research and holistic health,' as well as her outstanding achievements in the entertainment industry.

Cancer leads to a fractured sacrum in September. She has to learn to walk again, with excruciating pain. First treated with morphine, but changed to cannabis. Appears on Australian television shows talking about her cancer battles and her charity.

2019: Her brother, Melbourne-based physician Hugh Newton-John dies, aged 80. She has her 71st birthday with a quiet dinner at the hospital where she was being treated with radiation. Releases autobiography, '*Don't Stop Believin.*' Auction House sells more than 500 items, including the skin-tight black pants she wore in '*Grease*', at an auction in Beverley Hills. Auction raises $US 2.4 million, her '*Grease*' outfit selling for $US 405,700. Proceeds go to her Australian-based cancer treatment centre. With '*Grease*' co-star John Travolta revives their 'Sandy' and 'Danny' roles for a '*Meet n' Grease*' singalong in West Palm Beach, Florida. Puts her New South Wales farm and her southern California ranch up for sale. Instead of selling the ranch, transfers the title to husband John Easterling. Awarded Australia's highest honour, the Companion of the Order of Australia, in June in recognition for 'her work as an entertainer and philanthropist.' It is revealed that she is was among hundreds of artists whose material was destroyed in the 2008 Universal Studios fire in the San Fernando Valley area of Los Angeles County, California.

2020: Awarded Dame Commander of the Order of the British Empire (DBE) honour in Queen Elizabeth II's New Year's Honours List for her services to charity, cancer research and entertainment. Appears at the Fire Fight Australia charity fundraising benefit concert at ANZ Stadium Sydney on Sunday, 16 February to raise money for national bushfire relief after the 2019–20 Australian bushfire season, known as the 'Black Summer'. A related album by the various artists, *Artists Unite for Fire Fight: Concert for National Bushfire Relief* is released by Sony. It is her final public performance. Chloe appears as a contestant on '*Dancing with the Stars*' television program.

2021: Her final single, *Window in the Wall*, a duet about unity recorded with daughter Chloe Lattanzi, is released. The music video for the song peaked at No. 1 on the iTunes pop music video chart the week of its release.

2022: As her cancer worsens, she decides to spend her remaining time at the family ranch in California.

August 8: Dame Olivia Newton-John passed away peacefully at her Ranch in Southern California this morning, surrounded by family and friends. In keeping with her wishes, she was cremated, and her ashes scattered over Byron Bay, Australia, in parts of California and other places she loved.

Endnotes

Olivia's Afterlife Impact

1a. & 1b. Nov 9. 2024 Herald Sun V Weekend Gagazine. Grace Baldwin "Rock's New Hot Shots"

1b. Marie Claire/Remembering The Life Of Olivia Newton-John. Cameron Adams

2. https://www.hellomagazine.com/celebrities/20230307166063/whitney-houston-olivia-newton-john-ronnie-spector-advocates-for-women-international-womens-day/ March 7, 2023/ Justin Ravitz

3. Peter Ford * Sunrise Ch7 Entertainment reporter 2023 /Looking back on Olivia

4b/4c. https://www.theguardian.com/film/2022/aug/09/olivia-newton-john-was-a-trailblazer-in-the-art-of-pop-reinvention/ Wed 10 Aug 2022/ Angelica Frey

5. https://www.hellomagazine.com/celebrities/20230307166063/whitney-houston-olivia-newton-john-ronnie-spector-advocates-for-women-international-womens-day/ March 7, 2023/ Justin Ravitz

6. Album and single dates vary due to region. https://nypost.com/2022/08/09/olivia-newton-john-tops-charts-with-7-songs-after-her-death/

7. https://www.countryuniverse.net/2023/02/24/an-olivia-newton-john-retrospective-part-fourteen-2020-2022/

8a & 8b. "https://olivianewton-john.com/celebrate-the-season-with-four-time-grammy-winning-legend-olivia-newton-johns-

9. https://olivianewton-john.com/olivia-dolly-parton-team-up-for-new-duet-of-jolene/

10. https://people.com/olivia-newton-john-sings-about-her-dream-on-long-lost-recording-exclusive-8715550

11. https://7news.com.au/the-morning-show/olivia-newton-john-sings-about-her-dream-in-new-song-after-a-friend-found-late-stars-lost-music-c-16225988

12. OnlyOlivia.com

13a. https://www.thecoast.net.nz/news/olivia-newton-john-s-daughter-chloe-lattanzi-releases-new-song-in-tribute-to-her-mum/

14. https://www.adelaidefestivalcentre.com.au/media-centre/media-releases/tottie-goldsmith-joins-adelaide-cabaret-festival-line-up-with-hopelessly-devoted-a-celebration-of-olivia-newton-john

15. https://www.theguardian.com/film/2022/aug/09/olivia-newton-john-was-a-trailblazer-in-the-art-of-pop-reinvention/ Wed 10 Aug 2022/ Angelica Frey

16a &16b. Marie Claire/ Remembering The Life Of Olivia Newton-John/ Cameron Adams

17. https://www.theguardian.com/film/2022/aug/08/your-impact-was-incredible-hollywood-mourns-the-loss-of-olivia-newton-john
18. Marie Claire/Remembering The Life Of Olivia Newton-John. Cameron Adams
19. https://www.forbes.com/sites/robinraven/2020/10/20/olivia-newton-john-shares-news-on-gaia-retreat--spa-and-her-new-foundation/
20. https://people.com/music/olivia-newton-john-daughter-chloe-lattanzi-on-grief-keeping-mission-alive/Janine Rubenstein March 3, 2023
21. https://www.walkforwellness.com.au/theonjcentre
22a &22b. https://www.walkforwellness.com.au 2024
23. https://people.com/music/olivia-newton-john-daughter-chloe-lattanzi-on-grief-keeping-mission-alive/ Janine Rubenstein March 3, 2023
24a. Melanie Macleod /WELLNESS EDITOR August 22, 2023 https://www.hellomagazine.com/author/melanie-macleod/
24b & 24c. By Serena Seyfort • Afternoon Editor/Feb 26, 2023 9news.com.au
25a & 25b. https://www.hellomagazine.com/celebrities/20230307166063/whitney-houston-olivia-newton-john-ronnie-spector-advocates-for-women-international-womens-day/ March 7, 2023/ Justin Ravitz
26. https://www.hellomagazine.com/celebrities/720683/olivia-newton-john-widow-honest-love-life-update/Beatriz Colon September 26, 2024
27a & 27b. https://people.com/author/erin-clements/

Part 1: Intro

1. *New Idea* Olivia special Aug 22. 2022
2. 'Legacy Lives on' Jane Rocca, Domain
3. Olivia Newton-John Cancer Wellness & Research Centre website
4. Olivia Newton-John's tale of two Sandy's *New Yorker* Aug 9, Rachel Syme
5. https://www.nbcnews.com/think/opinion/olivia-newton-john-grease-star-australian-icon-british-dame-was-tough-rcna42225 By Kelly Hartog,
6a *The Daily Mail* UK. Online Oct 2022
6b https://www.nbcnews.com/think/opinion/olivia-newton-john-grease-star-australian-icon-british-dame-was-tough-rcna42225 By Kelly Hartog,
7. https://amnplify.com.au/media-statement-from-australian-women-in-music-awards-in-recognition-of-honor-role-inductee-olivia-newton-john/
8. Vicki Gordon, Founding AWMA https://amnplify.com.au/media-statement-from-australian-women-in-music-awards-in-recognition-of-honor-role-inductee-olivia-newton-john/
9a https://www.theaustralian.com.au
9b *SMH* Hopelessly devoted:Olivia was the queen of my childhood Jordan Baker
9c Recent *Herald Sun* article on Melbourne Rock and roll Hall of Fame. Nui Te Koha 6/11/2022
10. Vicki Gordon, Founding AWMA https://amnplify.com.au/media-statement-from-australian-women-in-music-awards-in-recognition-of-honor-role-inductee-olivia-newton-john/

11. https://www.nbcnews.com/think/opinion/olivia-newton-john-grease-star-australian-icon-british-dame-was-tough-rcna42225 By Kelly Hartog, journalist, editor and book coach NBC
12. *Woman's Weekly* Olivia special Oct 2022
13. Vicki Gordon, Founding AWMA https://amnplify.com.au/media-statement-from-australian-women-in-music-awards-in-recognition-of-honor-role-inductee-olivia-newton-john/
14. Only Olivia.com/AWIM/Wikipedia/Online bios
15. https://www.nbcnews.com/think/opinion/olivia-newton-john-grease-star-australian-icon-british-dame-was-tough-rcna42225 By Kelly Hartog, journalist, editor and book coach
16. *SMH* Hopelessly devoted: Olivia was the queen of my childhood Jordan Baker Aug 9
17. 1981 Album and Single of healing music '*Grace And Gratitude*'
18. 2007 Singapore interview REUTERS/Sulastri Osman
19. Australian musician and actor Rick Springfield.

Chapter 1: Childhood, Cambridge and Heritage blood
1. Olivia Google quotes
2. https://blog.12min.com/dont-stop-believin-pdf-summary/
3. Olivia Newton-John Interview 30 August 1994 Over lunch at Shelley Beach, Ballina, NSW © Debbie Kruger
4. https://lostcambridge.wordpress.com/2020/06/15/brinley-newton-john-headmaster-of-the-cambridgeshire-high-school-for-boys-today-hills-road-sixth-form-college/
5.-7. https://blog.12min.com/dont-stop-believin-pdf-summary/
8. Bio details from collected sources Biography channel/ Wikipedia / Australian Dictionary of Biography/ Onlyolivia.com /AMIMUSic Newton-John, Brinley (Brin) (1914–1992) by John Stowell and Jill Stowell
9. https://blog.12min.com/dont-stop-believin-pdf-summary/
10. https://adb.anu.edu.au/lifesummary/newtonjohn-brinley-brin-18243
11-12. https://blog.12min.com/dont-stop-believin-pdf-summary/
13. Olivia co-founded Gaia Retreat & Spa and Retreatment Botanics, retreatmentbotanics.com.
14. Olivia Newton-John Interview. 30 August 1994
Over lunch at Shelley Beach, Ballina, NSW© Debbie Kruger
15-17. https://blog.12min.com/dont-stop-believin-pdf-summary/
Don't Stop Believin' Viking/Penguin Random House 2019
18. https://www.ed.ac.uk/about/people/plaques/born#:
19. https://www.scottishdailyexpress.co.uk/celebrity-news/olivia-newton-johns-scottish-family-27690664
20. https://www.univerlag.uni-goettingen.de/bitstream/handle/3/isbn-978-3-86395- 3867/born beyond.pdf

21-23. https://blog.12min.com/dont-stop-believin-pdf-summary/
Don't Stop Believin' Viking/Penguin Random House 2019
24. https://blog.12min.com/dont-stop-believin-pdf-summary/
Don't Stop Believin' Viking/Penguin Random House 2019

Chapter 2: Address all Newton-John mail to Melbourne, Australia.

1 *Herald Sun* / Melbourne Rock and roll Hall of Fame/ Nui Te Koha 6/11/2022
2. https://www.traveller.com.au/melbourne-the-music-town-
3. https://beat.com.au/its-official-melbourne-declared-live-music-capital-of-the-world/
4. https://lens.monash.edu/2018/04/17/1347608/the-beating-heart-of-melbourne-.
5.Amazon reviews
6. https://lens.monash.edu/2018/04/17/1347608/the-beating-heart-of-melbourne-
7a https://theculturetrip.com/pacific/australia/articles/the-10-best-music-artists-from-melbourne/
7b. https://www.smh.com.au/culture/music/so-what-is-the-melbourne-sound-local-musicians-have-some-thoughts-20211122-p59b06.html
7c. Phoebe Bennett https://www.abc.net.au/doublej/music-reads/features/50-game-changing-women-australian-music/13215104
7d. https://www.smh.com.au/entertainment/music/melbourne-puts-rock-icon-chrissy-amphlett-on-the-map-20150218-13i9jv.htmlThe late Divinyls singer Chrissy Amphlett
8a and 8b. https://www.theage.com.au/national/victoria/what-is-it-that-makes-melbourne-the-music-capital-20220812-p5b9di.html/ Jon Faine
9. https://www.heraldsun.com.au/news/victoria/melbourne-in-danger-of-losing-reputation-as-live-music-capital/news-story
10. https://themusicnetwork.com/michael-gudinski-melbourne-achiever-award/
11. Olivia Quotes/Google
12. https://blog.12min.com/dont-stop-believin-pdf-summary/
13. https://blog.12min.com/dont-stop-believin-pdf-summary/
14. https://adb.anu.edu.au/biography/newtonjohn-brinley-brin-18243
15 -17. https://blog.12min.com/dont-stop-believin-pdf-summary/\
18. *Don't Stop Believin'* CH1.VikingPenguinRandom House 2019
19. https://uk.style.yahoo.com/much-demand-little-remembering-dame-
20. *SMH* Aug 11 Anthony Segaert
21 -24. *Don't Stop Believin'* CH1.VikingPenguinRandom House 2019
25. Olivia Newton-John Interviewhttp://pocketoz.com.au/afe/pop-migrants.html
26. *Don't Stop Believin'* CH1.VikingPenguinRandom House 2019
27. https://www.thelist.com/960606/the-stunning-transformation-of-olivia-newton-john
28. Olivia Quotes/ Google

29. https://www.dailymail.co.uk/tvshowbiz/article-11093335/How-Lovely-Lizzy-charmed-Australia-Olivia-Newton-John
30. https://www.nowtolove.com.au/celebrity/celeb-news/olivia-newton-john-best-moments-74653

Chapter 3: The UK Sixties World Beckons

1. *Don't Stop Believin'* Viking Penguin Random House 2019 p27
2. Olivia Newton-John Google quotes
3. https://www.historic-uk.com/CultureUK/The-1960s-The-Decade-that-Shook-Britain
4. *Don't Stop Believin'* Viking/Penguin Random House 2019
5. 7 news.com
6. *Don't Stop Believin'* Viking/Penguin Random House 2019
7. https://en.wikipedia.org/wiki/Olivia_Newton-John
8. Chris McLeod researcher
9. https://www.onlyolivia.com/aboutonj/irene/
10. https://www.onlyolivia.com/aboutonj/irene/
11.The Inspiring Women Who Shaped Olivia Newton-John Marie Claire / 5 Nov 2019
12. https://news.yahoo.com/underappreciated-singer-olivia-newton-john-162233919
13. Onlyolivia.com fan website
14. https://www.australian-information-stories.com/olivia-newton-john.html
15. https://au.rollingstone.com/music/music-news/olivia-newton-john-rob-sheffield-
16. https://www.nytimes.com/2022/08/08/arts/olivia-newton-john-dead.html
17. https://www.savingcountrymusic.com/olivia-newton-john-played-a-pivotal-role-in-country-music-rip/ with-a-song-covered-by-joe-pernice/ By Martin Jones.

Chapter 4. Country Music Star

1. https://outsider.com/american-entertainment/music-2/how-olivia-newton-john-became-an-important-figure-in-country-music/
2. https://outsider.com/american-entertainment/music-2/how-olivia-newton-john-became-an-important-figure-in-country-music/
3. https://www.abc.net.au/doublej/music-reads/features/50-game-changing-women-australian-music/13215104
4. Wikipedia
5. https://drum.lib.umd.edu › handle › umi-umd-2312
6. https://drum.lib.umd.edu › handle › umi-umd-2312
7. https://www.rollingstone.com/music/music-news/olivia-newton-john-rob-sheffield-1394426/
8. www.wideopencountry .com/olivia Newton John

9. https://rhythms.com.au/the-country-credentials-of-olivia-newton-john-r-i-p-
10a, 10b. NME https://www.nme.com/en_au/features/film-features/olivia-newton-john-obituary-grease-eurovision-physical-3286604
11. https://www.savingcountrymusic.com/olivia-newton-john-played-a-pivotal-role-in-country-music-rip/ with-a-song-covered-by-joe-pernice/ By Martin Jones.
12. https://www.savingcountrymusic.com/olivia-newton-john-played-a-pivotal-role-in-country-music-rip/ with-a-song-covered-by-joe-pernice/ By Martin Jones.
13. Wikipedia
14. https://www.nbcnews.com/think/opinion/olivia-newton-john-grease-star-australian-icon-british-dame-was-tough-rcna42225 By Kelly Hartog,
15. https://www.smh.com.au/culture/music/why-did-olivia-newton-john-make-it-in-the-us-when-so-many-others-didn-t-Michael Dwyer
16. *Don't Stop Believin'* Viking/Penguin Random House 2019 P 52
17.
18. https://www.rollingstone.com/music/music-news/olivia-newton-john-rob-sheffield-1394426/
19. Wikipedia
20. https://www.thelist.com/958114/what-you-never-knew-about-olivia-newton-john
21. Andrew Kayhttps://www.nationalworld.com/culture/music/olivia-newton-john-sandy-grease-country-singers-1970s-3799366
22. https://www.smh.com.au/culture/celebrity/a-woman-for-all-seasons-olivia-will-remain-something-specific-and-personal-to-each-of-us-20220809-p5b8hv.html
23. https://www.smh.com.au/culture/celebrity/a-woman-for-all-seasons-olivia-will-remain-something-specific-and-personal-to-each-of-us-20220809-p5b8hv.html
24. https://www.irishmirror.ie/showbiz/celebrity-news/olivia-newton-john-almost-turned-27711677
25. https://www.smh.com.au/culture/celebrity/a-woman-for-all-seasons-olivia-will-remain-something-specific-and-personal-to-each-of-us-20220809-p5b8hv.html
26. https://www.savingcountrymusic.com/olivia-newton-john-played-a-pivotal-role-in-country-music-rip/ with-a-song-covered-by-joe-pernice/ By Martin Jones.

Chapter 5: Grease –Ms Sandra Newton-John

1. https://www.nme.com/en_au/features/film-features/olivia-newton-john-obituary-grease-eurovision-physical-3286604
2. *Don't Stop Believin'* Viking/Penguin Random House 2019 p109
3. Wikipedia

4a. https://www.abc.net.au/news/2022-08-09/analysis-olivia-newton-john-bent-hollywood-to-her-whim/10679984
4b. http://www. nytimes.com 1978/6/ 11 archives
5. https://www.abc.net.au/news/2022-08-09/analysis-olivia-newton-john-bent-hollywood-to-her-whim/10679984
6. https://www.nbcnews.com/think/opinion/olivia-newton-john-grease-star-australian-icon-british-dame-was-tough-rcna42225 By Kelly Hartog,
7. https://www.abc.net.au/news/2022-08-09/analysis-olivia-newton-john-bent-hollywood-to-her-whim/10679984
8. The Guardian Peter Bradshaw 9 Aug 20200
9. New York times.com
10. Wikipedia
11. https://www.irishtimes.com/culture/film/grease-at-40-i-can-no-longer-hate-the-film-i-despised-in-1978-1.3471090
12. https://www.onlyolivia.com/memorabilia/presscut/70s/78-08-19-au-tv_week-01.htmlOlivia vows them at Grease Ball by Christine Richter and Molly Meldrum
13. 7news.com
14,15,16. *Vanity Fair* February 2016 issue/ How Grease Beat the Odds and Became the Biggest Movie Musical of the 20th Century
17. https://www.abc.net.au/news/2022-08-09/analysis-olivia-newton-john-bent-hollywood-to-her-whim/10679984 and she was one of
18. a &18 b https://7news.com.au/entertainment/inside-olivia-newton-john-and-john-travoltas-forbidden-love-they-werent-acting-c-7811496
19. Olivia Quotes Google
20. Watch What Happens Live with Andy Cohen "'Greased Lightning"' round of questions
21. https://www.smh.com.au/culture/celebrity/a-woman-for-all-seasons-olivia-will-remain-something-specific-and-personal-to-each-of-us-20220809-p5b8hv.html
22 & 23. https://www.newyorker.com/culture/postscript/olivia-newton-johns-tale-of-two-sandys
24. *Don't Stop Believin'* Viking/Penguin Random House 2019p99 p101
25. CrimeWiki
26. https://www.nbcnews.com/think/opinion/olivia-newton-john-grease-star-australian-icon-british-dame-was-tough-rcna42225 By Kelly Hartog,
27. https://www.abc.net.au/doublej/music-reads/features/50-game-changing-women-australian-music/13215104
28. E news/ and Host of A Life Of Greatness podcast
29. https://www.independent.co.uk/arts-entertainment/films/news/olivia-newton-john-grease-sexist-b1796196.html
30. *Don't Stop Believin'* Viking/Penguin Random House 2019 p 98
31. https://www.nowtolove.com.au/celebrity/celeb-news/olivia-newton-john-in-australia-62510

32. https://www.theguardian.com/film/2022/aug/08/olivia-newton-john-grease-xanadu-cult-classics-cherished-by-fans Peter Bradshaw 9 Aug 20200
33. https://decider.com/2022/09/16/olivia-newton-john-publicist-reacts-emmys-in-memoriam-snub/
34. https://www.washingtonpost.com/lifestyle/2022/08/09/olivia-newton-john-appreciation-essay/

Chapter 6: The Magic of Xanadu

1. https://www.nbcnews.com/think/opinion/olivia-newton-john-grease-star-australian-icon-british-dame-was-tough-rcna42225 By Kelly Hartog
2. *Vanity Fair* February 2016 issue / How Grease Beat the Odds and Became the Biggest Movie Musical of the 20th Century
3. Olivia Newton-John Google Quotes
4. New York times .com
5. https://www.onlyolivia.com/memorabilia/presscut/10s/18-10-22-us-popmatters.html
6. Wikipedia
7. https://www.theaustralian.com.au/the-oz/lifestyle/olivia-newtonjohn-is-our-great-music-chameleon/news-story/c8a72
8. https://citynews.com.au/2022/an-iconic-pop-culture-figure-olivia-newton-john-remembered/
9. https://www.newidea.com.au/olivia-newton-john-relationships
10a and 10b. Wikipedia
11. https://celebrity.nine.com.au/latest/olivia-newton-john-10-things-you-didnt-know-about-80s-film-xanadu
12. https://americansongwriter.com/meaning-xanadu-olivia-newton-john-song-lyrics/
13. https://celebrity.nine.com.au/latest/olivia-newton-john-10-things-you-didnt-know-about-80s-film-xanadu/
14a-14b. https://americansongwriter.com/meaning-xanadu-olivia-newton-john-song-lyrics/
15. https://www.washingtonpost.com/lifestyle/2022/08/09/olivia-newton-john-appreciation
16. Wikipedia
17 & 18 & 19. https://celebrity.nine.com.au/latest/olivia-newton-john-10-things-you-didnt-know-about-80s-film-xanadu/
20. Olivia Newton-John, quoted in The Billboard Book of Number One Hits by Fred Bronson
21. Onlyolivia.com   fan website
22. https://www.nytimes.com/2022/08/09/arts/music/olivia-newton-john-grease-physical.html Wesley Morris/
23. https://celebrity.nine.com.au/latest/olivia-newton-john-10-things-you-didnt-know-about-80s-film-xanadu/

Chapter 7: Trailblazing and Heady Years

1 & 2. https://www.theguardian.com/film/2022/aug/09/olivia-newton-john-was-a-trailblazer-in-the-art-of-pop-reinvention
3. https://www.6pr.com.au/the-uncanny-fact-about-olivia-newton-johns-video-for-hit-song-physical/
4a. Onlyolivia.com fan website
4b. https://www.nme.com/en_au/features/film-features/olivia-newton-john-obituary-grease-eurovision-physical-3286604
5. https://www.vogue.com/article/olivia-newton-john-most-memorable-roles
6. Saluting our seminal woman rockers/ Australian Musician Nov 29, 2007 Artists, Special Features/ November 29, 2007 | Author: Claire Hedger
7. https://www.nytimes.com/2022/08/09/arts/music/olivia-newton-john-grease-physical.html Wesley Morris/
8. https://en.wikipedia.org/wiki/Olivia_Newton-John_videography
9a and 9b. https://www.mediaweek.com.au/mercado-on-tv-remembering-olivia-newton-john-and-her-aussie-tv
10a and 10b. https://parade.com/852559/paulettecohn/delta-goodrem-on-her-real-life-friendship-with-olivia-newton-john-for-
11. https://www.hellomagazine.com/fashion/celebrity-style/20220809147714/olivia-newton-john-most-iconic-fashion-moments/
12. https://www.latimes.com/archives/la-xpm-1988-05-20-li-3848-story.html
13. https://www.abc.net.au/news/2022-08-09/olivia-newton-john-twists-and-turns/101313822
14. https://www.80sfashionworld.com/olivia-john-newton-outfits/Olivia
15. https://www.smh.com.au/lifestyle/fashion/from-grease-to-physical-and-koala-blue-olivia-newton-john-s-fashion-legacy-20220809-p5b8b3.html
16 & 17. The Lycra Legacy of Olivia Newton-John's 'Physical' https://www.nytimes.com/2022/08/09/style/lycra-olivia-newton-john-physical.html
18.https://www.australianmusicvault.com.au/music%20stories/read/olivia%20newton-john/
19. https://toofab.com/2019/12/11/olivia-newton-john-breaks-down-fan-returns-sandy-jacket-bought-auction/
20. https://www.hellomagazine.com/fashion/celebrity-style/20220809147714/olivia-newton-john-most-iconic-fashion-moments

Chapter 8: Lets Get Physical

1a. https://www.nbcnews.com/think/opinion/olivia-newton-john-grease-star-australian-icon-british-dame-was-tough-rcna42225 By Kelly Hartog
1b. Carl Arrington People Mag February 15, 1982
2. https://www.smh.com.au/culture/music/how-olivia-newton-john-guided-us-from-blissful-am-radio-to-raunchy-mtv
3. https://www.nytimes.com/2022/08/09/arts/music/olivia-newton-john-grease-physical.html Wesley Morris/

4. Salon.com By Alison Stine
5. Carl Arrington People Mag / February 15, 1982
6. Glenn A Baker . https://www.2hd.com.au/2022/08/09/rock-music-expert-glenn-a-baker-on-the-passing-of-olivia-newton-john/
7. https://www.nytimes.com/2022/08/09/arts/music/olivia-newton-john-grease-physical.html Wesley Morris/
8a. Wikipedia
8b. https://themusic.com.au/news/pink-tribute-olivia-newton-john/
9. Olivianewtonjohn.com.au
10. https://www.washingtonpost.com/lifestyle/2022/08/09/olivia-newton-john-appreciation-essay/
11. https://www.abc.net.au/doublej/music-reads/features/50-game-changing-women-australian-music/13215104
12. https://www.today.com.health
13. https://www.washingtonpost.com/lifestyle/2022/08/09/olivia-newton-john-appreciation-essay/
14. https://onlyolivia.com
15. https://www.theaustralian.com.au/the-oz/lifestyle/olivia-newtonjohn
16. Entertainment Weeklyhttps://ew.com/article/2008/04/07
17. https://www.smh.com.au/culture/music/why-did-olivia-newton-john-make-it-in-the-us-when-so-many-others-didn-t-Michael Dwyer
18. *Soul Kiss* Wikipedia

Chapter 9: Wellness Journey

1a. https://www.wellbeing.com.au/at-home/the-lasting-legacy-of-olivia-newton-john.html
1b. https://www.theguardian.com/film/2020/oct/26/olivia-newton-john-i-dont-wish-cancer-on-anyone-else-but-for-me-it-has-been-a-gift
2. Onlyolivia.com fan website
3. https://www.popmatters.com/olivia-newton-john-physical/4
4 & 5. Onlyolivia.com fan website
6a. https://people.com/music/olivia-newton-john-people-covers-through-the-years/2000.
6b. *Don't Stop Believin'* Viking/Penguin Random House 2019p166
7. https://www.countryuniverse.net/2018/08/28/an-olivia-newton-john-retrospective-part-ten-1987-1992/
8. https://www.thelist.com/958114/what-you-never-knew-about-olivia-newton-john/?utm_campaign=clip
9a. https://www.looktothestars.org/news/2067-exclusive-interview-look-to-the-stars-talks-to-olivia-newton-john
9b. Onlyolivia.com fan website
10. https://9now.nine.com.au/a-current-affair/olivia-newton-john-death-obituary-australias-sweetheart/410d3ba7-0876-421e-

11a. The Austin Health Foundation and The Olivia Centre
11b. https://www.theguardian.com/film/2022/aug/09/this-was-her-dream-olivia-newton-johns-legacy
12. People Mag 2013 Olivia Newton-John
12b. Michael Rowland interview ABC TV in 2017
13. Onlyolivia.com fan website
13b. https://www.theguardian.com/film/2020/oct/26/olivia-newton-john-i-dont-wish-cancer-on-anyone-else-but-for-me-it-has-been-a-gift /plant-based medicine
14. https://olivianewton-john.com/pre-order-physical-deluxe-edition/
15. https://www.wellbeing.com.au/at-home/the-lasting-legacy-of-olivia-newton-john.html
16a. News.com Aug 10 / The Post.
16b. https://www.heraldsun.com.au/entertainment/confidential/olivia-n
17. The Austin Health Foundation and The Olivia Centre
18, 19 & 20. https://www.theguardian.com/film/2022/aug/09/this-was-her-dream-olivia-newton-johns-legacy
21. https://www.heraldsun.com.au/news/victoria/onj-cancer-research-institute-announces-cancer-breakthrough/Olivia Cancer Research Institute announces cancer breakthrough
22. https://www.hellomagazine.com/celebrities/20221010153447/olivia-newton-john-niece-tottie-promise-letter/

Chapter 10: Earthmother

1a. https://www.gaiaretreat.com.au/a-message-from-the-gaia-team
1b. https://www.countryuniverse.net/2018/08/28/an-olivia-newton-john-retrospective-part-ten-1987-1992/
2. https://www.jaehakim.com/entertainment-reviews/music-reviews/olivia-newton-john-fine-tuned- Chicago Sun-Times September 3, 1999
3. OnlyOlivia.com
4. 1994 30 Aug / Olivia Newton-John Interview/ Over lunch at Shelley Beach, Ballina, NSW Debbie Kruger
5. jeremyhelligar.medium.com/olivia-newton-john-pops-first-female-chameleon
6. jeremyhelligar.medium.com/olivia-newton-john-pops-first-female-chameleon
7 & 8. OnlyOlivia.com
9. https://news.yahoo.com/underappreciated-singer-olivia-newton-john-Los Angeles Times.
10. https://au.rollingstone.com/t/olivia-newton-john/ 11. 11ahttps://news.yahoo.com/underappreciated-singer-olivia-newton-john-Los Angeles Times.
12a & 12b. OnlyOlivia.com
13. https://www.floridatoday.com/entertainment/2015/02/04
14. https://www.popmatters.com/olivia-newton-john-physical/
15a. Wikipedia

16.https://www.popmatters.com/olivia-newton-john-physical
17 & 18. https://www.looktothestars.org/news/2067-exclusive-interview-look-to-the-stars-talks-to-olivia-newton-john check
19, 20 & 21. OnlyOlivia.com
22. Social Media Death Notice by John Easterling August 10, 2022, 24.
23. https://au.rollingstone.com/t/olivia-newton-john/
24 & 25. https://jeremyhelligar.medium.com/olivia-newton-john-pops-first-female-chameleon- NPR and music critic Ann K Powers
26. Glenn A Baker https://www.6pr.com.au/the-uncanny-fact-about-olivia-newton-johns-video-for-hit-song-physical/
27. Newton-John explained on *The Rosie O'Donnell Show* in 1998. http://www. nytimes.com 1978/6/ 11 archives
28. https://au.rollingstone.com/t/olivia-newton-john/

Chapter 11: Legacy

1. Google
2a. https://www.nytimes.com/2022/08/09/arts/music/olivia-newton-john-grease-physical.html Wesley Morris/
2b. https://www.australianmusicvault.com.au/music/john/release 2019
3. https://www.nme.com/en_au/artists/olivia-newton-john
4. Dan Andrews/ https://www.reportdoor.com/olivia-newton-john-to-be-given-state-funeral-
5.. *Herald Sun* News. P6.3/02/2023 Olivia Newton John Memorial
6. https://celebrity.nine.com.au/latest/olivia-newton
7. Dan Andrews/ https://www.reportdoor.com/olivia-newton-john-to-be-given-state-funeral-
8. https://themusic.com.au/news/pink-tribute-olivia-newton-john/
9. https://themusic.com.au/news/pink-tribute-olivia-newton-john/ via *Rolling Stone*
10. https://www.smoothradio.com/artists/olivia-newton-john/mariah-carey-duet-hopelessly-devoted-to-you-1998-video/
11. https://www.jaehakim.com/entertainment-reviews/music-reviews/olivia-newton-john-fine-tuned-
12a. https://www.thelist.com/958114/what-you-never-knew-about-olivia-newton-john/
13a. Onlyolivia.com fan website
13b. https://jeremyhelligar.medium.com/olivia-newton-john-pops-first-female-chameleon-1008fbb26a71
14. Onlyolivia.com fan website
15. https://www.dawsonsgardenworld.com.au/product/hedging-rose-floribunda-olivia-newton-john
16. https://be.chewy.com/pet-parenting-pet-lovers-olivia-newton-john-devoted-to-animals/
17. Olivia Quotes Google

18. https://www.gaiaretreat.com.au/our-story/awards/
19a, 19b 19c. https://www.musicbusinessworldwide.com/primary-wave-music-publishing-strikes-partnership-with-olivia-newton-john/As a three-
20. https://www.australianmusicvault.com.au/music
21 & 22. https://www.smoothradio.com/artists/olivia-newton-john/mariah-Carey-duet-hopelessly-devoted-to-you-1998-video/
23. https://www.smoothradio.com/artists/bee-gees/abba-olivia-newton-john-rod-stewart-andy-gibb-duet/
24a and 24b. Neil Pharaoh @ProBonoNews
25. https://www.sandiegouniontribune.com/sdut-olivia-newton-john-reaches-conditional-settlement-2007dec04-story.html
26. https://www.smoothradio.com/artists/olivia-newton-john/new-song-daughter-chloe-lattanzi-duet
27. https://celebrity.nine.com.au/latest/olivia-newton-john-daughter-chloe-lattanzi-wrote-song-for-mum/52a5dbe4-ebcd-449a-8ae3-0d40bbce4753
28. www.dailymail.co.uk/MARTA JARY FOR DAILY MAIL AUSTRALIA
29. *Woman's Weekly* article oct 2022
30. https://forward.com/culture/421444/the-secret-jewish-history-of-olivia-newton-john/2019
31. 7news.com. 2022-10-02
32. OnlyOlivia.com

Part two: Introduction
1. https://www.theguardian.com/film/2022/aug/09/olivia-newton-john-was-a-trailblazer-in-the-art-of-pop-reinvention
2. *Don't Stop Believin'* Viking/Penguin Random House 2019
3. https://www.theaustralian.com.au/olivia
4. 1980 Aug *Countdown* interview tapes
5. https://www.nowtolove.com.au/celebrity/celeb-news/olivia-newton-john-in-australia-62510
6. Saluting our seminal woman rockers/ Australian Musician Nov 29, 2007 Artists, Special Features/ November 29, 2007 | Author: Claire Hedger

Chapter 12: Her Place amongst Women In Music
1. This episode written by Claire Hedger and produced by Tony Wyzenbeek. Series https://www.acmi.net.au/works/95003--love-is-in-the-air-eps-1-2/
2. *SMH* Hopelessly devoted: Olivia was the queen of my childhood Jordan Baker Aug 9
3. https://www.nbcnews.com/think/opinion/olivia-newton-john-grease-star-australian-icon-british-dame-was-tough-rcna42225 By Kelly Hartog
4. https://www.ilikeyouroldstuff.com/news/remembering-our-kings-queens-of-pop/David Laing
5. https://www.abc.net.au/doublej/music-reads/features/50-game-changing-

women-australian-music/13215104/ Dorothy Markek
6. Saluting our seminal woman rockers/ Australian Musician Nov 29, 2007 Artists, Special Features/ November 29, 2007 | Author: Claire Hedger
7. https://www.nme.com/en_au/news/film/rebel-wilson-pays-tribute-late-olivia-newton-john-3287048
8. https://www.thetoptens.com/music/artists-were-influenced-by-olivia-newton-john/
9. https://www.nfsa.gov.au/collection/curated/kylie-minogue-and-olivia-newton-johnotes by Beth Taylor
10b. https://www.abc.net.au/doublej/music-reads/features/50-game-changing-women-australian-music/13215104/ Dorothy Markek
11. https://themusicnetwork.com/double-j-iwd-music-list/
12. https://themusicnetwork.com/double-j-iwd-music-list/
13. https://themusicnetwork.com/double-j-iwd-music-list/ Nkechi Anele
13b. https://en.wikipedia.org/wiki/Chains_
14. http://musicfeeds.com.au/news/sia-might-be-rethinking-her-no-touring-policy/
15. http://musicfeeds.com.au/news/sia-might-be-rethinking-her-no-touring-policy/
16. https://www.news.com.au/entertainment/tv/morning-shows/emotional-vanessa-amorosi-stops-live-sunrise-interview/
17. Gab Burke/https://themusicnetwork.com/double-j-iwd-music-list/
18. https://www.escdaily.com/interview-jessica-mauboy/
19. WA NewsEntertainment https://www.perthnow.com.au/news/wa/jessica-mauboy-is-woman-of-the-hour-ng-72760d32da73272721eca63b09a9b561
20 & 21. https://www.oversixty.com.au/entertainment/music/first-look-at-delta-goodrem-as-olivia-newton-john
22. https://parade.com/852559/paulettecohn/delta-goodrem-on-her-real-life-friendship-with-olivia-newton-john-for-the-biopic-hopelessly-devoted-to-you/hen
23. https://uk.style.yahoo.com/olivia-newton-john-dannii-minogues
24. https://news.yahoo.com/underappreciated-singer-olivia-newton-john-
25. Olivia Newton-John Interview/ 30 August 1994/Debbie Kruger
26 & 27. https://jeremyhelligar.medium.com/olivia-newton-john-pops-first-female-chameleon
28. https://music.apple.com/au/playlist/inspired-by-olivia-newton-john
29. https://www.last.fm/music/Helen+Reddy/+wiki/ Fred Bronson's The Billboard Book of Number One Hits
30. https://www.mi.edu/news/18-quotes-women-music-industry-career-feminism/
31. May Ask an Aussie series/ Olivia Newton-John /Taipei on Saturday 7 May.
32. Sky News Australia 9 Aug 2022 Reporter Chloe Melas CNN Ent
33. Jim Bright, FAPS /Professor of Career Education

https://www.smh.com.au/business/workplace/who-do-you-aspire-to-be
34. https://www.forbes.com/sites/andreabossi/2021/03/26/these-are-3-of-the-biggest-reported-drivers-of-gender-inequality-in-music
35. 1994 30 Aug / Olivia Newton-John Interview, Ballina, NSW Debbie Kruger
36, 37, 38, 39. https://womeninmusicawards.com.au/honour-roll/

Chapter 13: Chloe: Family love is why we are here

1. Olivia Newton-John Interview 30 August 1994/Debbie Kruger
2. Olivia Newton-John Google quotes
3. https://www.marieclaire.com.au/olivia-newton-john-inspiring-women Nov 2019 - by Alley Pascoe
4. *Don't Stop Believin'* Viking/Penguin Random House 2019
5 *Don't Stop Believin'* Viking/Penguin Random House 2019
6. https://www.heraldsun.com.au/entertainment/celebrity/missed-out-a-lot-how-fame-took-toll-on-olivia-newtonjohns-daughter/news- Sarah Grynberg's
7. https://www.news.com.au/entertainment/celebrity-life/chloe-lattanzi-opens-up-about-conquering-her-mental-health-battles
8a. https://www.heraldsun.com.au/entertainment/celebrity/missed-out-a-lot-how-fame-took-toll-on-olivia-newtonjohns-daughter
8b. Olivia Newton-John Interview 30 August 1994/Debbie Kruger
9. https://www.heraldsun.com.au/entertainment/celebrity/missed-out-a-lot-how-fame- took-toll-on-Olivia-newtonjohns-daughter
10. https://www.heraldsun.com.au/entertainment/celebrity/missed-out-a-lot-how-fame-took-toll-on-olivia-newtonjohns-daughter
11. 2016/60 Minutes
12a & 12b. https://www.news.com.au/entertainment/celebrity-life/chloe-lattanzi-opens-up-about-conquering-her-mental-health-battles/news-story/236a4ca
13. interview /10 News First /2020
14. Wikipedia
15. https://www.heraldsun.com.au/entertainment/celebrity/missed-out-a-lot-how-fame-took-toll-on-olivia-newtonjohns-daughter
16. https://www.heraldsun.com.au/entertainment/celebrity/missed-out-a-lot-how-fame-took-toll-on-olivia-newtonjohns-daughter
17, 18, 19, 20. Chloe Social Media (chloelattanziofficial)
21a. 7news.com.au /sunrise
21b. https://www.jaehakim.com/entertainment-reviews/music-reviews/olivia-newton-john-fine-tuned- Chicago Sun-Times September 3, 1999
22. *Women's Weekly* Oct 2022-09-14
23. https://www.marieclaire.com.au/olivia-newton-john-inspiring-women Nov 2019 - by Alley Pascoe
24. Olivia Newton-John Google quotes
25. A Life of Greatness podcast in 2021
26. Social Media/Tottie Goldsmith

27, 28, 29. https://www.heraldsun.com.au/entertainment/confidential/olivia-n Digital /Toby Newton-John Wellness walk
*All Sources: WikiTree, Australian Dictionary of Biography, www.imdb.com, onlyolivia.com, obituaries in various newspapers.

Chapter 14: Boys Boys Boys …

1. *Don't Stop Believin'* Viking/Penguin Random House 2019
2. *SMH* Aug 11 2022 https://www.smh.com.au/culture/celebrity/
3. *SMH* Aug 11 https://www.smh.com.au/culture/celebrity/Anthony Segaert
4 & 5. www.dailymail.co.uk/tvshowbiz/articleIt's
6. https://www.hitc.com/en-gb/2022/08/09/olivia-newton-john-was-engaged-to-bruce-welch-but-they-never-made-it-down-the-aisle/
7. https://www.thesun.co.uk/tvandshowbiz/19486885/olivia-newton-john-crazed-stalker/
8, 9 &10. https://www.hitc.com/en-gb/2022/08/09/olivia-newton-john-was-engaged-to-bruce-welch-but-they-never-made-it-down-the-aisle/
11. https://www.thesun.co.uk/tvandshowbiz/19486885/olivia-newton-john-crazed-stalker/
12a. Olivia Newton John Wikipedia
12b. https://www.onlyolivia.com/memorabilia/presscut/80s/82-02-15-us-people.html/People Mag
12c. Olivia Newton John Wikipedia
13. https://www.onlyolivia.com/memorabilia/presscut/80s/82-02-15-us-people.html/People Mag
14 & 15. *Don't Stop Believin'* Viking/Penguin Random House 2019
16. https://www.onlyolivia.com/memorabilia/presscut/80s/82-02-15-us-people.html/People Mag
17. *Don't Stop Believin'* Viking/Penguin Random House 2019
18a. https://www.onlyolivia.com/memorabilia/presscut/80s/82-02-15-us-people.html/People Mag
18b. NBC News Think piece/ Aug. 10, 2022 / Kelly Hartog,
19. This Is Your Life TV files
20. *Don't Stop Believin'* Viking/Penguin Random House 2019
21a. https://www.thesun.co.uk/tvandshowbiz/19486885/olivia-newton-john-crazed-stalker/
21b. https://www.marieclaire.com.au/olivia-newton-john-boyfriend-missing
22. April 27, 2007. reuters/sulastri osman by jacqueline wong singapore
23. Olivia Google Quotes
24 & 25a .https://www.thelist.com/958114/what-you-never-knew-about-olivia-newton-john
25b. Olivia Newton John Foundation website
26. CH Nine Today Show/Olivia Newton-John.
27. John Easterling Instagram

28. Olivia Quotes /Google
29. *Don't Stop Believin'* Viking/Penguin Random House 2019
30a. https://www.bluemountainsgazette.com.au/story/7855744/katoomba-environmental-campaigner-remembers-friendship-with-olivia-newton-john/
30b. https://www.looktothestars.org/news/2067-exclusive-interview-look-to-the-stars-talks-to-olivia-newton-john
31. Bindi Irwin Instagram
32a. https://sports.yahoo.com/cliff-richard-shares-moving-tribute-104235256.html
32b. Chris McLeod /Wilkinson Publishing research
33. https://www.auspop.com.au/2016/10/john-farnham-olivia-newton-john-friends-christmas/
34. https://www.smoothradio.com/artists/olivia-newton-john/john-travolta-relationship-dating-grease/
35. Mamma Mia No Filter podcast in 2018,
36 & 37. https://www.foxnews.com/entertainment/olivia-newton-john-defied-all-odds-before-death-says-best-friend-jane-seymour-she-wasnt-afraid
38. https://www.dailymail.co.uk/tvshowbiz/article-11107727/Olivia-Newton-Johns-best-friend-Susan-George-pays-moving-tribute-late-Grease-star.html

Chapter 15: Musicologists and the LGBTQIA+ love

1. https://www.rollingstone.com/music/music-news/olivia-newton-john-rob-sheffield-1394426/
2. Neil Pharaoh | @ProBonoNews
3. Andy Bentley https://www.quora.com/What-is-the-importance-of-musicology-and-how-is-it-useful-in-society M.Mus in Musicology & Franz Liszt (composer), University of Cape Town (Graduated 1995)
4. Andy Bentley https://www.quora.com/What-is-the-importance-of-musicology-and-how-is-it-useful-in-society
5a. Melbourne University.com staff online
5b. Salon.com By ALISON STINE
6. Salon.com By ALISON STINE
7. LogoTV in 2008.
8. Wikipedia
9. AtlantisCruises jan 2018
10. Salon.com By ALISON STINE
11. https://www.pinknews.co.uk
12. Star Observer online/ Olivia Newton John
13. Neil Pharaoh | @ProBonoNews/
14. Wikipedia
15. https://www.smh.com.au/national/love-is-love-olivia-newton-john-backs-gay-marriage-20120123-1qdaq.html
16a & 16b. https://www.smh.com.au/national/love-is-love-olivia-newton-john-

backs-gay-marriage-20120123-1qdaq.html
17. LogoTV

Separate References provide by Dr Kat for her essay: '*When I heard the news of Olivia Newton-John's death*'
Encarnacao, J (2022) 'Three lessons Olivia Newton-John taught me about music - and life'. The Conversation. Online at: https://theconversation.com/three-lessons-olivia-newton-john-taught-me-about-music-and-life-188446 (accessed 7 September 2022).

Homan, S (2008) 'Playing to the thinkers or the drinkers? The sites and sounds of Oz Rock,' in Homan, S and Mitchell, T (eds.). Sounds of then, sounds of now: Popular music in Australia. ACYC Publishing, University of Tasmania.

Strong, C (2022) 'Pop Icon Olivia Newton-John was the rare performer whose career flourished through different phases'. The Conversation. Online at: https://theconversation.com/pop-icon-olivia-newton-john-was-the-rare-performer-whose-career-flourished-through-different-phases-188428 (accessed 7 September 2022).

Turner, G (1992) 'Australian Popular Music and its Contexts,' in Hayward, P (ed) From Pop to Punk to Postmodernism: Popular Music and Australian Culture from the 1960s to the 1990s. Allen and Unwin, Sydney.

Chapter 16: Australia- Olivia's 'Heart Home'
1. https://www.dailymail.co.uk/tvshowbiz/article-7133375/Olivia-Newton-John-cries-awarded-Companion-Order-Australia
2a. https://7news.com.au/the-morning-show/olivia-newton-john-receives-the-companion-of-the-order-of-australia-c-164248
2b. https://www.smh.com.au/national/hopelessly-devoted-olivia-was-the-queen-of-my-childhood-
2c. https://www.abc.net.au/news/2022-08-13/olivia-judith-archie-loss-legacy-giants-australia-music
3. https://www.nbcnews.com/think/opinion/olivia-newton-john-grease-star-australian-icon-british-dame-was-tough-rcna42225 By Kelly Hartog
4. Double J broadcaster Zan Rowe 50 list https://themusicnetwork.com
4b. https://www.nbcnews.com/think/opinion/olivia-newton-john-grease-star-australian-icon-british-dame-was-tough-rcna42225 By Kelly Hartog
5. Interview Magazine/https://www.thelist.com/960606/the-stunning-transformation-of-olivia-newton-john/?utm_campaign=clip
6. https://www.washingtonpost.com/archive/lifestyle/1982/07/31/australian-invasion/e05b181c-c886-46fa-ad9c-04ea7c036bb3/
7. https://probonoaustralia.com.au/news/2022/09/learning-from-olivia-newton-

john/
8a & 8b. https://twitter.com/SkyNewsAust/status/1557337162500038657
9. Wikipedia
10. https://blog.12min.com/dont-stop-believin-pdf-summary/
11. Better reading Autobio Don't Stop Believing review
12, 13, 14. https://www.heraldsun.com.au/news/victoria/olivia-newtonjohns-special-connection-to-melbourne
15. https://www.dailymail.co.uk/tvshowbiz/article-11094377/How-Olivia-Newton-John-Aussie-star-start-Byron-Bay-craze.html
16. https://womangoingplaces.com.au/Olivia Newton-John – My Top 5 Places
17. https://www.dailymail.co.uk/tvshowbiz/article-11094377/How-Olivia-Newton-John-Aussie-star-start-Byron-Bay-craze.html
18. News.com.au / Aug 15 / Seven special Spotlight Olivia – A Magical Life
19. Michael Dwyer August 13, 2022 / https://www.smh.com.au/culture/music/why-did-olivia-newton-john-make-it-in-the-us-when-so-many-others-didn-t-20220811-
20. Olivia Newton-John Interview/30 August 1994/, NSW/ Debbie Kruger
21, 22, 23. Michael Dwyer August 13, 2022 https://www.smh.com.au/culture/music/why-did-olivia-newton-john-make-it-in-the-us-when-so-many-others-didn-t-20220811-
24. https://www.heraldsun.com.au/news/victoria/olivia-newtonjohns-special-connection-to-melbourne
25. Michael Dwyer August 13, 2022 https://www.smh.com.au/culture/music/why-did-olivia-newton-john-make-it-in-the-us-when-so-many-others-didn-t-20220811-
26. https://www.smh.com.au/culture/celebrity/they-were-her-secret-ingredient-the-australians-who-helped-olivia-newton-john-conquer-the-world
27a, 27b. Wikipedia
28. https://www.heraldsun.com.au Olivia Newton-John: Actor Special connect to Melbourne
29. Music Network https://themusicnetwork.com/olivia-newton-johns-biggest-hits/
30. https://www.nbcnews.com/think/opinion/olivia-newton-john-grease-star-australian-icon-british-dame-was-tough-rcna42225 By Kelly Hartog

Chapter 17: Molly and Livvy

1. https://www.heraldsun.com.au/news/victoria/olivia-newtonjohns-special-connection-to-melbourne
2. *The Never, Um, Ever Ending Story* Ian Molly Meldrum. Life, *Countdown* and everything In Between with Jeff Jenkins in 2014
3. p120 *The Never, Um, Ever Ending Story* Ian Molly Meldrum. Life, *Countdown and everything In Between* with Jeff Jenkins in 2014
4. *Stellar* Magazine *Herald Sun*

5. August 1978 /https://www.onlyolivia.com/memorabilia/presscut/70s/78-08-19-au-tv_week-01.html. Olivia vows them at Grease Ball by Christine Richter and Molly Meldrum
6. August 1978 /https://www.onlyolivia.com/memorabilia/presscut/70s/78-08-19-au-tv_week-01.html. Olivia vows them at Grease Ball by Christine Richter and Molly Meldrum
7 to 13. Taken from both the *Countdown* Files ABC websites and Hey Hey It's Saturday online and Molly's memory.
14. Daryl Somers/ a sad dual loss for the nation @hey hey it's saturday facebook page

Chapter 18: Behind The Scenes 'Our Livvy' Recollections

1a. http://www.amiright.com/artists/olivianewtonjohn.shtml
1b. https://people.com/music/olivia-newton-john-remembered-by-fellow-music-and-film-stars-following-her-death-at-73/
2. https://radiotoday.com.au/ten-questions-richard-wilkins/https://www.bloomentertainment.com.au/djs-mcs/richard-wilkins
3. Today.com.au Olivia news Taken from *Women's Day* Magazine, *Today Show*
4. https://outsider.com/american-entertainment/people/today-shows-richard-wilkins-plays-heartbreaking-voicemail-from-olivia-newton-john-daughter-after-actress-death/
4b. https://www.foreignminister.gov.au/minister/julie-bishop/transcript-eoe/today-show-sydney-interview-richard-wilkins
5 to10. https://www.onlyolivia.com/news/events/06/laday/

Brett Goldsmith footnotes

1. https://www.scottholleran.com/interviews/interview-brett-goldsmith-hotel-sessions-olivia-newton-john/
2. Interview: Brett Goldsmith on 'Hotel Sessions' by Olivia Newton-John
Apr 29, 2014 | Scott Holleran
3. https://www.yahoo.com/news/olivia-newton-john-nephew-recalls-160838378.html
4. https://www.yahoo.com/news/olivia-newton-john-nephew-recalls-160838378.html

Chapter 19: Tributes

1. John Lennon *Rolling Stone*
2 & 3. NSW GIV.com Premier Dominic Perrottet and Minister for the Arts Ben Franklin
4 https://www.smh.com.au/national/hopelessly-devoted-olivia-was-the-queen-of-my-childhood
5. *Variety* magazine/Olivia .
6. https://www.heraldsun.com.au/entertainment/celebrity/missed-out-a-lot-

how-fame-took-toll-on-olivia-newtonjohns-daughter/news- Sarah Grynberg's A Life of Greatness podcast in 2021
7 & 8. Elvis Australia/Source: FECC/August 28, 2022 Elvis Articles, Elvis Interviews, Elvis Biography, Video and Audio, Elvis News/ text of an interview with Olivia Newton-John in 1974 broadcast on WGN Radio.
9. https://www.theaustralian.com.au/life/uniqueness-of-olivia-newtonjohns-voice-made-her-stand-out-
All Tributes @ sources Twitter/Instagram/Facebook/Radio/ABC and World News networks

Part three: Introduction
1. Google Olivia Quotes
2. Olivia tells TV WEEK from her home in California.
3. ABCNews.com
4. *Don't Stop Believin'* Viking/Penguin Random House 2019 p280
5. Salon.com By Alison Stine
6. https://www.smh.com.au/culture/celebrity/a-woman-for-all-seasons-olivia-will-remain-something-specific-and-personal-to-each-of-us-20220809-p5b8hv.html
7. Only Olivia.com Fan Website
8. Google Olivia Quotes
9. Listener Why did Olivia Newton-John make it in the US when so many others didn't? By Michael Dwyer August 13, 2022
10 & 11. Interesting articles of discovery via Olivia's early covers Showbiz from March 2004/ OnlyOlivia.com
12. https://www.theaustralian.com.au/

'You stood in awe of her welcoming beauty, and you basked in the feeling that she was connecting to you alone. But when she opened her mouth to sing, you knew instantly you'd have to share her with the world'.

– Melissa Etheridge

'Grace And Gratitude'

Olivia Newton John Lyrics

All I have and all I feel
Is all because of you
All I reap is all I sow
And love is our living proof

Thank you for life
Thank you for everything
I stand here in Grace and Gratitude
And I thank you ...

Seasons come and seasons go
No matter what we choose
A thousand names
A thousand roads
All lead to one simple truth

Thank you for life
Thank you for everything
I stand here in grace and gratitude
And I .. I thank you